100 NEW DISCOVERIES OF THE THIRD NATIONWIDE SURVEYS OF CULTURAL HERITAGE

第三次全国文物普查

百大新发现

国家文物局　编

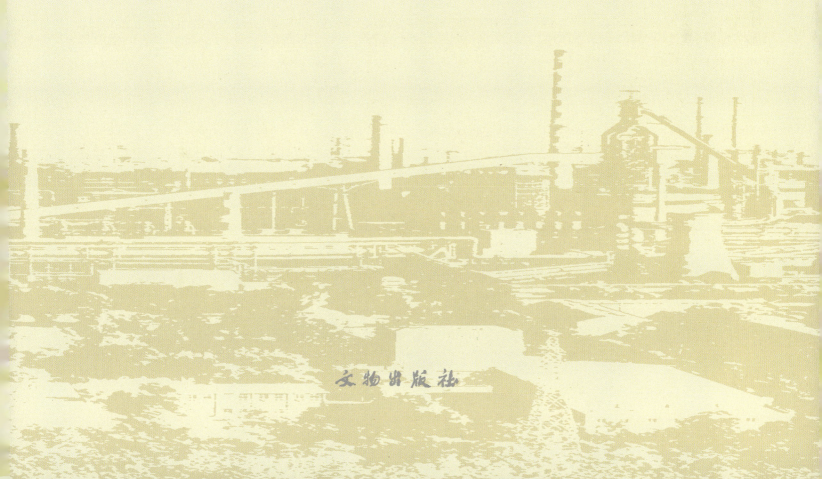

文物出版社

鸣谢单位

国务院第三次全国文物普查领导小组成员单位：

中华人民共和国国家发展和改革委员会

中华人民共和国民政部

中华人民共和国财政部

中华人民共和国国土资源部

中华人民共和国住房和城乡建设部

中华人民共和国交通运输部

中华人民共和国水利部

中华人民共和国商务部

国家统计局

国家林业局

国家宗教事务局

国家测绘地理信息局

中国人民解放军总后勤部基建营房部

中共中央党史研究室

支持单位

北京市第三次全国文物普查办公室

天津市第三次全国文物普查办公室

河北省第三次全国文物普查办公室

山西省第三次全国文物普查办公室

内蒙古自治区第三次全国文物普查办公室

辽宁省第三次全国文物普查办公室

吉林省第三次全国文物普查办公室

黑龙江省第三次全国文物普查办公室

上海市第三次全国文物普查办公室

江苏省第三次全国文物普查办公室

浙江省第三次全国文物普查办公室

安徽省第三次全国文物普查办公室

福建省第三次全国文物普查办公室

江西省第三次全国文物普查办公室

山东省第三次全国文物普查办公室

河南省第三次全国文物普查办公室

湖北省第三次全国文物普查办公室

湖南省第三次全国文物普查办公室

广东省第三次全国文物普查办公室

广西壮族自治区第三次全国文物普查办公室

海南省第三次全国文物普查办公室

重庆市第三次全国文物普查办公室

四川省第三次全国文物普查办公室

贵州省第三次全国文物普查办公室

云南省第三次全国文物普查办公室

西藏自治区第三次全国文物普查办公室

陕西省第三次全国文物普查办公室

甘肃省第三次全国文物普查办公室

青海省第三次全国文物普查办公室

宁夏回族自治区第三次全国文物普查办公室

新疆维吾尔自治区第三次全国文物普查办公室

我国是历史悠久的文明古国，在漫长的历史进程中，各族人民创造了极为丰富的文化遗产。保护、管理、利用好祖国的文化遗产，对于维系中华民族血脉、弘扬优秀传统文化、增进民族团结、振奋民族精神、促进社会主义和谐社会建设、推动人类文明进步，具有重要的现实意义和深远的历史意义。

第三次全国文物普查是新中国成立后，国家进行的最大规模的不可移动文化遗产资源调查工作。在国务院第三次全国文物普查领导小组的正确领导和各级人民政府的悉心组织下，历时5年余，经过准备工作、实地调查、资料整理三个工作阶段，耗资近20亿元，建立各级普查组织机构3000余个，汇集普查工作者近5万人，登记不可移动文物近77万处，其中登记新发现不可移动文物54万余处。

为了向社会集中展示第三次全国文物普查所取得的丰硕成果，国家文物局决定在全国进行第三次全国文物普查百大新发现评选活动。经过31个省、自治区、直辖市普查领导机构的认真遴选、推荐，共计报送参评项目305项。中国文物报社专门组织了具有广泛代表性的评委，对各地报送的参评项目进行了仔细、认真的研究和比对，最终以投票方式选出了这100项第三次全国文物普查新发现。

透过百大新发现，我们可以看到，正是由于我国优越的社会主义体制，使各地能够在较短时期内及时建立普查领导机构，动员和汇集近5万人参与此项工作，为普查工作的顺利开展提供了有力的组织保证；正是由于改革开放以来，我国社会经济的迅速发展，财力的充盈，为普查工作的顺利开展提供了坚实的物质保证；正是由于国民素质的大大提高，一大批优秀的专业人员参与，为普查工作的顺利开展提供了可靠的技术保证。

透过百大新发现，我们可以看到，随着对文化遗产认识的不断深化，保护理念的提升，大大拓展了文化遗产的领域，使保护文化遗产的视野更加宽泛，一些新的遗产品类被纳入了调查范围；随着人民生活水平的不断提高，促进了社会对传统文化的渴求，使这次普查得到了社会各界和民众无私的关心和支持，保护祖国文化遗产的意识正日益深入人心；随着科学技术的发展，大量先进的技术手段应用于这次普查工作，提高了工作效率，普及了科学知识，强化了文物工作者队伍的整体素质。

透过百大新发现，我们可以看到，每一项新发现都凝聚着一线普查队员辛勤的劳动，每一幅照片都浸沁着他们勤劳的汗水。正是他们，田野调查阶段不畏艰难、栉风沐雨；资料整理阶段客观求实、科学严谨，执着地发掘着祖国宝贵的财富，为我国文化遗产保护事业做出了不可磨灭的贡献，也为这次第三次全国文物普查百大新发现的评选提供了准确详实的资料。

窥一斑而见全豹，这100项第三次全国文物普查新发现，就是普查成果中古遗址、古墓葬、古建筑、石窟寺及石刻、近现代重要史迹及代表性建筑、其他6个方面经典体现。

国务院第三次全国文物普查领导小组办公室
2011年11月

China is an ancient civilization with time-honored traditions. Over the sweep of Chinese history, the people of all her ethnic groups have created rich and diverse cultural heritage resources. Protecting, managing and utilizing these cultural patrimonies in a proper manner is of both historical and realistic importance to continuing the identity of the Chinese nation, promoting the best of her traditions and culture, strengthening her national solidarity, invigorate her national spirit, facilitating her harmony-oriented social development and moving forward the progress of humanity.

The Third Nationwide Surveys of Cultural Heritage is the largest campaign of surveying and inventorying sites and monuments that the Central Government has ever launched since new China was founded in 1949. Under the proper guidance by the State Council Steering Group and with the well-planned organization by governments at various levels, the five-year campaign has successfully proceeded through three scheduled phases, including preliminary preparations, on-site surveys and data sorting out. Nearly 2 billion RMB was spent on this unprecedented project, with 3000 or so survey agencies established and nearly 50,000 surveyors mobilized to fulfill surveying and inventorying work. As a consequence, nearly 770,000 sites and monuments have been inventoried, among which 540,000 are newly-discovered ones.

In order to display to the public the remarkable achievements scored in the Surveys, the State Administration of Cultural Heritage launched event to select the 100 New Discoveries of the Third Nationwide Surveys of Cultural Heritage. With attentive selection and recommendation, 305 nomination files were submitted by 31 provinces, autonomous regions and municipalities directly under the Central Government. China Cultural Heritage News organized a judge panel whose members come from various professional circles. The experts from the judge panel made careful studies and comparisons and selected by voting the 100 New Discoveries of the Third Nationwide Surveys of Cultural Heritage.

China's socialist system made it possible to establish surveying agencies throughout the country only within a short period of time and mobilize nearly 50,000 surveyors to join in this national census. Meanwhile, China's economic strength and sufficient fiscal grants provided material guarantees for the Surveys' smooth proceeding and the voluntary work done by a great number of outstanding professionals made this nationwide campaign technically possible.

Thanks to ever-deepening understanding about cultural heritage and continued development of conservation concepts, the scope of cultural heritage has been significantly expanded. As a result, our vision on cultural heritage conservation has been broadened and new types of cultural heritage have been included as survey targets. Thanks to continued improvement of Chinese people's life and the whole society's increasing needs of traditional culture, the Surveys has gained unreserved attention and support from all walks of life and the awareness of cultural heritage conservation continues to increase. Advanced technologies were widely used in the Surveys, making significant contribution to increasing working efficiency, spreading expertise on cultural heritage conservation and improving professional quality of cultural heritage conservators.

In this nationwide census, surveyors working in the forefront have made tremendous efforts and overcome numerous difficulties in field surveys and data sorting out. Each new discovery and each photo crystallize their hard work and embody their pursuit of science and professionalism. They have made indelible contribution to China's noble cause of cultural heritage conservation and provided accurate and detailed information as references for the selection of the 100 New Discoveries of the Third Nationwide Surveys of Cultural Heritage, which are classified into six major categories, including historic sites, historic tombs, historic buildings, grotto temples and stone inscriptions, important historic sites and representative buildings of modern China, and others.

The General Office of the State Council
Steering Committee for the Third Nationwide
Survey of Cultural Heritage
2011.11

近现代重要史迹及
代表性建筑
IMPORTANT HISTORIC SITES
AND REPRESENTATIVE
BUILDINGS OF MODERN CHINA

其他
OTHERS

附录（参评项目）
APPENDIX

第三次全国文物普查百大新发现

100 NEW DISCOVERIES OF THE THIRD NATIONWIDE SURVEYS OF CULTURAL HERITAGE

古遗址
ANCIENT SITES

翻译：李新伟（中国社科院考古研究所）
Translator: Li Xinwei

古遗址类的新发现共评选出27项。这些遗址广泛分布在全国24个省、自治区和直辖市，门类丰富，时代跨度长。不仅包含了传统的聚落遗址、城址和衙署遗址，还入选了一些独具特色的古遗址门类，如反映各个历史时期农业、手工业发展状况的水利设施、造纸、制盐作坊遗址；反映历代交通的文化线路遗址；反映历代民间宗教信仰的古遗址；反映古代军事设施的烽燧遗址等。这些古遗址的年代跨度从新石器时代一直到清代，从不同角度和不同层面反映着我国古代社会生活的若干细节，为我们提供了研究古代社会历史不可多得的实物遗存史料，对于中国古代文明研究具有重要意义。

在聚落遗址中，内蒙古赤峰魏家窝铺遗址总面积达9.3万平方米，是一处保存较好、规模较大的红山文化早、中期聚落遗址，现已揭露出的28座房屋遗址皆为圆角方形半地穴式，面积不等，带有门道和瓢形的火灶，出土遗物也十分丰富，为研究红山文化时期原始居民的生活方式、聚落形态以及社会组织结构等方面提供了重要的新材料，是我国史前新石器时代考古的一个新收获。青海省都兰县发现的夏尔雅玛可布遗址是青铜时代诺木洪文化中十分重要的一处遗址，过去在自察汗乌苏至格尔木约700公里的青藏沿线仅发现过三处诺木洪文化的遗址，这次新的发现弥足珍贵。遗址的堆积特点、包含物以及与当地自然环境、民族迁徙的关系都值得做进一步的深入研究，在边疆考古领域具有重要意义。四川省的阿梢脑遗址位于九寨沟境内，是一处具有一定规模的汉代聚落遗址，发现泥墙建筑、灰坑、踏面、灰烬层等大量遗迹现象，出土了汉式铁器、铜器、彩陶残片、骨质装饰品以及大量的动物骨骼，表明早在汉代中原文化的影响已经到达九寨沟地区，为认识"华夏边缘"地带融入中原文化体系的历史进程提供了新的证据。新疆巴里坤红山口遗址发现大型的石围居址，结构复杂，遗址周围发现岩画和墓葬共存，拓展了研究古代游牧民族的生计与居住方式的学术视野。重庆市渝中区老鼓楼发现的南宋衙署遗址是一处保存较好的夯土包砖式高台建筑，部分城砖上有阴、阳模印的纪年铭文，它的发现不仅在研究重庆市的城市沿革变迁和宋代的营造技术等方面具有重要的学术价值，也为宋元时期流行的山城防御体系的来源问题提出了新线索。

反映各个历史时期农业、手工业发展状况的水利设施、造纸、制盐作坊遗址历来因数量稀少而弥显珍贵。此次发现的浙江省余杭彭公水坝遗迹是一处良渚文化时期的水利设施遗址，其堆筑方式是下部用草裹青淤泥堆筑，上部用黄土堆筑，形成山体之间长达数公里的人工屏障，达到使山洪改道的目的，反映出史前时期良渚古城外围的防洪治水系统的一个生动断面。浙江省杭州市发现的宋代泗洲造纸作坊遗址总面积达1.6万平方米，现揭露出摊晒场、沤料池、灰浆池、抄纸房、焙纸房等作坊遗址，基本上反映出当时造纸工艺的全过程。江西省宜春市华林造纸作坊遗址历经宋、元、明时期，共发现此类与造纸相关的遗迹28处，也可以完整再现古代造竹纸的整套工序。山东省黄河三角洲盐业遗址、陕西省镇坪古盐道遗址等则从不同的侧面对古代盐业生产的制作、贩运等情况有所反映，成为当前学术界给予高度关注的"盐业考古"的重要资料。

文化线路是近年来随着我国文化遗产保护事业的不断推进，提出的一个新的遗产门类。本次入选"百大"新发现的古遗址中，作为文化线路的代表，最具代表性的可举北京市门头沟区唐末至清代的西山古道，历经800多年，成为京师联系山西、内蒙古草原的主要道路。古道上还分布着众多的文物古迹，蕴含着丰富的文化内涵。黑龙江省海西东水陆城站是明代奴儿干都司境内的两大交通驿道之一，始建于明代永乐七年（1409年），全长2500公里，是明代东北地区六条驿道中最长的一条，分为水陆两道，不但加强了明中央政府对东北地区的经营管理，同时也促进了各民族之间的经济文化交流。

以往对于时代较为晚近的民间宗教信仰遗址关注度不高，此次入选"百大"的古遗址当中，湖南省鬼仔石像遗址群尤其引人注目。江永县、道县等地，流行一种高度仅30多厘米的石刻雕像，放置在偏僻之所，每处雕像多达数十上百尊，其中鬼仔井遗址的石像更是数以千计。这类石像的用途十分神秘，有的还与古

树等并存一处，在民间有不同的解释。湖南省文物考古工作者联合宗教学、民俗学等方面的专家，对这一遗址群进行了深入调查，初步判明其主要流行于宋、明、清，其性质与当地原始宗教信仰、祭祀活动以及民族迁徙有关。

吉林省乾安县发现的辽春捺钵遗址群地处松嫩平原西部，古代曾是游牧之地，遗址群由成片的土台基构成，其中最大的台基面积达3000余平方米。据研究，春捺钵是辽代独有的政治制度，四时捺钵不仅是契丹族的风俗，也是其笼络女真、稳定后方的一项重大政治活动所遗留下来的遗址。

古代军事遗址的发现历来是西北地区古遗址调查发现的重点领域。甘肃省敦煌市发现的一棵树烽燧遗址，就是一处十分重要的西汉时期的军事遗址。此处烽燧修建在敦煌西湖湾窑盆地中部，其中最为重要的发现是从F5号房屋遗址中出土的完整的封检，其形制为竖长方形，胡杨木质，长44.3厘米，宽6厘米，厚2.2厘米，上半部中间有供封泥缠绳打结的凹槽，上面的封泥还保存完整，呈暗红色，封泥上有篆书阳刻钤印，印文的字迹已模糊不清。凹槽的上端正面竖行书写墨书三行，下端正面竖行墨书五行，它的发现对于认识汉代边郡符信的种类、形制等均具有重要的意义。

霍巍

四川大学历史文化学院院长 考古系博士生导师

16

Totally 27 ancient sites in 24 provinces, autonomous regions and municipalities directly under the Central Government, are listed in the "100 Discoveries of the Third Nationwide Surveys of Cultural Heritage" . They consist of not only settlements, walled sites and ancient governmental yards, but also special remains including water conservancy facilities, paper making workshops, salt manufacture sites, ancient roads, ritual sites and beacons, which exhibit the development of agriculture, crafts, transportation, folk religions and military in different time. These sites cover a long time period from the Neolithic time to the Qing Dynasty, and provide valuable data for the detailed research on ancient societies from different perspectives and in different aspects. In a word, they are significant for the understanding of ancient Chinese civilization.

Among the settlement sites, the 9.3 ha large Weijiawopu site in the Hongshan District, Chifeng City, Inner Mongolia is a relatively large and well preserved settlement of Early and Middle Hongshan culture. The 28 semi-subterranean houses unearthed at the site are round-corner-square in shape but different in sizes. They all have passages and gourd ladle-shaped hearths. A large number of artifacts had been found on their floors. This important discovery of prehistory archaeology in China, with its abundant fresh new data, sheds light on the research on the subsistence economy, settlement pattern and social structure of the Hongshan societies. The Xiaeryamakebu site in the Dulan County, Qinghai Province is an important settlement of the Bronze Age Nuomuhong culture. Only three Nuomuhong sites had been recorded along the 700 km long road from Chahanwusu to Geermu before. Hence the discovery of this new site is really valuable, and is important for the interpretation on ancient environment and movement of peoples in this frontier area. The Ashaonao site in Jiuzhaigou, Sichuan Province is a relatively large settlement of the Han Dynasty with mud architectures, pits, roads and ash deposits. The Han style iron tools,

bronze objects, painted pottery, bone ornaments and large amount of animal bones unearthed at the site indicate the strong influence from the center of the Han in the Central Plains area. It is a new sample for the research on the integration of frontier areas into the central Han cultural system. The large settlement with stone walls found at Hongshankou in Balikun, Hami, Xinjiang is complex in structure. More important, rock arts and burials were also discovered near the site, which provide a chance to conduct a more comprehensive interpretation of the life of ancient nomadic people. The Southern Song Dynasty government yard in the Yuzhong District, Chongqing City is a relatively well-preserved high-platform architecture complex made of rammed earth and bricks. Inscriptions of the dates of the construction were found on some bricks. The yard is not only valuable for the research on the history of Chongqing as a central city and the architectural techniques of the Song Dynasty, but also significant for the exploration of the origin of mountain city defence system which was popular in the Song and Yuan Dynasties.

The sites of water conservancy facilities, paper making workshop and salt manufacture which reflect the development of agriculture and crafts in different time are small in number and hence high in value. The dam found at Penggong in Yuhang, Hangzhou City, Zhejiang Province was a water conservancy facility of the Liangzhu culture. Its lower part was made of mud wrapped up by grass, while its upper part was piled with yellowish soil. The several kilometers long dam was a man-made defence work to change the way of the flood, and an important part of the flood protection system surrounding the Liangzhu walled city. The Sizhou paper making workshop found in the Hangzhou City, Zhejiang Province is 1.6 ha in size. A recent excavation uncovered the sun drying ground, the pool for soaking the raw material, the large pot for boiling the raw material, the pool for lime slurry washing, the room for tearing off papers and the room for paper baking, exhibiting almost all the processes of paper making at that time. The Hualin paper making workshop in Yicun City, Jiangxi Province had been operating in the Song, Yuan and Ming Dynasties. The 28 features show a complete picture of bamboo paper making. The salt manufacture sites in the Yellow River Delta in Shandong, the Zhenping ancient salt road in Shaanxi provide important data in different aspects of salt production and transportation in ancient time, which deserves high attention of the archaeologists focusing on "salt archaeology".

Cultural routes is a new type of cultural heritage in the continually developing cultural heritage protection development in China. Among the "Top 100" new discoveries, the ancient road system in western Beijing is a good representative. It had been the main passage connecting Beijing with Shanxi and the Mongolian steppe in an 800 long time period from the Tang to the Qing Dynasties. The ancient heritages along the roads exhibit a colorful picture of local cultures. The Haixidong courier lines was one of the two main courier lines of the Ming Dynasty Nuergan dusi. Established in the seventh year of the Yongle reign (1409), the 2500 km long line was the longest among the six courier lines in the Northeast region. It is not only important for the management of the Northeast region by the Ming central government, but also for the communication between different nationalities.

The folk religion in later historic time has been neglected for a long time. Hence the "Ghost guys" stone statues listed in the "Top 100" is especially attract the gaze of archaeologists. Those 30 cm high statues were found at remote locations in the Jiangyong, Daoxian of Hunan. Each location usually has several dozens or more than 100 statues. The Guzaijing site has more than 1000. At some sites, the statues are set beside old trees. The local people have different explanations on these secret statues. Local archaeologists of the Hunan Province, together with the specialists on religion and folk customs,

had conducted a intensive survey of all the sites with these stone statues. Their primary conclusion is that the statues might have been made during the Song, Ming and Qing Dynasties for religious purposes and sacrifice ceremonies. The distribution of these sites might indicate the movement of peoples.

The site complex of the Chunnabo spring excursion the Liao royal court. consists of four groups of earth foundations and more than 3000 in area. The western Songnen plain where the site is located was the pastureland of nomadic peoples in ancient time. The "Sishinabo (Four seasonal excursions)" was an important political strategy to strengthen the relationship with the Jurchens in order to stablize its back yard. The discovery of the site complex is significant for the research on this political strategy and related activities.

The ancient military sites are always the focus of archaeological surveys and researches in northwestern China. The Yikeshu fire beacon is a very important military site of the Western Han Dynasty. It is located in the Xihu Wanyao Basin of the Dunhuang City. The most significant discovery at the site is the well-preserved mail box unearthed in house F5. This charb poplar made box is rectangular in shape, 44.3 cm long, 6 cm wide and 2.2 cm thick. It was tied by a cord, the knot of which was put in a concaved groove and sealed with a piece of dark-red clay. Stamp can be recognized on the clay. However, the characters on it are too misty to read. Three lines of characters were written at the top of the groove. Another five lines of characters were found at the bottom of the box. This discovery is important for the researches on the types and shapes of the fuxin token in the frontier prefectures of the Han Dynasty.

Huo Wei

Dean of Institute of History and Culture, Sichuan University

西山古道
Ancient Roads in Western Beijing

　　西山古道位于北京市门头沟区，是京西山区通往京师的重要交通干线。历经金、元、明、清、民国，长达800多年，特别是明代以来古驿道再经修建，成为联系山西、内蒙古草原的主要道路。

　　西山古道按功用可分为：商旅通行道路，如玉河古道；军用道，如西奚古道；进香道，如卢潭古道、庞潭古道。

　　西山古道分为北中南三路。中道又称玉河古道，东起麻峪，过河经大峪、东、西辛房到圈门；或从三家店经城子、龙门到圈门，经门头口、龙凤坡、三店、梁桥、横岭、天桥浮、拉拉湖到官厅村，上十八盘至峰口庵，一路经十字道、小店子、白道子、赵家庄到葛坡，一路经黄石港、花沟、南岭、北岭、官道到葛坡，并合后到王平口，最后至大寒岭关城，全长约20余公里。是门头沟区运煤业的重要道路，蕴含有丰富的煤炭文化资源，其中在峰口庵关城往西南行百余米，可以看到以前留下的密布的蹄窝。古道上还有圈门戏楼、过街楼、窑神庙、天桥浮碉堡群、大寒岭关城等文物古迹。

　　西山古道与北京的历史和社会发展也有着很多关联，门头沟地区也在古道的基础上逐渐发展形成了多条重要的交通干线和枢纽。此外，古道上还有众多文物古迹，蕴含着丰富的文化内涵。

　　　　　（文：北京市门头沟区普查办　摄影：齐鸿浩）

西山古道蹄窝
Nest Shoes in the Ancient Roads

圈门过街楼
Quanmen Guojielou

卢潭进香道
The Lutan Worship Road

The Ancient Roads in the Mentougou District of Beijing has an 800 years history started from the Jin Dynasty, and since then had been important transportation lines between the capital city and the mountain areas in its west during the Yuan, Ming, Qing Dynasties and the reign of the Republic of China. From the Ming Dynasty, it also had been an important road connecting the capital with Shanxi Province and the Mongolian steppe.

This road system consists of the business roads (such as the Yuhe ancient road), the military road (such as the Xixi ancient road), the worship road (such as the Lutan ancient road and the Pangtan ancient road).

These ancient road system in western Beijing had played an significant role in the history and social development of Beijing and makes the Mentougou District an important hub of communication and transportation. The ancient heritages along the roads exhibit a colorful picture of local cultures.

妙峰山进香道
The Mount Miaofeng Worship Road

西辽城村遗址
Xiliaocheng Village Site

西辽城村遗址位于河北省邯郸市涉县辽城乡。其所在的清漳河西岸台地，地势西高东低，原为坡地，现为梯田。遗址东西长约250米，南北宽约200米，面积约5万平方米。遗址暴露有文化层和丰富的遗物，文化层顶部距地表约0.5米，堆积厚1～2米不等，内含烧土、陶片、残骨和蚌类。遗物以陶器为主，质地有细泥、泥质和夹砂三类，有红、灰、褐三色，部分陶器（红顶钵）口部有橙色条带，纹饰有线纹、绳纹、弦纹和附加堆纹，可辨器形有红顶钵、碗、鬲、盆、罐等。根据遗物推断，该遗址包括了新石器时代仰韶文化、龙山文化和商周等多个时期。

清漳河上游自然环境优越，适于古人类生存。目前在该区域已发现新桥、东辽城村等多处早期古遗址，与西辽城村遗址共同构成了一个大规模的遗址群。西辽城遗址是其中的典型代表之一，其面积大、堆积厚、遗物丰富、延续时间长。它的发现对深入研究冀南太行山东麓史前文化面貌，完善清漳河流域考古学文化序列具有重要意义。

（文：河北省普查办　摄影：刘洋）

20

遗址地貌
Xiliaocheng Village Site

西辽城村遗址
Xiliaocheng Village Site

遗址出土标本
Objects from the Site

遗物暴露情况
Cultural Deposit

The Xiliaocheng Village Site is located in Liaocheng Township, Shexian County, Handan City, Hebei Province. Cultural layers and artifacts can be easily found at the site. The cultural deposit is about 0.5 m under the surface and 1m to 2 m in thickness, and contains burnt earth, ceramics, bones and shells. The unearthed artifacts include red rim bo bowls, wan bowls, li tripods, basins and pots, covering a time period from the Neolithic Yangshao culture, Longshan culture to the Shang and Zhou periods.

The site is large in size, thick in cultural deposit, abundant in artifacts and long in occupation history. Discoveries from the site are important for further researches on prehistoric cultures along the eastern foot of the Taihang mountains in southern Hebei and the local development in the Qingzhang River valley.

魏家窝铺遗址
Weijiawopu Site

魏家窝铺遗址位于内蒙古自治区赤峰市红山区文钟镇。遗址总面积约9.3万平方米，是一处保存较好、规模较大的红山文化早、中期聚落址。2008年文物普查时发现。2009年7月，内蒙古文物考古研究所和吉林大学考古系联合对该遗址进行了发掘，揭露面积约5000平方米，共发现房址28座、灰坑83个、灶址3个、墓葬2座、沟1条。房址皆为圆角长方形半地穴式，面积8~60平方米，门道在南侧，大部分为生土居住面，瓢形灶多位于房址中部。灰坑一般为圆形筒状，也有椭圆形的。出土遗物主要为陶器和石器。陶器有筒形罐、红陶钵、几何纹彩陶钵、斜口器等；石器有耜、锄、斧、刀、磨盘、磨棒等。

该遗址发现较多的房址和丰富的遗物，对研究红山文化时期的生活方式、经济形态及聚落分布等方面提供了较为重要的实物资料，且对深入探讨红山文化的社会结构、组织方式、文明程度以及与周边文化的关系等方面提供了更为可靠的资料。

（文/图：内蒙古赤峰市红山区普查办）

圜底釜
Pottery Fu

22

发掘现场
Excavation-site

出土遗物
Objects from the Site

陶罐
Pottery Bowl

房址
House Foundation

The Weijiawopu Site is located in Wenzhong Township, Hongshan District, Chifeng City, Inner Mongolia. It is 9.3 ha in size and in one the well preserved and relatively large site of the Early and Middle Hongshan culture in this area.

House foundations and a large quantity of artifacts found at the site provide us fresh data for the interpretation of the subsistence economy, inner settlement pattern, as well as the social structure, social development stage of the Hongshan culture. Some artifacts show the communication between this famous culture and her neighbors.

青山沟小城子山城
Xiaochengzi Mountain Fort

　　青山沟小城子山城位于辽宁省丹东市宽甸满族自治县青山沟乡。建在小城子山主峰一处平地上，海拔430米。平面略呈椭圆形，南北长约400米，东西宽约200米，西高东低，东侧、北侧均为悬崖峭壁，西侧、南侧皆以高句丽特有的楔形块石筑墙。西面城墙长约400米，底部存宽约4米，顶部存宽约2米，残高1.5～6米。南面城墙现已倒塌。

　　山城的东南角和西北角各设有一座城门，东侧有两个大致相同的半圆形豁口，宽约6米，根据结构和位置判断，应是两个泄水用的水门。城中靠近南侧有一段东西长约200米，底部存宽约4米，顶部存宽约2米，残高1.5～2米的墙体将山城分割成南、北两部分。北城较大，其中央有一口水井现已被淤平，大致可以看出轮廓。南城较小，根据山城的结构布局初步认为，南侧较小的区域应是一座瓮城，是为防守而修筑的设施。

　　山城虽历经2000余年风雨沧桑，但至今仍保存较好。它和牛毛坞的小城子山城（现为省级文物保护单位）同名，相隔不到6公里，与高句丽早期都城——五女山城距离也不远，小城子之称估计就是相对五女山城而得名，所以这两座山城或为五女山城的卫城。青山沟小城子山城可能稍早于牛毛坞的小城子山城。青山沟小城子山城的发现对研究早期高句丽民族的山城结构和文化内涵，以及辽东地区高句丽诸山城间的布局及内在联系具有非常重要的价值。

24

（文：辽宁丹东市普查办　摄影：王海）

水井遗迹
Well in the Fort

The Xiaochengzi Mountain Fort is located at the peak of the Xiaochengzi mountain in Qingshangou Township, Kuandian Manchu Autonomous County, Dandong City, Liaoning Province, which is 430 m above sea level. It is 400 m from south to north and 200 m from east to west, and guarded by the cliff on its eastern and northern sides, and the typical Koguryo stone walls made of wedge-like stones on its western and southern sides. The western wall is 400 m in length, 4 m in bottom width, 2 m in top width, and 1.5 m to 6 m in height. There are two gates at the southeast and northwest corner of the fort.

The discovery of the fort is important for the research on early Koguryo history and the regional pattern of Koguryo fort in the Liaodong area.

楔形块石
Wedge-like Stones

石筑墙
Typical Koguryo
Stone Walls

山城远景
Distant View
of the Fort

辽春捺钵遗址群

The Chunnabo (Spring Excursion) Site Complex of Liao Dynasty

　　辽春捺钵遗址群位于吉林省松原市乾安县赞字乡、余字乡。遗址群地处松嫩平原西部，地势低洼，是白城内流区的南缘，古代曾是游牧之地。文物普查时发现大量人工堆筑的台基，土层剖面和地表发现辽代陶片、瓷片、石器残片、铁器残片、兽骨、灶台，采集到北宋铜钱。地表可见广泛分布的红烧土颗粒，符合辽代春捺钵的临时营地、毡帐式居住、野炊等基本要素要求。

　　遗址群由成片的土台基构成，共有四区，保存较完整，规模巨大。查干湖畔的一区北自地子井村西开始，向西南绵延4千米，宽1千米，在近4平方千米的范围内，发现土台基530余处；二区在一区之南2千米处，藏字井村北，为1平方千米的近方形区域，发现土台基340余处；三区在二区东4千米滕字井村西，范围约1平方千米，发现土台基150余处。四区在花淖尔湖边，分布范围3.4平方千米，有土台基520余处。台基形状有圆形、长方形两大类，其中长方形居多，有些还有附台。最大的台基在四区中部，面积达3000余平方米。各区台基大小不一，区内还有再分区的迹象。一般台基面积以20～60平方米为多，高0.5～3米不等。

　　四时捺钵是辽代独有的政治制度，其中的春捺钵不仅是契丹族的风俗，也是辽统治者笼络女真、稳定后方的重大政治活动。遗址群的发现，再现了这一历史活动的盛景。

（文：吉林省普查办　乾安县普查办　摄影：王中军）

26

遗址群
Chunnabo (Spring Excursion) Site Complex

遗址台基清理发掘断面
The Section of a Foundation after Rain,
Exhibiting the Cultural Layers

The Chunnabo (Spring Excursion) Site Complex of Liao Dynasty consists of four groups of earth foundations located in the Zanzi Township, the Yuzi Township, Qianan County, Jilin Province. Totally 1540 man made round and rectangular earth foundations were discovered, together with Liao period pottery, porcelain, stone and iron artifacts, bones, hearths, and coins of the Northern Song Dynasty. Large area of burnt earth was also found. The earth foundations are different in height and regularly ranged. These evidence indicate that the site might be the remains of temporary campsite of the Chunnabo spring excursion the Liao royal court.

The Sishinabo (Four seasonal excursions) was a special custom of the Khitan royal court. It was in fact an important political strategy to strengthen the relationship with the Jurchens. According to ancient texts, the Liao emperors had visited the site for 29 times. The discovery of the site complex makes it possible to reconstruct some details of the special custom.

海西东水陆城站
Haixidong Waterway and Land Road Courier Stations

　　海西东水陆城站位于黑龙江省佳木斯市、汤原县、桦川县、富锦市、同江市、抚远县。海西东水陆城站，是明代奴儿干都司境内的两大交通驿道之一。其始建于奴儿干都司创设之年，即永乐七年(1409年)，全长2500公里，为明代东北地区六条驿道中最长的一条，自古以来就是三江地区先民与外界进行商贸和文化交流的通道，堪称"中国东北方的丝绸之路"。

　　海西东水陆城站：水路从吉林市松花江段出发，顺江而下，直抵奴儿干都司；陆路从海西底失卜站（今黑龙江省双城市石家崴古城）出发，基本沿松花江、黑龙江下游两岸45个驿站东北而行，到亨滚河口北岸的终点——满泾站（在奴儿干都司城附近）。共经10城与45站，合为55城站。目前大多数城站都已遭到破坏，位于佳木斯辖区内的6城多为后世所沿用，保存较好。

　　海西东水陆城站位于佳木斯辖区内有13个，具体为6城7站。按自西向东的路线，依次为：托温城、满赤奚站（今汤原县香兰镇东北六里的桃温万户府故城）——阿陵站（今佳木斯市西郊敖其镇）——柱邦站（今佳木斯市桦川县创业乡堆峰里）——弗思木城、古佛陵站（今桦川县东北20公里的瓦里霍吞古城）——弗踢奚城、弗能都鲁兀站（今富锦市上街基乡嘎尔当村西200米、松花江南岸的嘎尔当古城）——考郎兀城（今同江市乐业镇团结村西南1.5公里的图斯克古城）——乞勒伊城、乞列迷站（今同江市勤得利农场一分场西南约4公里的勤得利古城）——莽吉塔城（今抚远县城东北10公里，黑龙江右岸的城子山上）——药乞站（今抚远县通江乡黑瞎子岛上的木克得赫村）。

　　海西东水陆城站，不但加强了明朝政府对东北的管理，同时也促进了各民族之间的经济文化交流和社会经济的发展。这条驿道在巩固多民族国家的统一，开发东北边疆发挥了重要作用。

（文：黑龙江佳木斯市文物管理站　摄影：张亚平）

图斯克古城东侧、北侧城垣
Tusik Walled City

嘎尔当古城东侧城垣
Gerrdang Walled City

28

勤得利古城东垣
Qindeli Walled City

第三次全国文物普查百大新发现

The Haixidong Courier Lines was established in the seventh year of the Yongle reign (1409) of the Ming Dynasty, the same year of the founding of the Nuergan dusi. With the total length of 2500 km, it was the longest among the six courier lines the Ming Dynasty established in the northeastern region, stretching in today's Tangyuan County, Huachuan County, Fujin City, Tongjiang City and Fuyuan County in the Jiamusi City, Heilongjiang Province. Waterway of the courier line started from the Songhuajiang River near the Jilin City, running downstream directly to the Nuergan dusi. Its land road started from the Dishibu station in Haixi (Shijiawai walled city site in the Shuangcheng City, Heilongjiang Province), running northeastward along the banks of the Songhuajiang River and Heilongjiang River, passing 45 stations, and ending at the Manjing station (near the walled city of Nuergan dusi). The whole line consists of 10 walled cities and 45 stations.

Most of the walled cities and stations had been destroyed now. The six walled cities in the Jiamusi City had been used in later time, and relatively well preserved.

临江处的柱桩（泡子沿村西南二号遗址）
Pings near River

北水关遗址
Northern Water Gate Site

北水关遗址位于上海市嘉定区嘉定镇，嘉定故城护城河内侧、横沥河北端。2009年7月嘉定老城区泵闸改建工程北门泵闸施工时发现，上海市文物管理委员会进行了抢救性发掘。

北水关始建于明嘉靖年间，为嘉定故城四座水关之一。遗址曾遭多次破坏。此次发掘在水关西半部进行，遗址下部结构较完整，南北长14米，东西现宽9.3米，残高1.5米左右。

北水关遗址不仅是水利设施，同时还具有军事防御功能，历史上曾为抵御倭寇侵入发挥过重要作用，对研究嘉定人文历史、水利城防设施等具有重要价值。

（文/图：上海市嘉定区普查办）

木桩细部
Details of Pings

木桩俯视图
Overview of Pings

北水关遗址（摄影：陈启宇）
A Panoramic View of the Gate Site

北水关南面
South of the Gate Site

北水关西面
West of the Gate Site

The Northern Water Gate Site is located in Jiading Township, Jiading District, Shanghai. It is just on the inner bank of the moat of the ancient Jiading city and the northern end of the Henglihe River. A recent salvage excavation demonstrates that the gate was built in the Jiajing reign of the Ming Dyansty as one of the four water gate of the ancient Jiading. Although having been destroyed for several times, the lower part of the gate, which is 14 m from south to north, 9.3 m from east to west and 1.5 m in remained height, is still almost complete.

This gate was not only an important part of the water conservancy facility, but also functioned as millitary defence work, and had played an signigicant role in the fights with Japanese pirates. The discovery of the gate is valuable for the researches on the lcoal history of Jiading.

影山头遗址
Yingshantou Site

影山头遗址位于江苏省泰州兴化市林湖乡。现存面积约5～7万平方米，为江淮地区面积最大的一处新石器时代遗址。文化层堆积较厚，现水面以上部分即有两个文化层，堆积厚度约2米左右。在遗址上采集的文化遗物有石器、陶器、骨角器，器形有石斧、石刀、石纺轮、陶鼎、陶釜、陶盂、陶豆、陶三足盘、陶罐、陶壶以及骨笄、骨镞等；自然遗物有陆生的大型动物麋鹿、家猪和水生的丽蚌、蓝蚬等，其中部分陆生动物骨骼已形成亚化石。根据江淮地区原始文化的分期，应属江淮地区原始文化的中期，距今约6300～5500年。

影山头遗址是兴化市已知最早的新石器时代遗址，也是泰州市境内最早的新石器时代遗址。它的发现对研究江淮地区史前文化具有重要意义。

(文：江苏省普查办　图：兴化市普查办)

标本
Objects of the Site

遗址局部
Part of the Site

遗址全貌（摄影：杨爱国）
A Panoramic View of the Site

第三次全国文物普查百大新发现

The Yingshantou Site is located in Linghu Township, Xinghua City, Jiangsu Province. It is now about 5 ha to 7 ha in size and among the biggest sites in this area. According to a natural section on the river bank, the cultural deposit is about 2 m in thickness and consists of two layers. A surface survey at the site collected quite a number of stone axes, knives and spindle whorls, ceramic ding tripods, fu cooking pot, he vessels, dou stemmed plates, plate tripods, pots, hu vessels, and bone hair pins and arrowheads. Animal bones were also discovered. The date of the site is about 6300 to 5500 BP.

沿河断面
Natural Section on the River Bank

泗洲造纸作坊遗址
Sizhou Paper Making Workshop Site

泗洲造纸作坊遗址位于浙江省杭州富阳市高桥镇。遗址东西长约145米，南北宽约125米，总面积约1.6万平方米，分作坊区和生活区两大区块。遗址埋藏较浅，现揭露出的遗迹主要为摊晒场、浸泡原料的沤料池、蒸煮原料的皮镬、浆灰水的灰浆池、抄纸房和焙纸房等；另有石砌的道路、排水沟、水井和灰坑等。遗址南部还发现一条东西向古河道。基本反映了从原料预处理、沤料、煮镬、浆灰、制浆、抄纸、焙纸等造纸工艺流程。

目前暴露的遗迹主要为南宋时期，遗址中出土的"至道二年"、"大中祥符二年"等纪年铭文砖，可将遗址的时代上推至北宋初期。南宋时为全盛期，元代时仍在使用，此后废弃。20世纪中期此处成为农田。

该遗址为研究宋代中国南方乃至世界造纸工艺的传承和历史提供了重要的实物资料。

（文：江苏富阳市文物馆　摄影：杨金东）

34

铭文砖
Brick Inscription

缸
Cylinder

抄纸槽
Papermaking Slot

The Sizhou Paper Making Workshop Site is located in Gaoqiao Township, Fuyang City, Zhejiang Province. It consists of working area and living area and totally 1.6 ha in size.

The site had the remains of almost all the processes of paper making. A recent excavation uncovered the sun drying ground, the pool for soaking the raw material, the large pot for boiling the raw material, the pool for lime slurry washing, the room for tearing off papers and the room for paper baking. Other features include the stone road, ditch, well and pit. An ancient streamway was also found. The workshop might have been established as early as in the early Northern Song Dynasty. However, it was the Southern Song Dyansty who witnessed its prosperous. It still operated in the Yuan Dynasty, yet had been abandoned after then.

凤凰山发掘点清理出来的沟和池遗迹
C3 and G2 of Site T3

遗址全景
A Panoramic View of the Workshop Site

彭公水坝遗迹
Penggong Dam Site

彭公水坝遗迹位于浙江省杭州市余杭区瓶窑镇。2009年12月，浙江省文物考古研究所与良渚遗址管理所对彭公一带进行了初步调查，发现并确认包括岗公岭在内的6处人工堆筑的遗迹，拦水坝顶宽现存约10～18米，底宽现存约50～80米，高约10～20米。堆筑平面呈条形，剖面呈梯形。初步判断岗公岭、秋坞、石坞、老虎岭等遗迹应为良渚时期人工堆筑的水坝遗存，这些水坝实际上是在几座山体之间的山谷位置进行人工拦截，使这些分散的山头连成一体，形成一道长达数公里的屏障，从而达到使山洪改道的目的。推测它们应该与良渚古城外围的防洪治水系统有关。

2010年初经过对岗公岭遗址的进一步调查，发现其堆筑营建方式为：下部用草裹青淤泥堆筑，上部用黄土堆筑，这种营建的方式是莫角山等高台遗址普遍采用的方法，因此对认识和复原良渚人的大型工程的营建工艺和过程具有十分重要的意义。同时也反证出岗公岭等遗迹应该是良渚文化的营建工程。2010年7月，浙江省文物考古研究所将草裹泥样品送北大^{14}C实验室进行了测年，经测定年代为距今4300年左右（未校正），进一步确认了该拦水坝遗迹为良渚文化中期营建。

（文：浙江省文物考古研究所）

秋坞地点水坝断面草裹泥痕迹（摄影：费国平）
The Mud Wrapped Up by Grass of Qiuwu Site

岗公岭水坝断面草裹泥暴露情况（摄影：费国平）
The Mud Wrapped Up by Grass of Ganggongling Site

秋坞段局部（摄影：兰廷成）
Part of Qiuwu Site

36

马家山到密峰垅段俯拍（摄影：兰廷成）
A Bird's-eye View of the Site from Mount Majia to Mifenglong

The Penggong Dam Site is located in Pingyao Township, Yuhang District, Hangzhou City, Zhejiang Province. It consists of six man-made dam-like features at Ganggongling, Qiuwu, Shiwu and Laohuling, 10 m to 18 m in top width, 50 m to 80 m in bottom width, and 10 m to 20 m in height. These features might be parts of a dam built by the Liangzhu people to defend the flood from the mountains. Carbon dating of the features is about 4300 BP. Its lower part was made of mud wrapped up by grass, while its upper part was piled with yellowish soil. This was a typical way of large constructions (such as the city wall and the Mojiaoshan platform) in the Liangzhu time. This discovery makes it possible to reconstruct the process of large architecture building.

岗公岭段纵剖面（摄影：贾国平）
Section of the Ganggongling Site

浦溪河流域遗址群
Sites in Puxihe River Valley

　　浦溪河流域遗址群位于安徽省黄山区甘棠镇、耿城镇。浦溪河流域在黄山主峰之北的皖南山区腹地之中，近于长江流域和新安江流域的分水岭。在河流两岸仅50平方公里范围，分布有从新石器时期至商周时期乃至秦汉六朝的文化遗迹。在2009年的三普调查中，共发现12处先秦遗址，其中浦溪河东岸9处（查家商周遗址、蒋家山新石器遗址、董湾商周遗址、梅花群山商周遗址、团箩山商周遗址、饶家塝商周遗址、黄荆村新石器遗址、弯头山商周遗址、狮形山新石器～商周遗址），西岸3处（城澜刘家商周遗址、官山新石器遗址、张埂商周遗址）。汉至南北朝墓葬群1处，位于浦溪河的西岸。遗址之间距离最大不超过2.5千米，最小距离300米。

　　浦溪河流域遗址群以蒋家山遗址面积最大，原有面积至少在6万平方米以上，现存面积超过3万平方米，是皖南山区目前仅见的一处较大型遗址；而遗址群的分布密度也是整个皖南山区少见的。出土物以石器为主，占小件出土物总数的80%以上，其中镞的数量居多，次为锛、网坠，其他器类数量很少。此外还有极少量玉饰，在红烧土块中发现了稻谷痕迹。据^{14}C测定，出土物年代在距今5000～4800年左右。

　　蒋家山遗址中出土了一定数量的鱼鳍形鼎足，与浙江钱山漾遗址、上海广富林遗址的典型鱼鳍形鼎足相同，但年代较早，这为寻找钱山漾遗存、广富林遗存的来源提供了新线索；陶缸残片上的刻划日月符号，则是北方大汶口文化晚期最为典型的特征。

（文／图：安徽黄山区文物局）

狮形山遗址
Shixingshan Site

董湾遗址
Dongwan Site

弯头山遗址出土陶斝
Jia from Wantoushan

查家遗址
Chajia Site

第三次全国文物普查百大新发现

蒋家山遗址石器
Stone Objects from Jiangjiashan Site

The Sites in the Puxihe River Valley is in the deep mountains north of the main peak of the Huangshan mountains in southern Anhui Province. Totally 12 Neolithic, Shang, Western Zhou and Spring and Autuman periods sites were discovered on the banks of the river within an area of 50 sq km. The longest distance between the sites is 5 km, while the shortest distance is just 300 m. The Neolithic Jiangjiashan site (about 5000 to 4800 BP), which is 3 ha in area, is the largest one. It is the only large site ever found in the mountains of southern Anhui. Artifact found at the site include stone arrowheads, adzes, small yue axes, knives, net weights, jade ornaments and fin-shaped feet of ceramic ding tripods. Some pottery has the symbol of sun and moon. Rice remains were also found. These artifacts show the close relationship with the cultures in the Yangzi River Delta, the Dawenkou culture and the cultures in northern Jiangxi.

黄柏竹林坑遗址
Zhulinkeng Site at the Huangbai Village

黄柏竹林坑遗址位于福建省南平武夷山市武夷街道。遗址背靠连绵丘陵，自身向前突出相对独立，约呈馒头形，东西长约80米、南北宽约60米，相对高度约30米，面积约4800平方米。在山体东坡机耕道断面距地表深度约1米处，发现疑似残破窑炉2座，红烧土窑壁烧结面清晰可见。窑内径为1米，烧结面厚度达8～10厘米。在断面上还可见明显的文化层堆积，其中包含较多窑渣、红烧土粒以及原始青瓷残片。地表采集数量较多的原始青瓷残片，其中含有烧制黏结的青瓷器。青瓷器器形多为豆、罐、簋，灰胎，器表施青釉，釉色青中泛黄，胎釉结合紧密，火候足，质地坚硬。部分器表有方格纹、席纹等装饰，时代初步判定属西周时期。另在该遗址东侧100米处发现另一处遗址，地表也采集较多原始青瓷和窑渣烧土粒等遗物。

黄柏竹林坑遗址为研究原始青瓷器的起源和窑业技术提供了第一手田野资料。

（文：福建省普查办　摄影：赵爱玉 叶凯）

原始青瓷簋
Primary Porcelain Gui

窑址采集标本
Primary Porcelain Sherds

窑址采集标本
Primary Porcelain Sherds

40

遗址全景
A Panoramic View of the Site

The Zhulinkeng Site at the Huangbai Village is located on a small hill in Wuyishan Country, Nanping City, Fujian Province. On the section cut by a road on the eastern slop of the hill, cultural deposits including the remains of two damaged kilns 1 m under the surface and kiln rubbish (red burnt earth, primary porcelain sherds) can be easily recognized. The date of the remains might be the Western Zhou period. The kilns and large number of primary porcelain found at the site provide fresh data for the research on the origin of porcelain making technique and the development of kilns in the Northern Fujian area.

窑炉遗迹
Damaged Kiln

华林造纸作坊遗址
Hualin Paper Making Workshop Site

　　华林造纸作坊遗址位于江西省宜春高安市华林风景名胜区，在江西省开展全省文物普查时发现。2007年9～10月和2009年10～12月，江西省文物考古研究所、高安市博物馆联合组成考古队，对遗址进行了考古发掘，在周岭村福纸庙附近650平方米范围内发现各类与造纸相关的遗迹共28处，在周岭村清理水碓遗迹7座，西溪村清理水碓遗迹7座。揭露出宋代的沤竹麻塘和烧灰料的灰坑；元代的沤竹麻塘；明代的沤竹麻塘和烧灰料的灰坑、蒸煮竹麻的大片烧土块、浸碱堆腌的工作台以及清塘时产生的尾砂坑、舂打竹麻的水碓等大批与造纸工艺有关的遗迹。反映了从伐竹到沤料、煮料、腌料、舂料、配药制浆直至抄造成纸的一整套制纸流程。

　　华林造纸作坊遗址时代顺序清楚，功能相互关联，几乎可以完整再现明代宋应星《天工开物》所记"造竹纸"有关原料加工的工序。是目前我国发现的时代最早、延续生产时间最长的造纸作坊遗址，对研究我国古代造纸技术发展史有着非常重要的价值。

（文：江西省普查办　摄影：全国庆）

42

2号水碓遗址
No.2 Water-powered Trip-hammer

3号水碓遗址
No.3 Water-powered Trip-hammer

复原后的1号水碓遗址
No.1 Water-powered
Trip-hammer after
Reproduction

The Hualin Paper Making Workshop Site is located in Hualin District, Gao'an City, Jiangxi Province. Within the 650 sq m excavated area near the Fuzhimiao, were found 28 features pertaining to paper making. Besides, 14 water-powered trip-hammers were found, 7 in Zhoulingcun, 7 in Xixicun. The remains belong to the Song, Yuan and Ming Dynasties.

The site is the first paper making site excavated with scientific methods, and the earliest paper making workshop ever found in China. The discoveries at the site are significant for the research of paper making history in China.

福纸庙作坊发掘区
Excavation-site of the Fuzhimiao Site

黄河三角洲盐业遗址群
Yellow River Delta Salt Industry Sites

　　黄河三角洲盐业遗址群位于山东省广饶县、潍坊市滨海开发区、寿光县、昌邑县等地区。

　　潍坊滨海经济开发区发现4个由100余处古代盐业遗址组成的大规模盐业遗址群，其中龙山文化遗址1处、商代至西周早期遗址14处、东周遗址86处、金元遗址8处。昌邑盐业遗址群分布面积100平方千米，包括"火道——廒里"以及"东利渔"两处盐业遗址群共计202处，其年代由商周延续至明清时期，时代跨度近3000年，能够完整反映中国海盐生产的发展历程。广饶县南河崖盐业遗址群约5平方千米的范围内，共发现63处商至先秦时期的盐业遗址，商末周初的盐业遗址分布密度非常大，平均每平方千米就有12处，多数遗址相隔近50米。寿光县的双王城盐业遗址群面积达30平方千米，已发现古遗址84处，其中龙山文化时期遗址3处（属于龙山中期偏晚），商代至西周初期77处，东周时期4处，含有金元时期遗址6处。

　　此次考古调查，全面深入地了解了莱州湾地区盐业遗址的分布情况，填补了盐业考古的空白，对盐业遗址的规模、分布情况、堆积形态以及当时的制盐方式有了初步了解，对研究《管子》等文献所呈现的齐国规模化盐业生产水平、制盐方式等有重要意义。

　　（文/图：山东潍坊市普查办 寿光市普查办 昌邑市普查办 广饶县普查办）

44

遗址发掘近景
Excavation-site

宋金时期盐灶群
Salt Industry Sites of Song and Jin Period

2008年南河崖发掘现场
Excavation-site of the Nanheya Site in 2008

南河崖第9号遗址采集陶鬶
Pottery Gui from No. 9 of the Nanheya Site

火道—廒里盐业遗址群150号遗址（东周）
No.150 of Huodao-Aoli Salt Industry Sites

The Yellow River Delta Salt Industry Sites distribute in the so called "Yellow River Delta" area including the Guangrao, Weifang, Shouguang and Changyi of Shandong Province. They are large in number and sizes, and had been operating from the Shang and Zhou period to the Ming and Qing Dynasties, showing an almost complete history of sea salt industry in China. The discovery of these sites sheds light on a better understanding of the techniques and organization of ancient salt industry, especially the scale and methods of salt industry of the Spring and Autumn Period Qi State recorded in Guanzi.

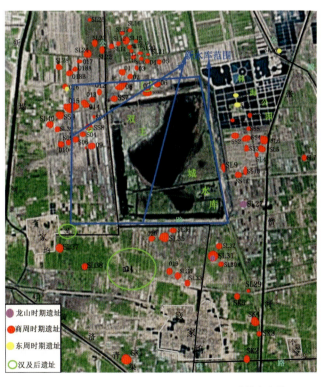

遗址分布图
Location of the Sites

陈庄城址
Chenzhuang Walled Site

陈庄城址位于山东省淄博市高青县花沟镇，周围属地势平坦的黄河冲积平原。遗址中部被一条南北向的水渠破坏，将遗址分成东、西两部分，南部压于小清河北大堤下。"三普"期间，发现地表有西周时期的陶片等遗迹现象，经勘探知，遗址东西约350米、南北约300米，总面积约9万平方米，其中城址面积近4万平方米，以西周早中期文化遗存为主，保存较好。

2008年10月～2010年1月，山东省考古研究所对该遗址进行了发掘，发掘面积近9000平方米，约占整个城址的四分之一，取得了包括城址、祭坛、车马坑等在内的一批重要成果。确认了该遗址为西周时期的城址及东周的环壕，并在城内清理了房基、灰坑、窑穴、道路、水井、陶窑等生活遗迹，尤其重要的是发现了多座贵族墓葬、车马坑以及祭坛。获取了大量的陶器及较多的蚌器、骨器等遗物，墓葬出土了一批重要青铜器及少量精美玉器。

陈庄西周城址所发现的成果填补了山东周代考古多项空白，具有十分重要的学术价值。其中，陈庄西周城址是目前山东地区所确认最早的西周城址，属西周早中期。夯土台基可能为祭坛，为山东周代考古的首次发现，为研究周代的祭祀礼仪提供了宝贵的实物资料。城址中发现的两座"甲"字形大墓当为西周时期高规格的贵族墓葬，对解读该城址的地位与属性具有重大意义。此外，城内还发现有直立跪伏车马坑、殉马坑、木架构水井等一批重要遗迹，具有重大价值。

（文：山东淄博市高青县普查办　摄影：高明奎）

46

遗址地貌
The Site

周代房基
House Foundation of the Zhou Period

马坑
Horse Burial Pit

M18铜簋底部铭文
Inscriptions on the Bottom of the Bronze Gui
from M18

The Chenzhuang Walled Site is located in Huagou Township, Gaoqing County, Zibo City, Shandong Province. The site can be divided into the eastern part and the western part. The recent excavation demonstrate that they are the Western Zhou period walled site and Eastern Zhou period settlement surrounded by a ditch . Within the wall, were found house foundations, pits, cellars, roads, wells and kilns, together with a large quantity of pottery, shell objects and bone tools. Several elite burials, horse-chariot pits and an altar were also unearthed. Offerings in the burials include bronze objects and finely made jade objects. The site is by present the earliest Western Zhou period walled settlement in the Shandong area.

东城墙解剖
Section of the East Wall

李家沟遗址
Lijiagou Site

　　李家沟遗址位于河南省郑州新密市岳村镇。遗址面积2万多平方米，是一处旧石器时代晚期向新石器时代早期过渡的文化遗存。出土石制品数以千计，还有数量较多的动物骨骼碎片及陶片等遗物。石制品为间接打制或者压剥而成，如端刮器、边刮器、雕刻器、石镞、残石叶、细石核、细石叶等。根据[14]C测年，新石器时代早期文化遗存距今8600～10000年（校正后数据），旧石器时代晚期文化遗存距今10300～10500年（校正后数据）。测年结果表明，李家沟发现的夹粗砂红陶片等遗物代表了中原地区最早的新石器早期文化。

　　尤为重要的是，该遗址南区的发掘揭示了从旧石器时代晚期到旧、新石器过渡时期再到裴李岗文化时期的连续堆积，堆积的特点及年代序列是中原地区的首次发现，为认识该地区史前人群、社会及行为文化的特点和变化提供了关键和丰富的资料。同时，成为以后在该地区继续寻找类似的遗址和考古材料的重要依据，为探讨中原地区旧石器时代晚期向新石器时代早期过渡及早期农业起源问题起着十分重要的作用。

（文：河南新密市普查办）

48

遗址全景（摄影：汪松枝）
A Panoramic View of the Site

新石器时代早期文化遗迹
（摄影：魏新民）
Cultural Remains of the
Early Neolithic Age

旧石器时代晚期细石器
（摄影：王羿）
Stone Artifacts of the
Early Paleolithic Age

端刮器与琢背刀
（摄影：魏新民）
Stone Artifacts

The Lijiagou Site, which is more than
2 ha in size, is located in Yuecun Township,
Xinmi County, Henan Province. Thousands
of stone artifacts, fragments of animal
bones, and ceramic sherds were unearthed
in the recent excavations. Both the artifacts
and the carbon dating results indicate
that the site can be dated to the transition
period between the Paleolithic Age and the
Neolithic Age. The discovery of the site
will improve the research on this transition
period, especially the origin of agriculture in
the Central Plains area.

新石器时代早期陶片
（摄影：王羿）
Pottery Sherds of the
Early Neolithic Age

南漳古山寨群
Nanzhang Ancient Fortified Mountain Villages

　　南漳古山寨群位于湖北省襄樊市南漳县板桥镇。南漳山寨群共包括300多座山寨，其中以卧牛山寨、春秋寨、樊家寨、青龙寨、尖峰岭寨和张家寨等最具代表性和典型性。

　　山寨始建年代不详，现存建筑主要为明清时期遗存。其中大部为进剿白莲教起义而筑。白莲教兴起之初，义军"所到之处，有屋舍以栖止，有衣食火药以接济，有骡马刍草以夺骑更换，有逼协之人为之向导负运"。但随着"团练寨堡"的兴起与逐步完成，义军与群众的联系被完全隔断，失去了兵马来源，也失去了粮秣、向导、负运来源，逐步陷入绝境而迅速衰弱并最终失败。

　　据《襄阳县志》、《团练条规》载，南漳山寨大多经过有经验的军人仔细选址，建前有施工规划图纸，大多修筑在临河、三面陡峭的绝壁峰顶以及关卡要塞处。形状因地形而异，平面多呈不规则椭圆形和条形，布局严谨。寨墙由片石或条石垒砌，设有马道、瞭望孔、箭垛等军事设施，功能齐全，设计巧妙，集雄、险、奇、秀于一体，单体山寨结构厚重而不失稳固。

　　以青龙、樊家、尖峰岭等为代表的山寨建筑，充分体现了冷兵器时代的战争特征，堪称山地建筑之奇观，反映了古人的聪明才智和高超的建筑艺术水平。

（文/图：湖北省普查办）

卧牛山寨西寨墙
West Wall of Woniu Village

樊家寨西寨墙
West Wall of Fanjia Village

张家寨西城楼
Gate Tower of Zhangjia Village

春秋寨全景
A Panoramic View of Chunqiu Village

第三次全国文物普查百大新发现

More than 300 Fortified Villages distributed in Banqiao Township, Nanzhang County, Xiangfan City, Hubei Province. The building time of them is not clear. Most of the remained architectures belong to the Ming and Qing Dynasties, probably built for defending the Bailianjiao rebellion. The villages were strategically located at the top of cliffs, steep bank of rivers and important passes, and difficult to access. The walls surrounding the villages were made of stones, and have military facilities such as horse roads, watching holes and arrow shooting blocks. The construction of these remarkable villages need wise design and high skills.

青龙寨中部通道
Pass Road of Qinglong Village

鬼仔石像遗址群
Ghost—guys Stone Statues

　　鬼仔石像遗址群位于湖南省永州市江永县、道县、江华瑶族自治县。是以自然神祇为祭祀主体,包含自发性个人行为和社群统筹行为的原始宗教信仰遗存,盛于宋代而衰于清末。

　　鬼仔石像遗址分为两大类。第一类为旷野型,石像遗址背倚土山,旁有溪泉,古木参天,环境清幽,如道县鬼仔井、江永消水眼、马蹄社、鱼口社、水口庙、江华亭路社、凤尾社等等;第二类为岩穴型,石山嶙峋,洞穴深邃,昔日多有暗河,如江永鬼仔岩、四方坛、岩寺社、白岩社之类。前者多设于村口村尾,后者则大多远离村落,环境颇为荒僻苍凉。 由鬼仔石像当前分布地的原住民及现居民的主要民族成分分析,可初步确认,鬼仔石像的产生及其变迁,与"平地瑶"亦即"盘瑶"的关系十分密切。

　　鬼仔石像均系地表式供奉而非坑式埋藏,石像原材料大多为本地河床中随处可见的砾石,雕制简约,主题多简单重复,表现出民间行为的总体特征;石像的大小、扁圆以及浅浮雕、高浮雕或圆雕类的雕刻方式,能大体反映出石像的发展脉络。

　　鬼仔石像遗址群的发现是湘南地区原住民"灾难性"变动的重要缩影,给苗、瑶同源找到了新证据,为研究瑶族文化的发展变革带来了新资料。

(文:湖南省普查办)

上甘棠白岩社内景(摄影:徐晓林)
Ghost—guys Stone Statues in Baiyanshe of Shangantang

鬼仔井遗址地表供桌及石像(摄影:杨雄心)
Ghost—guys Stone Statues in Daoxian on the Ground

鬼仔石像遗址分布总图
(采自Google Earth Map)
Location of the Site

江河鬼仔岩外景（摄影：陈永军）
Location of Guizaiyan of Jianghe

兰溪鼎天宫社王社母龛（摄影：吴顺东）
Ghost—guys Stone Statues of Dingtiangong,Lanxi

道县鬼仔井遗址探沟（摄影：何群）
Ghost—guys Stone Statues in Daoxian

The Ghost—guys Stone Statues were found in the Jiangyong, Daoxian, Jianghua in Hunan Province, some beside the hills in the open air and some in the caves. Though the lower parts of some statues have been buried by soil, they originally might have been set on the ground instead of buried in the pit. Raw materials of the roughly curved statues are just the pebbles in the local river beds. They might be the remains of ancient Yao nationality.

老鼓楼衙署遗址
Laogulou Government Yard

老鼓楼衙署遗址位于重庆市渝中区望龙门街道，遗址建筑规模宏大，纪年明确，推测可能是南宋四川制置使余玠组织抗蒙时期的衙署遗址。

2010年3月，渝中区文物管理所在"三普"中配合主城区危旧房改造工程调查发现该遗址。2010年4~7月，重庆市文物考古所对其进行了2000平方米的清理揭露，发现有宋元至明清时期的房址、道路、水井、灰坑、灰沟及礌石堆等遗迹25处，出土了一批保存较好的瓷器、瓦当、礌石、坩埚等遗物，取得了阶段性的重要收获。发掘区中心为一处保存较好的夯土包砖式高台建筑，现状略呈方形。高台内部以夹杂小型鹅卵石的黄灰沙土层层夯筑，四周砌筑护坡墙体。四面护坡墙均由下至上层层收分，墙体坡度79度左右，护坡墙及条石基础残高近10米。部分筑墙砖上发现有"淳祐乙巳（1245年）东窑城砖"、"淳祐乙巳西窑城砖"等阴、阳模印纪年铭文。在高台建筑周围发现有多处宋代房址、灰沟、礌石堆及大面积的夯土区。

老鼓楼南宋衙署遗址的发现，不仅对研究重庆城市沿革变迁、宋代营造技术具有重要的学术价值，同时也为山城防御体系找到了发源地，填补了重庆城市考古的重要空白。

（文/图：重庆市文物局）

青瓷碗
Celadon Bowl

礌石
Stone Missiles

54

高台建筑遗迹
High-profile Construction

发掘区全景
A Full View of the Excavation-site

The Laogulou Government Yard of the Southern Song Dynasty is in the Wanglongmen Sub-district, Yuzhong District, Chongqing City. The Chongqing City Institute of Cultural Relics and Archaeology had conducted an excavation at the site from April to July in 2010, during which were discovered 25 features from the Song and Yuan to Ming and Qing periods, including house foundations, roads, wells, pits, ditches and piles of stone missiles, together with well preserved porcelain, tile ends, stone missiles and furnaces. This Southern Song period government yard with clear record of its date is really large in size. It probably the office of Yu Jie, the Sichuan Zhishushi of the Southern Song during the fight he organized to defend the Mongolians. This discovery has not only provided fresh new data of the archaeological research in Chongqing, but also important for the investigation of the development of Chongqing city plans and local architectures, as well as the Song – Mongolian wars.

铭文砖
Brick Inscription

阿梢脑遗址
Ashaonao Site

　　阿梢脑遗址位于四川省阿坝藏族羌族自治州九寨沟县漳扎镇。遗址呈扇形分布，北宽南窄，东西长900米，南北宽150米，总面积13.5万平方米。在阶地各处断面上可见房屋墙体痕迹、灰坑、踏面、灰烬层等文化堆积。调查发现大量遗迹现象，并采集到陶片等遗物。初步认为该遗址的主体是一处具有一定规模的汉代聚落遗址，也包括可早到新石器时期的遗存。

　　发现的遗迹有泥墙建筑，残存外墙以及层内隔墙。墙体残长5.3米，宽2米，从剖面观察，距现地表深5米。建筑形式为泥土板夯，略有收分，内侧抹泥，经火烧，白灰地面，地面板结，硬度较高。灰坑口大底小，圆形，坑壁抹泥修整，坑内出土可修复的陶器多件，推测做窖藏使用。

　　出土遗物有铁器（锸、铁镰、铁环、铁削）、铜珠、石器、彩陶片、骨珠、陶片以及大量鹿科动物骨骼。铁器属于内地汉式风格的铁质生产工具。陶器有存储器和饮食器，多平底豆；夹砂红陶和夹砂灰陶；手制，慢轮或快轮休整；纹饰有压印纹、划纹等。制陶技术显得较为落后。另采集到施黑彩的黄褐色陶瓶口沿，似马家窑文化风格。

　　阿梢脑遗址是迄今为止在九寨沟藏羌地区调查发现最早的遗址。调查发现遗迹、遗物丰富，文化既具有本地土著民族特点，亦有汉式的铜铁生产工具和其他装饰，说明最迟在汉代，汉文化已影响到九寨沟，这为了解汉民族与藏羌民族的经济文化往来提供了重要资料。遗址中心房屋建筑和现在九寨沟县内抹地、大录等藏羌民族建筑形式相似，与岷江、大渡河其他藏羌民族地区建筑形式截然不同，说明本地藏羌民族流行的建筑形制及其渊源或可追溯到汉代或以前。

（文／图：四川阿坝藏族羌族自治州文物管理所　九寨沟县文体局）

56

出土的器耳
Ear of Utensil

铁镰
Iron Sickle

骨头切割痕
Cut Marks on the Bone

采集的彩陶片
Colorful Pottery Sherds

The Ashaonao Site is located in Zhangzha Township, Jiuzhaigou County, Sichuan Province. It is in the shape of a fan with a narrow south end and a wide north end, 900 m from east to west, 150 m from south to north, and 13.5 ha in area. Remains of house walls, pits, hard surfaces, ash layers can be recognized on the sections of the terraces. A large number of pottery sherds had been collected during a field survey. The site might have been a settlement during the Han Dynasty. It is by present the earliest site in the areas of the Tibetan and Qiang peoples in Jiuzhaigou.

断壁上暴露的陶片堆积
Pottery Sherds

暴露的板筑土墙夯层
Remains of House Walls

第三次全国文物普查百大新发现

锦江谷岸遗址群
Sites in the Jinjiang River Valley

锦江谷岸遗址群位于贵州省铜仁地区铜仁市。锦江是沅江一级支流辰水的上源，为贵州铜仁境内最大的河流。锦江流域铜仁段文物普查主要发现落鹅遗址、坳田董遗址、黄腊关遗址、落箭坪遗址、坳上坪遗址、新屋遗址、笔架冲遗址、磨刀湾遗址、茅溪遗址、锡堡遗址、宋家坝遗址、方田坝遗址等17处遗存（包括器物采集点3处），均分布在锦江干流的一级阶地上，遗址面积从数百至数万平方米不等。其中以黄腊关、新屋、茅溪、宋家坝、方田坝、龙井等遗址堆积最丰富，保存亦佳。主体应在商周时期，个别遗址早可至新石器时代，晚可至汉代。

调查共采集石制品、陶片数百件，征集铜钲1件。石制品分打制、磨制两大类，用河边砾石直接加工而成。打制石器有砍砸器、石片等；磨制石器有斧、锛、凿等。陶器的陶质有泥质、夹砂二种；陶色有红褐、黄褐、黑皮、灰色等；纹饰有篮纹、绳纹、方格纹、弦纹、附加堆纹、划纹等。可识别的器形有高领罐、凹底罐、梭形网坠、豆等。

通过调查获得了一批锦江流域先秦时期重要的考古学资料，为厘清该地区从新石器时代—商周时期—汉代的文化脉络提供了难得的实物资料，并将贵州铜仁地区的考古学文化与湘西地区的文化联系起来。

（文/图：贵州铜仁市普查办）

磨制石器
Polished Stone Implements

打制石器
Stone Artifacts

方田坝遗址
Fangtianba Site

58

落鹅遗址
Luoe Site

Totally 17 Shang And Zhou Periods Sites, including the Luoe, Aotiandong, Huanglaguan, Luojianping, Aoshangping,Xinwu, Bijiachong, Modaowan, Maoxi, Xibao, Songjiaba and Fangtianba, were recorded in a survey along the banks of the Jinjiang River. The Site in the Jinjiang River Valley is located in the Tongren City, Guizhou Province. Stone artifacts, ceramic sherds and a bronze zheng bell were collected in the survey.

The data is fresh new to the archaeology in the Tongren region, and had extended the local history to an earlier period.

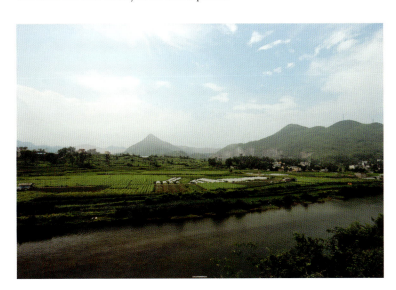

岩董遗址采集的陶片
Ceramic Sherds

茅溪遗址
Maoxi Site

第三次全国文物普查百大新发现

学山遗址
Xueshan Site

学山遗址位于云南省玉溪市澄江县右所镇。2008年，云南省文物考古研究所等单位对遗址进行了初步调查，2009年进行了系统考古勘探，随后进行了试掘。发现有半地穴式房屋，灰坑遗迹38个，面积1.6万平方米。据房屋地面和火塘内的陶片来看，为与金莲山墓地墓葬同时期的建筑遗址。结合勘探的情况，可判定学山遗址应为一处保存完好的古人类生活聚落遗址。2010年的发掘，除明清时期的建筑基址外，发现了石寨山文化的建筑基址，有半地穴式和干栏式的房屋，还有连接房屋的道路、灰坑等遗迹。

学山遗址是目前云南发现的唯一一处保存完好的青铜时代聚落遗址。为研究石寨山文化（即滇文化）的属性、特点和渊源提供了重要的资料和依据，对研究滇文化的村落形态和布局，及其他地区滇文化的演变和流向具有重要的学术研究价值。

（文：云南省普查办　摄影：蒋志龙）

石寨山文化的房址
F1 Houses Foundation of the Bronze
Age Shizhaishan Culture

60

遗址远景
A Distant View of the Site

发掘现场
Excavation-site

清理明代建筑内的建筑填充物
Architecture Foundations of the Ming Dynasty

The Xueshan Site is located in Yousuo Township, Chengjiang County, Yuxi City, Yunnan Province. Under the architecture foundations of the Ming and Qing Dynasties, were found foundations, semi-subterranean houses, post holes of stilt style buildings, roads connecting the houses and pits of the Bronze Age Shizhaishan culture. The site is the only well preserved Bronze Age settlement found in Yunnan by present, and is important for the researches on the characteristics and origin of the Shizhaishan culture, as well as the development of settlement pattern in the Yunnan area and the communication between local cultures and other regions.

柱洞
Post Holes

镇坪盐道遗址
Zhenping Ancient Salt Road

镇坪盐道遗址位于陕西省镇坪县。是古代四川巫溪宁昌井盐运销陕南、鄂西北等地的重要通道，最早开通于商周时期，至1970年代废弃。盐道起于今重庆巫溪县大宁厂，翻越陕渝交界鸡心岭后，在镇坪县境内沿南江河及其主要支流两侧分布，属秦巴古盐道起点，沿途有数处店铺、寺庙遗迹。后来的平镇公路及207省道镇坪段基本沿古盐道走向延伸。

现盐道大部分已被毁坏，遗存有鸡心岭、车湾、晒米溪、险子城、叮当沟、崖砭子、代安河等200多处遗址，总计长度153千米。除鸡心岭段沿山坡修筑外，其余依南江河东西两岸分布，一般距离河床高度2～20米不等。残存路面宽约0.8～1.5米不等，主要道路类型有在山岩上凿出的石镫道、石砭道，块石垒砌衬补的碥道，栈道等多种形式。除代安河450米栈道至今仍在使用外，其余20余处栈道仅存栈孔。从车湾和晒米溪两处道路遗迹看，盐道有多次开凿痕迹，部分碥道、栈孔已近水面或没于水下。

镇坪古盐道为陕南、鄂西北地区食盐运销及其沿革研究提供了重要资料，对研究鄂渝陕交界地区经济文化交往、民俗风情及地域文化形成等有一定的学术价值。

（文：陕西省普查办　摄影：施昌成）

鸡心岭盐道石台阶
Stone Stairs of Jixinling Salt Road

瓦子坪盐道内壁凿痕
Chiseled of Waziping Salt Road

老崖湾石砭道
Laoyawan Stone Road

The Zhenping Salt Road is loacted in Zhenping County, Shaanxi Province. It was an important ancient pass for salt transportation from the well salt center in Ningchang of Wuxi, Sichuan Province to southern Shaanxi and northwest Hubei. The road appeared as early as in the Shang and Zhou periods, and be abandoned in the 1970s. The road started at the Daningchang in the Wuxi County, crossing the Jixinling Mountain at the boundary of Shaanxi and Chongqing, and running along the Nanjiang River and its tributaries in the Zhenping County. In fact, it is just the beginning part of the long salt road connecting Northern Sichuan (or Ba) and Shaanxi (or Qin). Remains of several shops and temples were found along the road. The discovery of the road demonstrates the long history of salt exploration in this area. It is important for our better understanding of salt transportation as well as cultural communication among Sichuan, Shaanxi and Hubei.

钟宝盐道晒米溪栈道
Shaimixi Plank Road of Zhongbao Salt Road

谢家湾栈道
Xiejiawan Plank Road

代安河盐道栈桥桥面
Trestle on the Daianhe Salt Road

一棵树烽燧遗址
Yikeshu Fire Beacon

一棵树烽燧遗址位于甘肃省酒泉敦煌市南湖乡。烽燧用土坯夹芦苇砌筑，底部面积约18平方米，残高1.8米，向上内收。烽燧东南5米处为房屋建筑，房屋东西长约14米，南北宽约7.2米，约有6间。附近地面有大量汉代灰陶片。调查的主要收获均出自编号F2和F5的房间，有简牍12枚，无字素简4枚，其他木器残件有木勺、木篦子、木铲、木车轮等，还有丝绸、麻布、毡片、麻、苇编绳等物。其中出土简牍中有纪年的2枚，为西汉元康三年（公元前63年）封检、西汉初元四年（公元前45年）木简。

封检系胡杨木质，长44.3厘米、宽6厘米、厚2.2厘米，形制为竖长方形，其上半部中间有供封泥缠绳打结的凹槽，上面封泥保存完整，呈暗红色，封泥上有篆书阳刻钤印，印文字迹模糊不清。在凹槽上端正面竖行墨书三行，下端正面竖行墨书五行，有西汉"元康三年"纪年。

从新发现的简牍内容及所处险要位置分析，一颗树烽燧属汉龙勒县大煎都候官的辖区，其应领属于玉门都尉大煎都候官，为阳关西出的一重要关卡。封检简文所记文字对于探讨汉代边郡符信的种类、形制及使用和汉代龙勒县大煎都候官的候望燧次问题有重要研究价值，是研究汉代丝绸之路南道、北道交汇和军事防御体系的最新资料。

（文／图：甘肃敦煌市普查办）

麻布
Linen Cloth

房屋建筑
House Construction

木觚
Wooden Gu

西汉初元四年木简
Wooden Slip Recording the Date of the Fourth Year of the Chuyuan
Reign (45 BC) of the Western Han Dynasty Emperor Yuandi

西汉元康三年封简
Wooden Slip Recording the Date of the Third Year of the Yuankang
Reign (63 BC) of the Western Han Dynasty Emperor Xuandi

65

The Yikeshu Fire Beacon is located in Nanhu Township, Dunhuang City, Gansu Province. The beacon was built with adobes and reed. Clay tiles of the Han Dynasty were found on the surface around the beacon. Totally 16 wooden slips were unearthed, 12 of which have characters. Other artifacts found in the beacon include wooden objects, silk, linen cloth, felt, fiber and reed ropes. Two of the wooden slips record the date: the third year of the Yuankang reign (63 BC) of the Western Han Dynasty Emperor Xuandi, and the fourth year of the Chuyuan reign (45 BC) of the Western Han Dynasty Emperor Yuandi. The records on the slips provide new information on the types, shapes and usage of tally and the mail system in the frontier prefectures of the Han Dynasty. They also shed light on the research on the names and organization of the beacons under the control of the Dajiandu houguan officer in the Longle County, as well as the joint point of the southern and northern silk road and military defence system of the Han Dynasty.

F5封简出土
F5 Site

夏尔雅玛可布遗址
Xiaeryamakebu Site

　　夏尔雅玛可布遗址位于青海省海西蒙古族藏族自治州都兰县巴隆乡，东侧紧邻伊可高里河，西侧紧邻哈图河。几个砂包高耸在平坦的戈壁滩上，而且从卫星照片上看遗址周围似有一方形的古城痕迹。遗址南北长200米，东西宽50米，平面呈南北狭长的椭圆形，面积约1.2万平方米。发现有用河卵石堆砌的宽1米、高0.5米的石墙。遗址上有文化堆积分布，文化层厚60～90厘米，地表采集有夹砂红陶、灰陶等残片、石器及兽骨等，可辨器形有罐、盆及石斧等，应属青海青铜时代诺木洪文化遗址。

采集的遗物
Artifacts Collected on the Surface

　　诺木洪文化的遗址仅在1959年进行过试掘和调查，文化面貌一直不十分清楚，其来源和去向目前仍然是一个谜。自察汗乌苏至格尔木约700公里的青藏线沿线到目前为止只发现3处该时期的遗址。夏尔雅玛可布遗址规模大、保存好、遗物非常丰富，尤其是大量的有机质遗物保存相当完好，对开展多学科的综合研究十分有利。而其"包状堆积"又是一种比较独特的考古学文化堆积现象。

　　该遗址的发现成为研究柴达木盆地古代文明的兴衰与气候变迁、民族迁徙之关系的重要线索，也是研究青藏高原东部与西部地区曾经并存过的几种青铜时代考古学文化之间关系的重要遗址。

（文：青海省普查办　摄影：周安）

66

石墙基
Stone Wall Foundation

遗址全景
A Full View of the Site

The Xiaeryamakebu Site is located in Balong Township, Dulan County, Qinghai Province. It is ellipse in shape and 1.2 ha in area. There is a wall build with pebbles in the river bed, which is 1 m wide and 0.5 m high. The cultural deposit is 60 cm to 90 cm in thickness. Artifacts collected on the surface include sandy sherds of ware red pottery and gray pottery (pots and basins), stone tools (axes) and animal bones. The site is a settlement of the Nuomuhong culture, the origin of which is still a puzzle. The site is important for the research on the development of local cultures, environmental changes and the movement of peoples in the Chaidamu Basin.

石墙及文化层
Stone Wall and
Cultural Deposit

文化层
Cultural Deposit

小河湾遗址
Xiaohewan Site

陶鬲
Pottery Li

小河湾遗址位于宁夏回族自治区固原市彭阳县新集乡。遗址面积约48万平方米，现地表为农田，散见大量的绳文板瓦、筒瓦及陶器残片，另有少量的云纹瓦当和铁器等，在断崖崖壁发现灰坑、沟及文化层堆积等，文化层厚1.5米左右。

2009年7月，在西气东输二线工程建设中，宁夏文物考古研究所和彭阳县文物管理所沿管道线路对遗址进行局部发掘，发掘面积3000平方米，清理墓葬4座。发现遗迹主要有房址、灰坑、陶窑、水井、道路、壕沟等；出土的陶器有铲足鬲、袋足鬲、盆、罐、瓮、甑及云纹瓦当、板瓦等；铁器有斧、铲、犁铧，还有骨器、青铜器等，同时出土少量的带有"陶文"的器物。

瓦当
Vatan

小河湾遗址是宁夏首次发现面积较大的秦汉遗址，对今后研究战国至汉代王国制向郡县制的转变及宁夏彭阳地区秦汉时期的置县情况，探寻该地区秦戎文化面貌以及秦文化与西戎文化、北方草原文化的关系，提供珍贵的线索。同时，还发现了与该遗址相关的两处墓地，对它们的保护和研究，为认识宁夏南部地区秦汉时期文化的延续、秦至西汉墓葬的形制特征和断代分期提供了资料依据。

（文：宁夏固原市彭阳县文物管理所 摄影：杨宁国）

遗址远景
A Distant View of the Site

68

铁器
Iron Objects

地表堆积遗物
Surface Remmains

带陶文的器物
Ceramic Vessels Inscribed Characters

The Xiaohewan Site, which is 48 in area and can be easily recognized by the large amount of surface remmains, is located in Xinji Township, Pengyang County, Ningxia. An excavation was conducted in July 2009. Within the 3000 sq m exposed area, were found 4 burials, house remains, pits, kilns, wells, roads and ditches, as well as pottery and bronze objects. Some ceramic vessels have inscribed characters. This is the first large site of the Qin and Han periods ever found in Ningxia, and important for the research on the establishment of the prefecture-county system, the characteristics of the Qinrong culture, and the relationship between the Qin culture, the Xirong culture and cultures in northern steppe area.

遗址发掘
Excavation-site

红山口遗址
Hongshankou Site

红山口遗址位于新疆维吾尔自治区哈密地区巴里坤哈萨克自治县
红山农场。居址分布较集中，数量多，规模大。单体居址直径5～30
余米不等，其中石围居址规模都较大，而且很集中，多是双层石块堆
积而成，也有单层石块堆积或多层石圈的。居址以长方形为主，有单
间的、分间的以及多间相连的几种，有的中间被墓葬打破。据规模可
推测该遗址区是一处大型的聚落遗址。周围的基本建设对遗址造成了
一定程度的破坏。另外在遗址区周围还发现有很多墓葬和岩画。

墓葬分布较集中，规模从5～10余米不等，多数在4～7米之间。
墓葬形制丰富，以起封堆的、中心凹陷的、土石混合圆形封堆墓为
主，不起封堆的、围一圈石块的方形墓圹墓和圆形墓圹墓较少；有的
墓带墓祭堆，墓祭堆有一个的，也有多个的；有的墓带立石。

岩画也相对集中，数量很多，内容以刻画山羊为主，也有蛇、狼
形象，文字，花纹图案，人射箭狩猎山羊、骆驼、鹿、牛、马、人骑
马，车及车轮等形象。刻画技术有粗线条静态、细线条动态、静态剪
影式、动态剪影式等不同表现形式。

红山口遗址对于研究哈密早期考古学文化、尤其是古代游牧文化
有着重要的意义。

(文/图：新疆哈密地区普查队)

岩画
Rock Arts

遗址局部
Part-Section of the Site

The Hongshankou Site is located in Balikun County, Hami District, Xinjiang. House remains at the site are large in number, big in size and high in density. Most of the houses have two circles of stone wall, some has single circle or multi-circles stone wall. Besides, burials and rock arts were found in the surrounding area. Most of the burials are covered by a soil-stone mixed mound with a concave top. Some are square or round in shape and surrounded by a stone circle. Most of the rock arts depict the goat. The site is an early settlement in Xinjiang. It is significant for the research on early archaeological cultures in Hami. Furthermore, it provides a new perspective for the research on the development of nomadic cultures.

遗址区北部墓葬
Burials on the North of the Site

古道遗迹
Ancient Road Remains

遗址南部全景
A Full View of the
South of the Site

第 三 次 全 国 文 物 普 查 百 大 新 发 现
100 NEW DISCOVERIES OF THE THIRD NATIONWIDE SURVEYS OF CULTURAL HERITAGE

古 墓 葬

ANCIENT TOMBS

翻译：李新伟（中国社科院考古研究所）
Translator: Li Xinwei

古墓葬

此次参评的古墓葬共20处，涉及15个省、自治区，涵盖了从新石器时代至清代各历史时期。它们类型丰富，形制多样，呈规模分布，丰富和深化了古墓葬的考古学认识。既有分布于辽宁省朝阳市的车杖子积石冢群，也有位于河南省南阳市的寺坡汉代崖墓群和陕西省柞水县的杏园沟口崖墓，还有被盗后发现的陕西省甘泉县城关镇袁庄金代砖雕壁画墓。此外，包括单室墓、多室墓、砖室墓、石室墓、土坑竖穴偏洞室墓、长方形券顶砖室墓、券进式穹窿顶单室砖墓、长方形仿木结构砖砌单室墓等多种形制。而且在20处参评项目中，有16处是以"墓葬群"的形式进行申报的，分布面积均在3万平方米以上，包含墓葬最多的河南闰楼墓群达300余座。具有一定的分布规模是此次参评古墓葬的重要特点之一。

从遗存本身价值看，6处入选项目均在某一方面或几个方面具有突出价值，填补该类墓葬的年代、区域或学术研究空白。

河南正阳闰楼墓群是一处商周时期的贵族及贫民墓地，面积大，地形复杂，分西区、中区、东区三部分。通过调查共发现墓葬300余座，发掘149座，出土青铜器、玉器、陶器、骨器、石器275件，除商周时期的墓葬以外，还有少量的唐、宋、明、清时期的古墓。现有研究结果表明，闰楼古墓群是豫南地区新发现的一处十分重要的大型商代晚期贵族墓群，为探讨豫南淮河流域上游地区的晚商文化及淮夷集团的政治、经济、文化具有极高的学术价值。

山西翼城大河口墓群，是一处西周至东周时期的族墓地。土坑墓和车马坑内出土的青铜器、玉石器、漆木器和陶瓷器，数量多、种类全、规格高。特别是已发掘的1号大墓，出土了中原地区所见最早的木俑实物资料，棺椁之间随葬有大量的青铜容器、乐器、兵器和车马器，11个壁龛之内见有较多的漆器、原始瓷器和陶器，壁龛数量居目前西周考古发现之首，为研究晋南地区西周时期的埋葬习俗提供了一批新的资料。墓群西距天马—曲村晋国遗址约15公里，揭示的大墓规格较高，对于研究西周时期晋南地区的封国及其与晋国的关系具有十分重要的学术价值。

江西靖安李洲坳墓葬，是一座东周时期带封土的大型长方形土坑竖穴墓。墓室埋有棺木47具，为迄今发现时代最早、埋葬棺木最多、结构最为奇特的一坑多棺墓。该墓出土各类文物360余件、绝大多数保存完好。其中所见最早的方孔纱和面积最大的整幅拼缝织物以及密度最高、时代最早的织锦实物，为重新认识中国古代的纺织技术、织造史和文化史提供了弥足珍贵的资料。现存最早最完整的竹编席、最完美的彩绘木剑和最早的扇类实物，为研究古代竹、木、漆器的起源和工艺找到了难得的实物证据。花椒、果核、瓜子、植物茎叶的发现，对研究古代农业生产方式和当时的生态环境具有很高的价值。出土的人骨，填补了南方地区先秦时期体质人类学研究的空白。

安徽舒城县春秋塘茶林场墓群，是一处春秋时期高等级的贵族墓地。该墓地面积较大，墓葬形态一致，均为大型坟丘形墓葬，封土呈锥形或圆台形，保存完好。墓葬时代单一，两两相对，排列有序。舒城境内春秋时期分布着群舒的一些小国，它们是南北接通的枢纽，在沟通南北文化上起着重要的作用，但一直未能明确认定这些小国的具体方位。由此来看，春秋塘茶林场墓葬群的发现及其提供的考古资料，对于研究群舒方国的历史具有重要的参考价值。

甘肃张掖地埂坡墓群共发现魏晋时期墓葬30座，从甘肃省文物考古研究所和高台县博物馆清理发掘的5座来看，墓葬基本由墓道、照壁、墓门、前甬道、前室、后甬道、后室构成，随葬遗物主要为金博山、铜连枝灯构件、铜车马器构件、石龟、骨尺等。其中2座以原生黄土雕出仿木结构的墓葬，反映出深受中原传统建筑艺术和文化影响的痕迹，具有重要的建筑艺术研究价值。3座壁画墓中出现的胡人髡发、裹头等多种少数民族以及角抵、戴鼓等艺术形象，既是美术史、服饰史和乐器史研究中不可多得的实物资料，也为研究河西地区魏晋时期的中西文化交流、民族融合、丧葬礼俗等提供了珍贵的参考依据。

2010年清理的内蒙古锡林郭勒盟宝日陶勒盖墓群，是一座土坑竖穴偏洞室墓。据遗物特征判断，年代大致相当于北魏太和初年至迁洛以前（496年），属北方民族的贵族墓葬。该墓遗物丰富，器类珍贵，异域特征明显。出土陶器、金银器、铜器、玻璃器以及镶宝石首饰等200余件，其中玻璃碗等应为波斯舶来之物。北魏时期的随葬品，以前见于山西大同南郊的北魏墓葬，但出土较为零散。地处北方草原地区的宝日陶勒盖墓群，首次出土如此众多而珍贵的北魏遗物，不仅具有极高的文物价值，更为研究北魏时期北方草原地带的部族分布提供了宝贵的考古资料。

金旭东

吉林省文物局副局长 研究员

Totally 20 ancient cemeteries from 15 provinces joined the competition for the "Top 100 Major Discoveries" of the Third National Surveys of Cultural Heritage. The cemeteries cover a long time period from the Neolithic age to the Qing Dynasty. The various types and structures of the tombs largely improve our understanding of ancient mortuary practice based on archaeological data. They include the cairns at Chezhangzi in Chaoyang City, Liaoning Province, the Han Dynasty cliff burials at Sipo in Nanyang City, Henan Province, the cliff burials at Xingyuangoukou in Zuoshui County, Shaanxi Province, and the looted Jin Dynasty tomb with brick chamber and murals at Yuanzhuang, Chengguanzhen Township, Ganquan County, Shaanxi Province. Types of the tombs include single chamber tombs, multi-chambers tombs, brick chamber tombs, stone chamber tombs, side chamber tombs, rectangular arch ceiling chamber tombs, dome ceiling chamber tombs and rectangular brick chamber tombs imitating wooden structure. Sixteen of the 20 cemeteries are larger than 3 ha. The largest is the Runlou cemetery in Henan which has more than 300 burials. Large in area is a characteristic of these cemeteries.

Six cemeteries were selected as the "100 New Discoveries Of The Third Nationwide Surveys Of Cultural Heritage". They all have remarkable significance in one or several aspects.

The Runlou cemetery was a burial ground in the Shang and Zhou periods of nobles and commoners. The 300 burials in this large cemetery can be divided into three parts: the east, west and middle. Within the 1.8 ha excavated area, were found 149 burials of the Shang and Zhou period and the Tang, Song, Ming and Qing

Dynasties. Totally 275 pieces of bronze, jade, ceramic, bone and stone artifacts were unearthed. Current research indicates the cemetery is a very important graveyard of the elites in the Late Shang period. These discoveries is important for the research on the Late Shang cultures in the upper Huai River Valley in southern Henan, as well as the politics, economy and cultures of the Huaiyi peoples.

The Dahekou cemetery in Yicheng, Shanxi had been the clan burial ground from the Western Zhou to the Eastern Zhou period. The bronze, jade, stone, lacquer, wooden, ceramic and proto-porcelain artifacts found in burials and chariot-horses pits are large in number, various in types and high in standard. The large burial Center No.1 is especially astonishing for the bronze vessels, musical instrument, weapons, chariot parts and harness unearthed from it. The two wooden human statues found in the burial are the earliest in the Central Plains area. Totally 11 niches (at most in Western Zhou burials) were found in the walls of the burial pit with lacquer, proto-porcelain and ceramic objects in them. They are important for the research on Western Zhou mortuary practice in Southern Shanxi. Noticeably, this cemetery with large high level burials is just 15 km east of the Tianma – Qucun site of the Jin State. It is significant for our comprehensive understanding of the local state in Southern Shanxi and its relationship with the Jin State.

The Lizhouao Eastern Zhou Period tomb in Jing'an County, Jiangxi Province contains 47 coffins within a large rectangular shaft under the high earth mound. This is the first and earliest multi-coffins tomb ever found in China. The more than 360 pieces of burial offerings are mostly well preserved. The silks are especially important for the research of the history of silk manufacture in China. Other important artifacts include the earliest and most complete bamboo mat, the most complete color painting wooden sword and the earliest fan. They are valuable evidence for the researches on the development of ancient crafts. Remains of Chinese prickly ash, cores, melon seeds and plant branches and leaves are important for the researches on the practice of agriculture and natural environment. The human bones will sure improve the physical anthropological researches in southern China.

The Chunqiutang Tea Farm cemetery in Shucheng, Anhui is a high level grave ground of the Spring and Autumn period. The cemetery is large in area and the tombs were almost symmetrically ranged into two lines on a low hill. Each burial has a well-preserved cone-shaped or flat top cone-shaped earth mount. The cemetery might be a graveyard of the nobles of the Shu States in the Spring and Autumn period. Several small local states all having the surname Shu lived in the Shucheng area in the Spring and Autumn period. They had played an important role in the cultural communication between the south and the north. However, the details and even the exact locations of these states are still unclear. Hence the discovery of Chunqiutang Tea Farm cemetery is significant for the research on these local Shu states.

Totally 30 tombs were unearthed at the Digengpo cemetery in Zhangye, Gansu. Five of the 30 tombs in the cemetery had been excavated. The tomb consists of the passage, the zhaobi screen wall, the chamber gate, the front chamber, the chamber passage and the back chamber. Offerings in the tombs include the gold boshan mountain censer, the bronze tree-like lamp, the bronze chariot parts

and harness, the stone turtle and the bone ruler. Two tombs have wooden like beams, roof, posts and dougong corbel brackets directly curved on the loess walls, exhibiting the influence from the Central Plains area. The murals found in three tombs show the customs of several nationalities including the hu people, who shave off their hair on the top, and wear special head cloth. There are also the scenes of wrestling and drum knocking. These discoveries are valuable for the researches on cultural communication, ethnic groups integration and funeral custom in the Wei and Jin period in Hexi area.

The Baritaolegai Tomb in Zheng Xiangbaiqi Banner Xilinguole League, Inner Mongolia unearthed in 2010 consists of a pit shaft and a chamber in the side wall of the shaft. Artifacts found in it indicate that its date is between the first year of the Taihe reign of the Northern Wei Dynasty and the year the dynasty moving its capital to Luoyang (496 AD). Its owner might have been a noble of certain northern nationality. Burial offering in this tomb are large in quantity and high in quality, some are obviously exotic goods. More than 200 pieces of ceramic, gold, silver, bronze and glass objects and jewelry were unearthed from the tomb. The glass bowl might have been imported from Persian. Burial offerings of the Northern Wei Dynasty had been found in the Northern Wei burials in the southern suburb of the Datong City in Shanxi, yet small in quantity. Such noble tomb with abundant offerings is really rare in the northern steppe area and important for the research on ethnic groups of the Northern Wei.

Jin Xudong

Research Fellow and Deputy Head of Jilin
Provincial Administration of Cultural Heritage

大河口墓群
Dahekou Cemetery

　　大河口墓群位于山西省临汾市翼城县隆化镇。墓地坐落于两河交汇的三角地带，分布面积约10万平方米，是一处西周至东周的族墓群，还发现有车马坑。

　　墓地于2008年普查发现，随后进行了大规模科学发掘。墓葬为土坑竖穴，出土了大批青铜器、玉石器、漆木器和陶瓷器等。其中，1号墓发现了设置在墓壁四周的11个壁龛，里面放置着漆器、原始瓷器、陶器等；在墓室内的棺椁之间，发现了大量青铜容器、乐器、兵器、车马器等。根据青铜器铭文等判断，此墓主人为西周霸国侯伯级人物。

　　大河口墓群西距曲沃县天马—曲村晋国遗址约15公里，大墓规格较高，为研究西周早期晋南地区，特别是晋国周边的封国情况以及与晋的关系提供了重要资料；大河口大墓是继绛县横水西周大墓之后，在墓葬内再次发现壁龛，对研究西周晋南地区的葬制具有重要价值；此外，其随葬漆木俑也是目前中原地区出土最早的实物资料。

（文／图：山西省普查办）

1号墓墓圹
Tomb No.1

墓群远景
A Disntant View of the Cemetery

This 10 ha larger cemetery is located in Longhua Township, Yicheng County, Linfen City, Shanxi Province. It was a clan cemetery from the Western Zhou to Eastern Zhou period.

Within the pit shaft burials, were found large amount of bronze, jade, stone, lacquer, ceramic and porcelain offerings. A large burial in the center of the cemetery has 11 caches in the walls of its shaft for displaying lacquer, primary porcelain and ceramic vessels. The owner of this burial might have been a hou or bo level noble of Western Zhou. Chariot – horses pits were also found. Sherds of Eastern Zhou period gray ceramic basins with cord patterns were collected on the surface of the cemetery.

Discoveries from the cemetery are very important for the researches on local states in southern Shanxi and their relationship with the Jin State in the Western Zhou period.

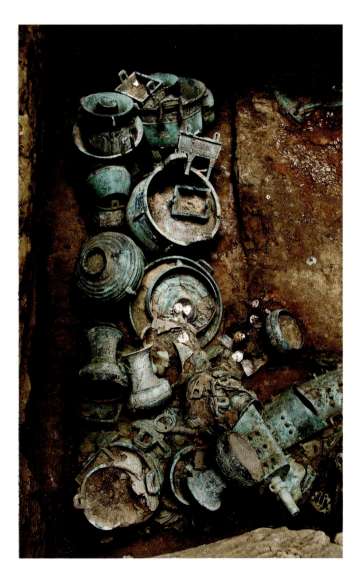

出土青铜器
Large Amount of Bronze

宝日陶勒盖墓群
Baoritaolegai Cemetery

宝日陶勒盖墓群位于内蒙古自治区锡林郭勒盟正镶白旗伊和淖苏木。2010年文物部门对该墓葬进行了清理。根据遗物特征判断，该墓葬的年代大致相当于北魏太和初年(477年左右)至迁洛以前（496年），应为北方民族的贵族墓葬。对于研究北魏时期北方草原地带的部族分布有着重要意义。

墓葬形制为土坑竖穴偏洞室墓，共出土文物200余件，主要有陶器、金银器、铜器、玻璃器以及镶宝石首饰等。出土文物较为珍贵，且异域风格明显，其中玻璃碗等为波斯舶来之物。此类北魏时期随葬品，曾见于大同南郊北魏墓，但出土较为零散。在北方草原地区，随葬如此多珍品的北魏墓葬，相当少见。

（文/图：内蒙古锡林郭勒盟正镶白旗普查办）

陶罐
Pottery Vessel

鎏金錾花银碗外部
Bowl Engraved Gilt

单个铜铺首
Single Bronze Pushou

金耳环
Gold Earrings

铜铺首
Bronze Pushou

玻璃碗
Glass Bowl

The Baoritaolegai Cemetery was found in Yihenao Sumu Township, Zheng Xiangbaiqi Banner, Xilinguole League, Inner Mongolia. It consists of a pit shaft and a chamber in the side wall of the shaft, within which were found more than 200 pieces of offerings including ceramic, gold, silver, bronze, glass objects and jewelries. The date of the tomb is between the first year of the Taihe reign of the Northern Wei Dynasty and the year the dynasty moving its capital to Luoyang (496 AD). Its owner might have been a noble of certain northern nationality. Such noble tomb with abundant offerings is really rare in the northern steppe area and important for the research on ethnic groups of the Northern Wei.

春秋塘茶林场墓群
Chunqiutang Tea Farm Cemetery

春秋塘茶林场墓群位于安徽省六安市舒城县城关镇。墓冢两两相对，沿西北—东南向在一条低矮岗地上排列，其中北部两墓冢巨大的封土完好无缺。墓葬均筑大型坟丘，封土形状呈方锥体或圆台形，其底径达几十米，高几米至十余米不等。2009年普查时发现确认的墓葬有4对（8座）。2010年对已发现的墓葬周边进行全覆盖式的区域系统调查，调查区域近5平方千米，初步判定现存墓葬总数42处，皆有锥形或圆台形封土。年代因未做钻探，暂根据2006年附近变电所输电塔施工时清理出土的春秋时期青铜龙柄盉、鼎等器物，定为春秋至汉代墓葬，且可能属于春秋时期高等级贵族墓地。

该墓地规模较大。到目前为止，可明确认定有春秋时期墓葬的岗地分布面积近3平方千米，墓葬封土大都保存完好。墓葬分布规律，大都分布在低矮的岗地（山脊）、近水、面临开阔地，同时排列较为有序，形态单一，年代应相差不远，可能是春秋时期群舒贵族墓葬。舒城境内春秋时分布着群舒方国的一些小国，它们是南北接通的枢纽，在沟通南北文化上起着重要的作用。但迄今为止不能明确认定这些小国的具体方位，此次调查发现的墓葬及出土的器物对探究春秋时期群舒方国有着重要意义。

（文/图：安徽六安市舒城县普查办）

墓葬环境
Cemetery Lining on a Low Hill,
Near the Water and Facing the
Open Field

墓群封土
Earth Mount of the Cemetery

The Chunqiutang Tea Farm Cemetery is located in Shucheng County, Anhui Province. The 42 tombs were almost symmetrically ranged into two northwest to southeast lines on a low hill, near the water and facing the open field. Each burial has a well-preserved cone-shaped or flat top cone-shaped earth mount, dozens of meters in diameter and several meters to more than ten meters in height. The cemetery might be a graveyard of the nobles of the Shu State in the Spring and Autumn period.

墓葬
The Cemetery

李洲坳墓葬
Lizhouao Tomb

李洲坳墓葬位于江西省宜春市靖安县水口乡。2007年普查发现并发掘，清理出土棺木47具，出土各类文物360余件。

该墓葬为一处有封土的大型土坑竖穴墓。原封土高约12米，分5层呈水平状夯筑，间隔有成片的石块。封土正中下方为墓穴，面积约160平方米。墓口至底部深约4米，墓葬东壁南端为东西向斜坡墓道，宽约3米，受现代公路的破坏，残长5米。墓底垫厚约40～60厘米的青膏泥，在膏泥上铺一层竹席，竹席上放置棺木47具，除主棺有棺有椁外，均为圆木小棺。48号墓坑为空置，原因尚不明。棺木以多层竹席包裹下葬，再用青膏泥覆盖，之后裹以厚约10厘米的黄土，夯打并火烤，形成致密的包裹层。该墓是迄今发现的全国罕见的一坑多棺墓葬。

墓葬出土文物包括竹木器144件、漆器12件、玉器13件、青铜器30件、原始青瓷器7件、金器1件、金属器5件、纺织品300余件，以及大量的人体骨骼标本、动植物标本、纺织工具。纺织品工艺复杂，织造精细，表现了相当高的技术；出土了中国最早的方孔纱、面积最大的整幅拼缝织物和中国密度最高、时代最早的织锦实物，为研究古代纺织技术提供了详实的资料。墓葬出土的人骨填补了南方地区先秦时期体质人类学研究的空白。

李洲坳东周墓葬所代表的一支具有深厚越文化因素，又受某些楚文化影响的新型青铜文化，也反映了春秋晚期，在赣西北地区可能存在一支具有高度青铜文明的大型政治集团。

（文：江西省普查办　摄影：刘新宇）

埋葬有47具棺的墓室
The Large Rectangular Shaft with 47 Coffins in the Chamber

织锦
Tapestry

织锦纹样
Tapestry Patterns

金质棺饰
Golden Decoration of the Coffins

The Lizhouao Tomb is located in Shuikou Township, Jing'an County, Yichun City, Jiangxi Province. Under the high earth mound of the tomb, there is a large rectangular shaft with 47 coffins in the chamber at the bottom. This is the first multi-coffins tomb ever found in China, and is significant for the research on the funeral practice as well as social life of the Eastern Zhou period. Burial offerings found in the tomb are large in number, various in types and finely made with outstanding skill. The silks are especially important for the research of the history of silk manufacture in China.

清理棺木表面
Cleaning Surface of the Coffins

墓葬远景
A Distant View of the Tomb

闰楼墓群
Runlou Cemetery

闰楼墓群位于河南省驻马店市正阳县付寨乡，主体为商周时期贵族及平民墓群。墓地面积较大，地形复杂，分为东、西和中部三个区。东、西两高岗呈长条形由南向北延伸至文殊河南岸边，两岗间一高台地为中部区，群众称此地为"二龙戏珠"。

墓地西部区北高南低，总面积67500平方米；中部区总面积58800平方米；东部区总面积为20万平方米。通过调查，发现有墓葬近300余座。2008年9月，对该墓群进行抢救性考古发掘，发掘总面积1.8万平方米，清理商周、唐、宋、明、清古墓葬149座，出土青铜器、玉器、陶器、骨器、石器共275件，发现遗迹有房基、灰坑、井、窑30余处。其中最为重要的是商代晚期贵族墓群的发现。

闰楼古墓群是近年来豫南地区新发现的一处重要的大型商代晚期贵族墓群。为研究豫南地区淮河流域上游晚商文化及淮夷集团的政治、经济、文化具有极高的学术价值。

(文：河南驻马店市正阳县普查办 摄影：刘群 周育红)

86

铜鼎
Bronze Ding

铜觚
Bronze Gu

腰坑及殉狗
Dog Burial Pit

墓地全景
A Full View of the Cemetery

铜钺
Bronze Yue

玉虎
Jade Tiger

The 20 ha large cemetery is located in Fuzhai Township, Zhengyang County, Zhumadian City, Henan Province. The nearly 300 burials in it cluster into three groups in the east, west and middle. Within the 1.8 ha excavated area, were found 149 burials of the Shang and Zhou period and the Tang, Song, Ming and Qing Dynasties. Totally 275 pieces of bronze, jade, ceramic, bone and stone artifacts were unearthed from the burials. Features include more than 30 house foundations, pits, wells and kilns. These discoveries is important for the research on the Late Shang cultures in the upper Huai River Valley in southern Henan, as well as the politics, economy and cultures of the Huaiyi peoples.

竖穴土坑墓
Pit Grave

100 New Discoveries of the Third Nationwide Surveys of Cultural Heritage

第三次全国文物普查百大新发现

地埂坡墓群
Digengpo Cemetery

地埂坡墓群位于甘肃省张掖市高台县罗城乡，墓地面积32万平方米，包含墓葬30座。2007年9～11月，甘肃省文物考古研究所和高台县博物馆在此清理发掘5座墓，基本由墓道、照壁、墓门、前甬道、前室、后甬道、后室等构成。3座墓绘壁画，其中2座以原生黄土雕出仿木结构的梁架、屋顶、立柱、斗拱等。M1南北壁各有用生土雕凿的梁柱、人字拱，长方形前室拱顶且附双耳室，近方形后室为覆斗顶并彩绘莲花藻井；M3彩绘照墙，雕绘龙头、兽头、熊面力士等；M4前室四壁均绘壁画，人物有胡人、汉人以及裹头和髡发的少数民族。墓内出土金博山、铜连枝灯构件、铜车马器构件、石龟、骨尺等。

这批墓葬为研究河西地区魏晋时期的中西文化交流、民族融合、丧葬礼俗等提供了珍贵资料。墓群中独特的生土雕凿仿木结构的墓葬形制和营造方式，显示了其深受中原传统建筑艺术和文化影响。壁画中出现的胡人髡发、裹头等多种少数民族以及角抵、敲鼓等艺术形象，是美术史、服饰史和乐器史研究中不可多得的重要研究资料。

（文/图：甘肃张掖市高台县普查办）

M3出土彩绘石龟
Stone Turtle from Tomb 3

M3墓室结构示意
Structure of Tomb 3

M4壁画
Mural of Tomb 4

88

墓群概貌
A Full View of the Cemetery

The 32 ha large Digengpo cemetery is located on the second terrace beside the Heihe River in Luocheng Township, Gaotai County, Zhangye City, Gansu Province. Five of the 30 tombs in the cemetery had been excavated. The tomb consists of the passage, the zhaobi screen wall, the chamber gate, the front chamber, the chamber passage and the back chamber. Two tombs have wooden like beams, roof, posts and dougong corbel brackets directly curved on the loess walls, three have murals. Offerings in the tombs include the gold boshan mountain censer, the bronze tree-like lamp, the bronze chariot parts and harness, the stone turtle and the bone ruler. These discoveries are valuable for the research on cultural communication, ethnic groups integration and funeral custom in the Wei and Jin period in Hexi area.

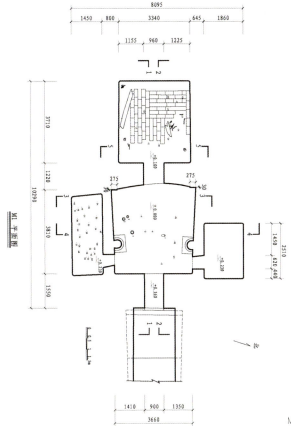

M1平面图
Plan of Tomb 1

第三次全国文物普查百大新发现
100 NEW DISCOVERIES OF THE THIRD NATIONWIDE SURVEYS OF CULTURAL HERITAGE

古 建 筑

ANCIENT ARCHITECTURE

翻译：刘红艳（北京工商大学）

Translator: Liu Hongyan

中国的古建筑在历史上多位于社会公众视线，是显著于史籍的文化遗产类型。在第三次全国文物普查过程中，新发现的古建筑占有重要的分量，它为完整认识我国古代建筑的基本文化面貌及其生存状态，科学制定其保护政策和中长期规划提供了科学依据；对于整合国家资源，促进国民经济全面协调可持续发展，均具有十分重要的意义。

与我国前两次文物普查情况相比，此次选入"第三次全国文物普查百大新发现"的古代建筑项目具有面貌全面、类型丰富、内涵典型的特点：

1. 文物覆盖范围广。此次参选的古代建筑项目，除港、澳、台地区外，全国31个省、自治区、直辖市中，有21个区域申报了古代建筑项目。

2. 文物时空跨度大。此次参选的项目中，既有春秋战国时期的军事建筑遗迹，也有宋、金、元时期的宗教建筑，还有明清时期不同类型的建筑遗存，纵向展示了中国古代建筑文化的发展脉络。

3. 文物类型丰富。乡土建筑、文化景观、文化线路、文化空间、老字号等这些在前两次全国文物普查中被忽视的新增文化遗产类型，在此次普查中得到了充分重视。此次参选的古代建筑项目，包括医院建筑、水利工程、交通建筑、仓储建筑、作坊、军事建筑、宗教建筑、纪念建筑、宅第、乡土建筑群、特色民居、壁画等十余种类别。其中具备典型乡土建筑群特征的项目15处，约占参选项目的1／3；分别代表着我国12个省区不同特色的乡土建筑文化面貌；涉及

少数民族建筑的项目约占1／3，分别涉及了藏、回、苗、瑶、侗、彝、佤族等民族的建筑。

4. 能体现区域文化的典型特色。此次各地参选的古代建筑项目，在古代分属不同的文化区域，其所反映出的文化信息，真实、完整地反映了中国不同区域、不同类型的古代建筑的历史面貌。

根据同比例入选的原则，此次被选入"第三次全国文物普查百大新发现"的古建筑为16项。

作为医疗机构性质的建筑，北京清太医院旧址，保留了听差茶房、科房、土地祠、铜神庙、医官办公东西厅、大堂、二堂、首领厅、医学馆、庶务处、教习室、诸生自修室等建筑设置，对研究古代医学科学、了解中国古代医疗管理制度与官式医疗建筑规制，均具有重要的学术意义。

水利是农业国度的命脉。明初，朝廷为安民养息，颁诏天下注重农耕，兴修水利。此次入选的两个明代水利工程——贵州鲍家屯水利工程、江苏相国圩护堤水牮分别代表了以引、蓄结合为特色的塘坝式和以拦、导、防御为主要功能的水利工程形式。

中国是一个地形复杂的国度，古代桥梁建筑十分发达。因各区域气候、建材资源的差异，古代桥梁的类型很多。在南方多雨地区，盛行建造能够遮蔽风雨的廊桥建筑。福建建瓯市迪口镇的黄村值庆桥，属于单孔木伸臂梁廊屋桥，始建于明弘治三年（1490年），它比建于明天启五年（1625年）、全国木拱廊桥中唯一的全国重点文物保护单位——浙江庆元如龙桥还早

135年，是我国现存的有确切纪年的、最早的木廊桥。

在古代中国，泛神崇拜的影响极为广泛，导致宗教建筑成为古代中国建筑的主要公共建筑类型。此次入选的河南济源市凤凰岭三皇殿、山西新绛县北池稷王庙、山西泽州县西顿济渎庙、西藏吉隆县恰芒波拉康等宗教建筑，前三项均位于中原文化的西北部，是纪念先贤、祭祀水神的建筑，与农耕文化有直接的联系；后者位于著名的西藏蕃尼古道上，反映了西藏宗教文化的融合。凤凰岭三皇殿，是目前为止发现的河南现存明代砖石无梁殿建筑中的孤例，其建筑价值不仅反映在用对比艺术手法所建造的糙砌的石墙与极为精致的檐下仿木构构件烧制与大量装饰图案上，而且在檐下平板枋、拱眼壁上还发现了以民间艺术表现形式雕刻的中华民族文明之祖伏羲、神农、黄帝等先贤教民射猎、捕鱼与生产，摆脱蒙昧、走向文明的画面。北池稷王庙，其建筑规模较大且保存完整，庙南临村民生活所依的清代泊池，池北台地建戏台与稷王殿等祭祀建筑，东为清嘉庆二十二年(1817年)的村门楼，如此完整的原生历史环境在山西省实属罕见。西顿济渎庙，据檐柱题记及碑文记载，创建于宋宣和四年（1122年），现存主体建筑保存了精美的宋金木、石遗构。恰芒波拉康，现存木构件的托木、梁架形制及其上的动物雕饰形象与风格，在目前西藏境内保存下来的建筑构件艺术风格与雕刻作品中至为少见。

与其他建筑类型相比，乡土建筑与人类生存所需要的资源、区位、气候、环境等自然要素和社会伦理道德、宗亲秩序、文化教育、宗教信仰、传统文化等社会要素结合得最为密切，反映了丰富多彩的地方文化、民族习性、生活习惯、气候特征以及时代特点。此次入选的四川犍为县清溪古建筑群、甘肃榆中县金崖古建筑群、湖南绥宁县大园苗族古村寨、广西南丹县蛮降屯白裤瑶族古村寨、云南沧源县翁丁佤族古村寨、陕西绥德县贺家石党氏庄园、广东始兴县长围村围屋等项目，分别代表了古村镇、少数民族聚落、庄园与围屋等三种乡土建筑类型，体现了中华文化的多元性。将乡土建筑纳入文物普查范围，是这次文物普查工作的重要突破，反映出国家文物管理部门对文化遗产内涵完整性的深刻认识，是我国文化遗产保护理念不断进步的体现。

中国古代建筑壁画装饰艺术始于有建筑之始，反映着古人对建筑艺术美的追求、对未来美好生活的企盼，同时也作为一种社会资料记录手段，起着历史档案的重要作用。此次入选"百大新发现"的河北蔚县关帝庙，其中的《百工图》应出自清末民间画匠之手，以其原生的民间艺术风格和手法，酣畅淋漓而又翔实地再现了清代民间百行作坊作业及其丰富的民俗与世情，勾勒出了彼时鲜活的人间。

杜启明

河南博物院副院长 研究员

Chinese ancient architecture has been under the focus of the public in the history, which is a more remarkable type of cultural heritage than historical records. A large number of ancient buildings are newly discovered in the Third Nationwide Surveys of Cultural Heritage. These buildings lead us to a better and thorough understanding of the general picture and the survival condition of the ancient buildings, providing us with the scientific basis for the protection measures and long-run planning. The ancient buildings also play a vital role to integrate national resources and to stimulate the comprehensive, coordinated and sustainable development of the national economy. Compared with the ancient architecture in the first two Nationwide Surveys of Cultural Heritage, the chosen ancient architecture projects in the "100 New Discoveries of the Third Nationwide Surveys of Cultural Heritage" displayed more intact appearances, variable types and typical contents.

Firstly, the ancient architecture projects cover a wide range of areas. The items submitted for approval include applications from 21 regions of China's 31 provinces, autonomous regions and municipalities, except for Hongkong ,Macao and Taiwan.

Secondly, there is a large span over time and space carried by cultural relics. Among these submitted projects, there are not only military architecture remains of Spring and Autumn Period and Warring States period, but also religious buildings of Song, Jin, Yuan Dynasties as well as different kinds of architectural heritage of Ming and Qing Dynasties, which display the cultural development process of the Chinese Ancient architecture in a longitudinal way.

Thirdly, the ancient architecture projects are featured by various types of cultural relics. Those new cultural relics that were omitted during the two previous national culture relic general surveys such as vernacular architecture, cultural landscapes, culture lines, culture places, time-honored brands, have drawn sufficient attention this time. More than 10 kinds of ancient architectures have been involved in the survey, including hospital architectures, irrigation engineerings, transportation constructions, storehouse buildings, workshops, military architectures, religious architectures, memorial architectures, mansions, vernacular architecture groups, featured folk-houses, wall paintings etc. Fifteen sites of vernacular architecture take up 1/3 of the involved achitecture projects, which are characterized by the features of classic folk-building groups, representing distinctive culture of vernacular architecture in 12 provinces and areas. About 1/3 of the constructions are representatives of ethic minorities, including architecture of Zang, Hui, Miao, Yao, Dong,

Yi, Wa nationalities.

Fourthly, the ancient architecture projects are endowed with typical classic features of region culture. The ancient architecture projects, which have been recommended by the local bureau, belonged to different culture sections in the old times. They are able to convey cultural context, showing a real and complete picture of different ancient buildings in various regions in China.

According to the principle of proportionality of enrollment, 16 sites of the ancient architectures have been chosen as "100 New Discoveries of the Third Nationwide Surveys of Cultural Heritage".

As a building of medical institution, the site of Beijing Imperial Hospital in the late Qing Dynasty retained various ancient buildings, such as the stand-by tea room, offices, Temple of the Earth God, Temple of the Bronze God, west and east offices of doctors, major hall, minor hall, leader's hall, medical library, errands bureau, teaching rooms, students' slef-study rooms etc, showing academic significance of studying ancient medical science and understanding the medical management and architecture construction of official medical institution in ancient China.

Water conservancy is the lifeblood of an agricultural country. In the early days of the Ming Dynasty, the imperial court formally proclaimed a notice to the public to declare the emphasis on farming and encourage water conservancy projects in order to pacify the masses and stock strength for rehabilitation. The two selected water conservancy projects of Ming Dynasty are Baojiatun Water Conservancy Project in Guizhou Province and the Water Dyke of Xiangguo Embankment in Jiangsu Province. The former stands for a pond style, which combined water diversion with water reserve. And the latter is a project whose main function is for water intercrept and defense.

As a country with complicated geographical conditions, China boasts of advanced ancient bridge architecture. Due to difference in climate and construction material resources, there are a large number of various types of ancient bridges. Arched corridor bridges which can be used to shelter rain and wind are quite popular among rainy areas in South China. Zhiqing Bridge of Dikou Town in Jian'ou, Fujian Province, built in Year 1490, the 3rd year of Emperor Hongzhi in Ming Dynasty, belongs to the type of the single-hole timber outrigger arch-beam bridge. The year of construction for Zhiqing Bridge is 135 years earlier than Rulong Bridge, Qingyuan, Zhejiang Province, the only timber corridor bridge granted the title of Key Cultural Relics Site Under the State Protection in China. According to literature review, Zhiqing Bridge is China's earliest extant timber arched corridor bridge which can be dated back to exact year of construction.

In ancient China, the extensive influence of adoration for Gods leads to the fact that religious architecture became the major type of ancient public architecture of China. This time, the elected religious architecture includes the Hall of Three Sovereigns in Jiyuan, Henan province, King Ji Temple in Beichi Village, Shanxi Province, Ji-du Temple of Xi Dun Village, Shanxi Province, Bya Mang Po Lha Khang in Tibet, among which the first three religious buildings, directly linked to the farming culture, are located at the northwestern part of Central Plains culture and are used for commemorating ancestors and offering sacrifice to the God of Water.

The latter one, Bya Mang Po Lha Khang, located on the famous ancient Fanni road of Tibet, reflects the merger of Tibetan Religious Culture. So far, the Hall of Three Sovereigns in Jiyuan, Henan province is the sole example of the extant masonry structures with beamless halls of Ming Dynasty in Henan Province, whose architectural value lies not only in the rough masonry stone wall expressing themselves in a contrastive artistic way, and in the extremely exquisite wood-like fire components under eaves and a large quantity of decorative designs, but also in the pictures carved either on square columns under eaves or the eye wall of arches, describing how Chinese sages, also named "Three Sovereigns", Fuxi, Shennong and the Yellow Emperor and so on, taught people to shoot and hunt, fish and cultivate land as well as how they made their way from ignorance to civilization. The pictures presented themselves in a rarely-seen folk art expression.

The King Ji Temple of Ming Dynasty, discovered at BeiChi village of Yangwang Town in Xinjiang County, Shanxi Province, is large in scale and preserved in good condition. The south of the temple is close to a pool built in the Qing dynasty for villagers to live by. The stage and?King Ji Hall and other buildings for offering sacrifice were constructed in the north of the pool, while the village gate tower built in 1817, the 22nd year under the reign of Qing Emperor Jiaqing, was located on the east of the pool. Such complete well-preserved historical environment is rarely seen in ShanXi Province. According to the inscriptions on peripheral columns and the records of epigraphs, the Ji-du Temple of Xi Dun Village, Shanxi Province, whose major body structure reserves delicate wood and stone structure of Song and Jin Dynasties, was built in Year 1122, the fourth year under the reign of Song Emperor XuanHe. Bya Mang Po Lha Khang in Tibet, with its wooden bolsters, wood beam frames and the image and style of carving animals, is exceptionally unique and rare among extant architectural elements and sculptures in Tibet.

Compared with other types of construction, vernacular architecture is closely related with natural and social factors needed for human survival such as resources, location, climate, environment and social ethics, clan order, culture, education, religion, traditional culture. The variety of native culture, as well as feaures of local nationalities, living habits, climate characteristics and characteristics of the times, have been represented by those vernacular buildings. Those selected projects, including the ancient architectural complexes in Qingxi Town, Sichuan Province, in Jinya, Gansu Province and in Miao Nationality Village of Dayuan, Hunan Province, Ancient Village of Baiku Yao Nationality——Manjiangtun Village, Guangxi Province, ancient buildings of Wa Nationality in Wengding, Yunnan Province, Dangshi Manor in Shanxi Province, Hakka Enclosed Houses in Changwei Village, Guangdong Province, etc., respectively stand for three kinds of rural building styles such as ancient towns and villages, minority settlements, manors and hakka enclosed houses, reflecting the diversity of Chinese culture. It is an important breakthrough to add vernacular architecture into the national culture relics survey. It reflects the deep understanding of national cultural relics management administration towards the integrity of the connotation for cultural heritage, as well as the continuous improvement in the ideology of China's cultural relics preservation.

Chinese ancient decorative art of murals could be dated back to the beginning of architecture construction. It reflects people's pursuit for the beauty of architecture at that time, and also their expectation for the promising future. As a means of recording social materials, murals play an important role in serving as historical archives. Painting of Hundred Professions from from the Hall of God of Wealth in the Temple of Lord Guan in Wei County, Heibei Provence is elected to be on the list of " 100 Greatest Discoveries " Created by by folk painters in late Qing Dynasty, in an original folk art style, the painting vividly describes the colorful life of common people and the working situations of workshops of various professions in the Qing Dynasty.

Du Qiming
Research Fellow and Vice President
of Henan Museum

清太医院旧址
The Site of Imperial Academy of Medicine in Qing Dynasty

　　清末太医院旧址位于北京东城区交道口街道。此地原为千祥寺，始建于元泰定年间（1324～1327年），明正统三年（1438年）赐名吉祥寺。1900年"八国联军"入侵北京，次年逼迫清政府划出东江米（交民）巷一带为使馆区。太医院被划入俄国使馆，原署拆平。光绪二十八年（1902年），清廷选择吉祥寺旧址改建为新太医院，医院于光绪三十年（1904年）建成。

　　现存建筑从东至西分为四路，总占地面积约7000平方米，古建筑面积约4000平方米。其中新太医院衙署的大门、正殿及两侧配殿于1968年被火焚毁，其余建筑保存基本完整。民国以后，太医院改为两吉女子中学，后为市立第二女中，其间还办过一个小学。新中国成立后为单位宿舍。

　　明、清中央级的衙署是皇都文化的重要组成部分，但至今没有遗留下一处完整的遗存。太医院作为当时全国医药行政主管机构，保存了清朝的中央官衙制度，其中的先医庙和药王庙（铜人庙）保存了中国古代的医药文化，具有重要的历史价值。现存古建筑基本完整，衙署部分虽然无存，但根据1952年地形图、1958年普查记录和有关文献，可以有效地进行保护。

（文：北京市东城区普查办　摄影：李仅录）

中路大殿
Middle Hall

中路大殿前廊井口天花
Ceiling of Middle Hall

The Site of Imperial Academy of Medicine in Qing Dynasty is located in Jiao Daokou Subdistrict, Dongcheng District, Beijing, the Imperial Academy of Medicine, originally named 'Qianxiang Temple', was built in the period between Year 1324 and 1327 under the reign of Emperor Taiding in the Yuan dynasty, and then was renamed as the Auspicious Temple in 1438, the third year under the reign of Emperor Zhengtong in the Ming Dynasty.

As the major part of the imperial capital culture, the central government office of the Ming and Qing Dynasty, however, has not left behind any well-preserved historic relics up to the present. The Imperial Academy of Medicine, as the department of national pharmaceutical administration at that time, kept the feudal official system of the Qing dynasty, in which the Xian Yi Temple and Yao Wang Temple (Tong Ren Temple) preserved the medicine culture of ancient China.

蔚县关帝庙
Temple of Lord Guan in Yu County

蔚县关帝庙位于河北省张家口市蔚县西合营镇。现存一进四合院，格局为前殿、东西厢房、正殿。正殿为单檐卷棚硬山布瓦顶，面宽三间，进深二间，前抱厦，为四檩悬山式，面阔一间，进深一间，现屋顶坍塌。东西厢房为单檐三檩硬山式，东厢房面宽三间，进深一间，供奉赵公明。西厢房面宽三间，进深一间，供奉比干、和合二仙等。

两厢房山墙有精美的"百工图"壁画。壁画为四行四列分布，每面墙绘制16幅，共有64幅图，均以墨线相隔，右上角有榜题，内容有：首饰楼、成衣局、仁义当、生药店、书籍斋、弓箭铺、银钱局、柳器店、酒缸行、读书林、剃头房、切烟铺、哑医堂、粟粮店；还有兑换金银、高唱古词、专理音乐、烟火炮铺、顽童耍货等等。其内容主要为"民间百行作坊作业"，内容丰富，画工精美、描绘细腻，是存世不多见的珍贵画本。

蔚县关帝庙创建于清代康熙五十三年（1714年），重修于清代光绪年间，庙内保存的清代"百工图"，真实反映了清代市井生活的状况，表现了64种社会行业的从业情况。

（文/图：河北省普查办）

壁画局部
Paitings

东配殿北壁壁画
Paitings of East Room

东配殿南壁壁画
Paitings of East Room

The Temple of Lord Guan is located in Xiheying Town, Yu County, Zhangjiakou, Heibei Provence. As the remaining part of the temple, the single-layered compound with traditional Chinese houses around a courtyard consists of the front chamber, the main hall and two wing-rooms, west and east.

Originally built in 1714, the 53rd year under the reign of Qing Emperor Kangxi, the Memorial Temple of Lord Guan was reconstructed under the ruling period of Qing Emperor Guangxu. Inside the temple, the artwork of Qing Dynasty, Painting of Hundred Professions, an authentic reflection of the citylife in Qing Dynasty by showing the working situations of 64 professions, has been well preserved and is treasurable for the study of Qing Dynasty from the perspective of society, politics, economy, humanity, custom, religion and belief etc.

壁画局部
Paitings

西配殿南壁壁画
Paitings of West Room

第三次全国文物普查百大新发现

西顿济渎庙
Ji-du Temple of Xi Dun Village

　　西顿济渎庙位于山西省晋城市泽州县高都镇。坐北朝南，一进院落，南北长36.11米，东西宽35.83米，占地面积1294平方米。据檐柱题记及碑文记载，庙始建于宋宣和四年（1122年），金大定二十八年(1188年)、清乾隆四十三年(1778年)重修。现存建筑正殿为宋、金遗构。沿南北轴线依次建有山门、正殿，轴线两侧依次建有角房、厢房、耳殿等。西耳殿、东西厢房均为1960年代新建，东西耳楼、西角房已改建。

　　正殿台基石砌，面阔三间、进深六椽有前廊，单檐悬山顶，屋顶布灰筒瓦，前檐柱为青石质八角柱，柱身有收分，斗拱为四铺作单杪双下昂，覆盆式莲花柱础，砖砌台明。

　　济渎庙为祭祀中国"四渎"之一——济水之神的庙宇，多见于河南、山东境内。晋城因临近济水之源的济源，因而保留了多座济渎庙，而西顿之济渎庙有宣和纪年题刻石础和宋、金遗构正殿为证，是国内现存济渎庙中建筑年代纪年最久者。是研究中国早期木构建筑的重要标本，也为研究济水神崇拜的分布范围和传神形态提供了重要资料。

（文：山西省普查办　摄影：王鹏飞）

100

正殿次间角柱题记
Inscriptions on the Column of the Post

正殿檐柱题记
Inscriptions on the Column of the Eaves

正殿
Main Hall

The Ji-du Temple of Xi Dun Village is situated in a town of Zezhou County in Jincheng, Shanxi Province, Ji-du temple sits on the north and faces south, with only one courtyard covering 1,294 square meters. According to inscriptions on the column of the eaves and record of the epigraphs, this temple was originally built in Year 1122, the 4th year under the reign of Song Emperor Xuanhe, and underwent renovations in 1188, the 28th year under the reign of Emperor Dading in Jin Dynasty as well as in 1778, the 43rd year under the reign of Qing Emperor Qianlong. The main hall of the extant building is the architectural relics of Song and Jin Dynasties.

Ji-du temple was designed to offer sacrifice to the God of Jishui River, one of the "Four Rivers" in China. As the earliest-built temple among the extant Ji-du temples in China, ji-du temple of Xidun village is an important specimen for the study of early Chinese wooden architecture and provides significant resources for defining distribution range of the worship of the God of Jishui as well as researching the lifelike countenance of the legendary god.

正殿明间补间斗拱
Brackets of Main Hall

正殿柱础
Column Bases of Main Hall

北池稷王庙
King Ji Temple in Beichi Village

北池稷王庙位于山西省运城市新绛县阳王镇。始建年代不详，据庙内梁脊板及现存碑刻载，明弘治、万历及清康熙、道光、光绪年间均有重修和扩建。现存建筑为明清遗构，坐北向南，占地面积1241平方米。四合院布局保存完整，中轴线上存有戏台、正殿，两侧有东西耳殿、配殿、土地庙及门楼。

正殿为稷王殿，面宽三间，进深五椽，单檐悬山顶，东山墙内壁有大幅毛主席画像及标语，为文革时期遗存。东西耳殿为关爷殿、圣母殿，东西配殿为天王殿、财神殿。戏台西侧建土地庙。

晋南地区自古就是我国重要的农耕文化区，稷王祭祀极为普遍。该庙主体建筑保留了明代特征，且有明确题记，总体布局完整，保存完好，为研究明清时期稷王庙的建制和道教诸神的源流提供了丰富的实物资料。

（文：山西省普查办　摄影：王军）

戏台后砖雕影壁
Stone Screen Wall

正殿梁脊板题记
Inscription Carved on the Extant Stele

戏台
Performance Stage

稷王庙全景
A Full View of the Temple

The King Ji Temple is located in Yangwang Town, Xinjiang County, Yuncheng, Shanxi Province and the time when it was built is unknown. The inner beam, trictum and the inscription which was carved on the extant stele show that the building had been rebuilt and expanded during the reign of Emperor Hongzhi, Wanli of Ming Dynasty and Emperor Kangxi, Daoguang, Guangxu of Qing Dynasty. As the extant building of architectual relics in Ming and Qing Dynasties, the King Ji Temple sits on the north and faces south, covering an area of 1241 square meters. Within the well-preserved layout of the quadrangle, there are a performance stage and main hall on the central axis and east and west ear halls, side hall, Land Deity Temple and Gate Tower on both sides.

The King Ji Temple in Beichi Village provides substantial object materials for the study of the construction system of the King Ji Temple built during Ming and Qing Dynasties and the origin of Daoist gods.

正殿
Main Hall on the Central Axis

相国圩护堤水牮

Water Dyke of Xiangguo Embankment

相国圩护堤水牮位于江苏省南京市高淳县砖墙镇。建于水碧桥至亮徒门闸水阳江岸，系古人为避皖南山区洪水下泻直冲相国圩而构筑。

相国圩为江苏省最早的围湖造田工程，距今已有2000多年。外部圩堤逐年加固，千百年来，圩堤遭受到无数次洪水的侵袭而安然无恙，故有"铁相国圩"之誉称。

关于水牮始建年代，据说明初朝廷为安民养息，颁诏天下注重农耕，兴修水利。水牮上自水碧桥、下至大花滩约7公里范围内，分别布设"九牮八档"，用土石构筑起挡水之牮，从上游水碧桥始名"头水牮"，其后称二水牮、三水牮等，各牮间距150～200余米不等，除分水牮外，其他规模逐渐小于头水牮。

头水牮，呈圆形，残高2.5米，平面纵横长16.5米，三面分别用长0.82米、宽0.32米、厚0.16米的青石块构筑，中间堆土。

分水牮，沿相国圩外的水阳江中，用青石外砌，高3.5米、宽约20余米，内填土层，形呈鱼嘴长条形，俗称"鳡鱼咀"。上游设分水尖，其作用是将上游江水分为二股，左入水阳江下泄，右归县内狮树，双桥渡至县城南官溪河段通航灌溉。

水牮作为古代防洪工程已不多见，更不为后人所知。相国圩护堤水牮对研究古代护堤治水，具有重要的意义。

（文：江苏省普查办　图：南京市高淳县普查办）

二水牮
The Second Dyke

头水牮
The First Dyke

鳡鱼嘴分水牮
Water-retaining Dyke

The Water Dyke of Xiangguo Embankment is situated in Zhuanqiang Town, Gaochun County ,Nanjing City of Jiangsu Province, the dyke stretches itself from Shuibi Bridge to Liangtu Sluice Gate on the bank of Shuiyang River. The dyke was constructed to prevent the flood rushing down from mountainous areas of south Anhui which posed threat to Xiangguo Embankment which was the first dam built in lakes to reclaim cultivated land in Jiangsu Province over 2000 years ago. The dyke was said to have been built aiming at rehabilitating people and contributing to the construction of water conservancy projects by the government of early Ming Dynasty. Within the distance of 7 kilometers from Shuibi Bridge to Dahua Beach, "Nine Dykes and Eight Shields "were set up. The water-retaining structure was made up of mud and stone with the range interval distance ranging from 150 meters to 200 meters. Water dykes, as an ancient flood control installation, are rarely seen in west Gaochun County, which belongs to water network region. Therefore, its preservation is of great significance to the research of ancient flood control by means of dams and dykes.

第三次全国文物普查百大新发现

相国圩
Xiangguo Embankment

黄村值庆桥
Zhiqing Bridge of Huang Village

黄村值庆桥位于福建省南平建瓯市迪口镇。明弘治三年（1490年）始建，最近一次大修为1954年，但整体结构基本保存了原貌。

桥为南北走向，单孔木伸臂梁廊屋桥。桥长30米、宽6米，桥面距水面高3米，跨径6.5米，占地面积180平方米。桥北端大部分建在硬地上，两侧桥台为块石垒砌，上铺井字形圆木，逐层出挑向河面中心延伸，以减小两墩之间的间距，最后铺长圆木连接两墩；桥面木板铺设，上覆廊屋。廊屋为重檐悬山顶，面阔八间，进深四柱，抬梁减中柱，中间三间屋顶高于两侧，形成重檐，檐下设风雨挡板。左侧加边廊，右侧尽间兼作过路方亭使用。廊屋用柱41根，两侧设栏杆和休憩长凳，中有神龛，两端靠下游处做木橱存放当地先民的尸骨罐。

该桥廊屋藻井内斗拱层层叠叠，装饰简洁、粗壮有力，很有美感。廊屋梁架处作大量粗大的丁字形斗拱，尤其是桥正中间平板天花饰彩绘图案，大梁皮下墨书："大明弘治三年岁次"。该桥是国内现存年代较早的梁式廊桥之一，建造方式上沿用了宋代营造法式做法，对研究福建省明代建筑、梁式木廊桥的演变有着重要意义。

（文：福建省普查办　摄影：唐瑞荣）

廊屋木结构
Wooden Frames of the Porch

值庆桥全景
A Full View of the Bridge

106

桥面
Surface of the Bridge

第三次全国文物普查百大新发现

Zhiqing Bridge of Huang Village is located in Dikou Town in Jian'ou, Fujian Province. It dates back to Year 1490, the 3rd year of Emperor Hongzhi in Ming Dynasty. Although the bridge had its latest overhaul in 1954, the overall structure of which remains unchanged in general. Running north and south, the 30-meter-long, 6-meter-wide bridge belongs to the single-hole timber outrigger arch-beam bridge. Under the caisson are corbel archs made layer upon layer and a large number of massive T-shaped corbel brackets have been built on the wooden frames of the porch. As an early-built arch-beam bridges among the extant ones, its construction follows the authentic architectural style of Song dynasty, which renders it a significant role in the study of architecture of Ming dynasty in Fujian Province and the evolution of timber arch-beam bridges.

廊屋藻井
Caisson of the Porch

凤凰岭三皇殿
Hall of Three Sovereigns on Phoneix Mountain

凤凰岭三皇殿位于河南省济源市五龙口镇，为明代道教建筑。

三皇殿面阔三间，进深一间，系单檐歇山无梁殿建筑，灰色筒板瓦覆顶。斗拱、大额枋、平板枋、檐檩等皆为砖石制作。在前檐平板枋上有凤凰、云纹、人物、禽兽等砖雕图案，东西稍间平板枋上所砌砖雕表现为"射猎"、"捕鱼"等生活场面。殿内放置的五个供案由硕大的青石凿成，并细线阴刻有人物、云龙、缠枝花卉、凤鸟等图案。殿前现存碑刻记载，明万历十三年（1585年）、崇祯十年（1637年）曾对三皇殿进行过重修。另在屋顶正脊上有"大明嘉靖三十四年（1555年）石殿一所"的题款，也佐证了该殿的建筑时代。

三皇殿属典型的中原地区明代中期地方建筑手法"无梁殿式建筑"。檐下斗拱、拱眼壁、大额枋、平板枋、挑檐檩、檐椽、飞椽、角梁、耍头等砖雕图案精美，在河南现存明代砖石无梁殿建筑中保留较少。该殿的斗拱形制、檩、椽、枋等结构特征均符合中原地区明代中期地方建筑做法，是研究中原地区、特别是研究河南省明代地方建筑手法的珍贵实物资料。

（文：河南济源市普查办　摄影：陈良军）

前檐东部
East of the Front Eaves

前檐斗拱
Brackets of the Front Eaves

远眺三皇殿
A Distant View of the Hall

三皇殿正面
The Hall

Hall of Three Sovereigns, a Taoist construction in Ming Dynasty, is situated on the top of Phoneix Mountain in Wulongkou Town, Jiyuan, Henan Province. With three wide rooms and one long room, it is a beamless-hall building of a single eave, with gable and hip roof with gray tube slate on rooftop. The Hall adopts the architecture style of beamless halls which was a representative style in the Central Plains region of the Mid-Ming Dynasty. There are brackets, buttresses, big architraves, square architraves, projecting eaves, eave-rafters, flying-rafters, cantilevered corner beams, and locusthead-shaped archs under the eaves, which are delicate in design. Due to their rareness in existing beamless halls of Ming Dynasty in Henan Province, the tile carvings are of great value in architecture and art.

前檐从东向西
East to West of the Front Eaves

大园苗族古村寨
Ancient Building Complex in Dayuan Miao Village

　　大园苗族古村寨位于湖南省邵阳市绥宁县关峡苗族乡。村寨占地面积6平方公里，是一个典型的苗族集聚地。

　　整座苗寨由四个聚居点组成。村寨内保存有宋、元时期的土地庙、嫣子屋、杨光裕墓、三公同心路等建筑。寨内有四条总长1800多米的铜鼓石铺的巷道，巷道上分布有单拱券石桥、水井、寨门、凉亭及33座砖木结构民居。现存古建筑总面积38200平方米。

　　大园苗寨始建于宋太平兴国年间（976～984年），明代初具村寨雏形，清代为发展的鼎盛时期。寨内不同时期的古建筑类型丰富，公共建筑大都完整，祭祀性建筑别具一格，防护性设施臻于完善。以民居建筑为主体的苗寨建筑群具有典型苗区特色。建筑多为面阔三间或五间、两侧厢楼布局的三合或四合庭院。内部房屋主体木构架，外观上为四向砖墙围合的封闭或非封闭式。

　　大园苗寨古建筑群历经宋、元、明、清、民国而经久不衰，各类建筑造型风格和特点突出，建筑内饰精巧灵活，窗、栏木雕花卉、卷草、戏曲典故、花鸟虫鱼等图案，构图朴实缜密，工艺流畅精致。

（文：湖南绥宁县普查办　摄影：蒋兴柏）

铜鼓石巷道
Stone Street

窨子屋前门
Front Door of Yinzi House

苗寨远景
A Distant View of the Village

The Guanxia Dayuan Village where Miao Nationality lives lies in Suining County, Hunan Province. Occupying 6 square kilometers, the extant ancient building complex, which consists of 4 clusters of dwellings, covers an area of 38,200 square meters in total. Dayuan Miao Village was first built under the reign of Song Emperor Taiping (from 976 to 984) and began to take shape in Ming Dynasty, reaching its heyday in Qing dynasty. In the village, the styles of the ancient buildings constructed in different periods of time vary greatly. Most of the public buildings are intact and the architecture used for holding sacrificial rites are constructed with a fairly unique design, with perfect protective facilities. The architecture complex, which centralizes on the residential dwellings, takes the typical characteristics of the inhabitation region of Miao Nationality.

窨子屋山墙
Gable of Yinzi House

民居山墙翘角
Gable of Dwellings

长围村围屋
Hakka Enclosed Houses in Changwei Village

长围村围屋位于广东省韶关市始兴县罗坝镇。由围楼和民居组成，坐北向南，建于清代。面阔52米，进深92.2米。围楼呈长方形，四层高15米。门楣有"人文蔚起"，大清咸丰五年（1855年）乙卯岁柱吉旦曾盛堂立。整座民居河石瓦木构筑。围内中间天井，二层四周出靠栏（走廊），有木梯可登楼。围墙牢固结实，底层外墙厚1米。民居青砖瓦木构筑，中间祖堂，三厅二井；两侧民居，二厅四房组合；地面铺青砖。整组建筑保存完好，是典型的客家围屋。

（文/图：广东韶关市始兴县普查办）

围楼大门
Door of Enclosed House

民居全景
A Full View of Residential Dwelling

瓦顶上的石狮
Stone Lion

围楼的窗户
Window of Enclosed House

围楼围内结构
Structure of Enclosed House

The Hakka Enclosed Houses in Changwei Village is situated in Luoba Town, Shixing County, Shaoguan, Guangdong Province. The Hakka Enclosed Houses, sitting on the north and facing south, were built in Qing Dynasty, consisting of enclosed houses and residential dwellings. Rectangle in shape, the four-storey Hakka Enclosed Houses are 52 metres in length, 92.2 metres in depth and 15 metres in height. The whole construction is made of river rock, tile and wood, with a patio in the middle of the surrounding buildings, railings forming the corridor which reaches out on the second floor, wodden ladder equipped for climbing upstairs. The enclosing walls are firm, and the bottom of the exterior wall is 1 meter thick. The residential dwelling is made of brick, tile and wood, with an ancestral hall in the middle and three halls and two patios. The rooms on two sides are a combination of two halls and four rooms, paved with thin grey bricks. This whole building complex is the typical Hakka enclosed house which has been well preserved.

蛮降屯白裤瑶族古村寨
Manjiangtun Village—An Ancient Village of Baiku Yao Nationality

蛮降屯白裤瑶族古村寨位于广西壮族自治区河池市南丹县里湖乡，是古老的自然村落。现居住白裤瑶族87户341人。蛮降屯白裤瑶民与其他白裤瑶民一样，处在一种典型的男耕女织自然经济状态。村寨地处岩溶峰丛地貌，寨子被茂密的植被和参天古树环绕，房屋错落有序，多为干栏式建筑

根据白裤瑶头人黎前当墓碑文"生于乾隆五十五年，殁于咸丰"，可以推断蛮降屯建寨时间为乾隆年间或更早。寨内有古树古藤、古井、古道，村民们沿着古道到远处农作；有用石块堆砌而成的寨门寨墙遗址，寨门保存完整。分布在村边的粮仓，由四根柱子顶立，禾仓有方、圆两种，其建筑造型别致美观。总体来看，蛮降屯民居与周围自然生态环境非常和谐。

蛮降屯是白裤瑶民族文化保留最完整的一个村落，由原始社会生活形态直接跨入现代社会生活形态，至今仍遗留着母系社会向父系社会过渡阶段的社会文化信息。蛮降屯妇女精于纺织，至今仍保留着一套完整的手工制作技术。蛮降屯的"砍牛"和"打铜鼓"是白裤瑶族葬礼习俗中最重要的活动，具有典型的民族特征。

（文：广西南丹县普查办　摄影：廖丹宁）

古寨门
Village Gates

岩洞葬
Tomb in the Caves

粮仓
Vines

114

村寨全景
A Full View of the Village

The Manjiangtun Village—An Ancient Village of Baiku Yao Nationality is located in Lihu Township, Nandan County, Guangxi Zhuang Autonomous Region.The ancient village of Baiku Yao Nationality boasts of old and precious trees, vines, wells, and ancient streets and histoical relics of village walls and well-preserved village gates piled up with stones. Manjiangtun Village, with karst and peak-cluster geographic landform, is surrounded by dense vegetation and towering ancient trees. The houses are designed in orderly layout, most of which are stilt style architectures. Manjiangtun Village is the most representative village with best-preserved Baiku Yao Nationality culture.

古道
Ancient Streets

清溪古建筑群
Ancient Architecture Complex in Qingxi Town

　　清溪古建筑群位于四川省乐山市犍为县清溪镇。南临马边河，背靠平畴沃野。东汉建武元年（25年）时设清溪驿，唐永徽元年（650年）置边关军镇——惩非镇，北宋大宗祥符四年（1011年）至明洪武四年（1371年）为犍为县治所，清末民初发展成远近闻名的商业重镇。

　　清溪古建筑群分布面积0.48平方千米，由24条街道构成。街面多为青石板铺筑。现有祠堂8处、会馆4处、寺庙3处、民居221处、牌坊1处，另有码头遗址和抗战时期国民职业学校旧址、水利设施清溪渠等近现代重要史迹及代表性建筑。其中古建筑220处，近现代史迹及代表性建筑37处。

　　古建筑群中的历史街区，具有典型的川南风格特色。会馆建筑，表现了不同的地域风格，汇集了包容南北、纵贯华夏的中华文化，形成了古镇特有的地方文化。寺庙的形制多为宫殿式建筑，气势恢宏壮观，展示了高超的建筑技艺。国民职业学校旧址，为清溪古镇注入了一段抗战文化的历史。清溪渠，是当年水利建设的重要设施。

　　清溪古镇不仅是一座古代建筑博物馆，也是一座古代社会生活博物馆。对于研究古代城镇的兴起与发展以及古代社会、经济、文化生活都具有重要价值。

（文：四川乐山市犍为县普查办　摄影：罗长安）

沉溪牌坊
Chenxi Memorial Arch

116

南华官
Nanhua Temple

俯瞰清溪古镇
A Panoramic View of Qingxi Town

第 三 次 全 国 文 物 普 查 百 大 新 发 现

古码头
Ancient Pier

The Qingxi Ancient Architecture Complex is located in Qianwei County, Leshan City, Sichuan Province and most of the extant buildings date back to the period from Ming Dynasty to Republic of China. Covering an area of 0.48 square kilometres and being composed of 24 streets most of which are paved with grey stone slates, the complex, according to an overall survey, consists of 257 certified immovable historical relics, 8 ancestral halls, 4 guild halls, 3 temples, 221 residential dwellings and one memorial arch. Besides, there are many significant modern historical relics and representative buildings, such as the site of quays, the former site of the National Vocational School in the Anti-Japanese War, and the water conservancy facility, Qingxi Canal. Qingxi ancient town is of significant value for the study of the rise and development of ancient towns, as well as for the better understanding of various aspects such as politics, economy and cultural life of the ancient society.

古街巷
Ancient Street

鲍家屯水利工程
Water Conservancy Project in Baojiatun Village

鲍家屯水利工程位于贵州省安顺市西秀区大西桥镇。始建于明洪武二年（1369年），距今已有630余年，属引蓄结合的塘坝式水利设施。它由横坝、顺坝和高低龙口组成，可以满足丰水与枯水期的引水、水量调节等需求，整个工程系统布局合理，设施简洁且功能完备。除灌溉外还有供水、排洪、水力利用等功能，使鲍家屯具有便利的农业与生活用水、粮食加工等条件。

延续了六百年的鲍家屯明代水利工程，周围至今仍然保持了完好的自然生态环境，绝无刀劈斧砍的痕迹。尤其是小青山脚下的回龙坝采用在水利工程较少见的"S"形坝，不但降低了洪水的冲击力，降低了洪涝灾害的危害，而且极具美感。这里也体现出鲍家屯村所具有的另一主要环境特色，即将江南神韵的"水口园林"结合到村落传统的入口区，达成山水、田园融为一体，园林、村落相互印衬。此外，在恬静的田园风光里，利用村落四周山林和自然水体组成的防卫体系巧妙地嵌入其间，景观内涵由此也变得更为丰富。

鲍家屯兼具水利工程遗产和农业文化遗产的双重属性。它是我国民间组织修建的、以满足农业灌溉和生活用水需求的农田水利设施。它既是研究我国水利和农业科技史的难得实物，也是研究我国农耕文化传播、演变和发展的重要物证。

（文/图：贵州安顺市西秀区普查办）

小青山—回龙坝
Xiaoqingshan-Huilong Dam

碉楼
Diaolou

118

鸟瞰
A Bird View of the Project

The Baojia Village Water Conservancy Project, dating back more than 630 years, was built in Year 1369, the second year under the reign of Ming Emperor Hongwu. Located in Daxiqiao Town, Xixiu District, Anshun, Guizhou Province, the water conservancy project adopts the dam-type irrigation system which combines the draining and the storage of water resources. It consists of transverse work, longitudinal dike and the top and bottom closure gap so as to be functional both in water diversion and in water regulation during wet and dry seasons. The whole project system is designed with reasonable layout, simple facilities with perfect functions. It could not only make contribution to irrigation but also several other goals such as water supply, flood drainage and hydraulic utilization. The project now provides material data for Chinese water conservancy and agricultural science and technology history.

大坝
Dam

翁丁佤族古村寨

The Vanacular Architecture Complex of Wa Nationality Group in Wengding Village

翁丁佤族古村寨位于云南省临沧市沧源佤族自治县勐角乡。地处云南省滇西南中缅边境走廊，始建于清代，世居民族为佤族，全村共有98户，距今已有350多年的历史。村落中还保留着浓厚的原始社会公社残余形态，沿袭佤族父系氏族时期的头人制，同时具有从原始公有制向私有制过渡的特征，沿袭了古老的生产生活方式及古老的民居建筑形式。

村道
Street of the Village

整个村落由"干栏式"建筑及寨门、寨桩、粮仓房、神林、图腾柱、撒拉房、祭祀房、木鼓房、剽牛桩、牛头桩等组成，寨内设有佤王府、民俗陈列室等，是佤族传统建筑风格保留最完整的原始村落。民居建筑风格统一，错落有致。材料均就地取材，结构多采用人字木架，屋顶多为歇山顶或四面坡，民居平面布局多为长方形，竹木结构，屋顶有草片铺盖，竹篱笆护墙、竹篱笆地板，利于排水通风散热，适宜当地气候。村寨中的围墙和道路均用石块垒砌、铺垫。翁丁佤族保留了较为原始的的农耕文化。

翁丁佤族古村寨是佤族传统历史文化的生态博物馆，是研究佤族文化、佤族历史乃至远古人类社会的活化石。

（文：云南临沧市文物管理所　摄影：邱开卫）

古村寨远景
A Distant View of the Village

俯瞰古村寨
A Panoramic View of the Village

村内寨桩
Stockades of the Village

The Weng-ding Village is located in Mengjiao Township, Cangyuan Wa Nationality Autonomous County, Lincang, Yunnan Province. The construction of the village began in Qing Dynasty. Following the Headman System in the paternal clan society, the village, at the same time, displays the changes in the transition from the primitive public ownership to the private ownership. Traditional life styles, modes of production as well as the ancient dwellings are remained in the village. The whole village consists of stilted architectural Vanacular complex and the gate and the stockades of the village, the granary, the magic woods, the totem poles, Sa-La House (a house symbolizing love in Wa ethnic minority group), sacrifice chambers, houses for wood drum, the sacrifice poles used for killing bulls and hanging bulls' heads and so on. Besides, there is an Imperial Mansion for the emperors of Wa Nationality in the village. As the best and intactly-preserved primitive village constructed in the traditional architectural style of Wa Nationality, Wending Village is deemed as the living fossil for the study of the culture and history of Wa ethnic minority group, or even of the primitive human society.

恰芒波拉康
Bya Mang Po Lha Khang

恰芒波拉康位于西藏自治区日喀则地区吉隆县差那乡。相传，最初的建筑是由藏医大师新宇拓·云登贡波（1126～1201年）出资，恰芒波地方的恰·桑杰噶玛伏藏师修建。从现存木构架雕刻看，具有12～13世纪时期的风格特征。原佛堂建筑为二层，经堂为一层。佛堂一层屋顶上仍残存有夯墙残断。

现存恰芒波拉康建筑以东西向分布，主要由一座殿堂、两间储藏室和一间厨房组成，建筑分布面积558平方米，门向正东。殿堂由后庭佛堂（主供殿）及前庭经堂（集会殿）构成。后庭佛堂前接经堂，佛堂后墙的里侧一半、左侧及其向东延伸至经堂内长5米的墙体、以及正门两侧墙保持有最初建筑的夯土墙。另外，经堂左侧靠近东北角处，也残存有长3.6米的一段夯土墙。现存两间储藏室当为文革后重修，厨房接建于大殿东南角。

恰芒波拉康的形制布局与初建时有了一些改变，但建筑内的木构件特征显示出其修建年代的久远。现存木构件的托木形制与风格、托木枋椽之上及门楣部位出檐木质卧狮等构架的整体形式，与吉隆县宗噶镇卓玛拉康、宗噶曲德寺的建筑构件形式均有着相似之处。目前西藏地区除了拉萨大昭寺、吉隆卓玛拉康、宗嘎曲德寺以外，其他地区的古建筑中很难见到保存如此好的木构架。

（文：西藏自治区普查办 摄影：达次）

梁架
Wooden Carving

木质卧狮
Wooden Carving

俯瞰恰芒波拉康
A Panoramic View of the Monastery

恰芒波拉康
The Monostery

The Bya Mang Po Lha Khang is situated in Chana Township, Gyirong County in Xigazè, Tibet Autonomous Region, Bya Mang Po Lha Khang, a monastery, is said to be built by a Tibetan master, Qia Sangjiegemafu, a Bya mang po native, with the fund sponsored by the master of Tibetan medicine named Xinyutuo Yundenggongbo（1126-1201）. With east to west distribution, the extant Bya Mang Po Lha Khang architecture consists of a monastery hall, two storerooms and a kitchen, which covers 558 square meters, with its door facing the east. The monastery hall is made up of a Buddha hall in the rear (where the shrine is placed) and a prayer hall (the assembly hall) in the front. The wooden carving is well-preserved, keeping the style of the 12th and 13th Century, which is exceptionally valuable in Tibet.

局部建筑
Part of the Monastery

贺家石党氏庄园
Dangshi Manor in Hejiashi Village

贺家石党氏庄园位于陕西省榆林市绥德县白家硷乡，占地面积6600余平方米。清嘉庆十九年（1814年），四世党盛荣始建，经五世阳字辈大兴土木（清道光年间），历经六辈人的逐步完善，历时近百年，终于建成竣工。

党氏特色民居，由城垛、城门、小单院、阳院、背院、上院、下院、左院、右院、坊院、碾磨院、马棚、猪圈、羊圈、草房、甬道、过桥、匾额、照壁等构成。建筑坚固，布局合理。上下相通，左右相连，属传统的三明两暗两厢房的典型建筑。

党氏庄园是黄土高原保存完整、独具特色的城堡式庄园。整个建筑群坐落在环境优美、风水宜人、地势险要的山环水抱处。根据地形，整体设计精巧、匠心独具、布局严谨。在建筑风格上，砖、木、石雕做工精细，华丽考究。其中尤以大门、影壁墙的设计、造型、图案、雕刻堪称一绝。同时在主体及局部的设计中蕴涵着家训、能文能武、期盼平安吉祥及传统建筑理念的道德风范。整体建筑气势雄伟，是黄土高原窑洞文化杰出的代表。

（文：陕西省普查办　摄影：乔建军）

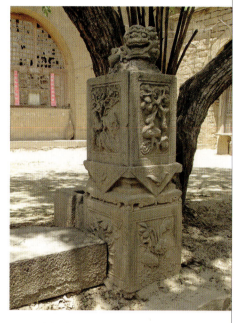

13号院右门墩石狮
Stone Lion of the Gate of No.13 House

8号院
No.8 Cave Dwelling

100 New Discoveries of the Third Nationwide Surveys of Cultural Heritage

第三次全国文物普查百大新发现

庄园全景
A Full View of the Manor

The Dangshi Manor in Hejiashi Village is situated in Baijiajian Township, Suide County, Shaanxi Province, Dangshi Manor was built in the period under the reign of Qing Emperor Jiaqing, covering an area of over 100 Mu. The completion of Dangshi Manor lasted for nearly 100 years. It can be said to be the largest, most complete, most distinctive castle-like cave dwellings made up of brick and stone in Loess Plateau. Both the design and carving of the gate and the screen wall are especially marvelous. With a rational layout, the achitecture complex is firm and interlinked up and down, left and right, which belongs to a traditional representative architecture with 3 bright rooms, 2 dark rooms and 2 wing-rooms. Leaning against the mountain, the cave dwellings, warm in winter and cool in summer, are constructed luxuriously and decorated elegantly and delicately. Moreover, both the bright roads and dark path are accessible and convenient. Following the terrain of plateau, the architecture complex is in good distribution, which is a typical representative of cave dwellings in north Shaanxi area.

8号院砖雕影壁背面
The Screen Wall of No.8 House

金崖古建筑群
Jinya Ancient Architectural Complex

金崖古建筑群位于甘肃省兰州市榆中县金崖镇，分布在内苑川河两岸的河谷阶地上绵延12公里范围内。现存主要古建筑有三圣庙、金崖驿站、手工水烟作坊（福元泰烟坊）、周家祠堂、永丰金氏家祠、郑家祠堂、黄家祠堂、谈家祠堂、张氏家祠、金崖金氏家祠、岳氏家祠、白马庙、雷祖庙、关帝庙、翠英寺、龙王庙等16处，集中分布的古民居50处，总占地面积26002平方米，总建筑面积8872平方米。

金崖毗邻省会兰州，是丝路古道上货通东西的旱码头。明清以降，金崖逐渐成为兰州水烟的主产区和集散地，成为苑川河流域政治、经济、文化的中心，一大批祠堂、庙宇、驿站、会馆和四合院等建筑也随之诞生。现存古建筑及民居群多建于清晚期；新中国成立后，所有祠堂、庙宇、驿站等均收归国家或集体所有，曾一度成为政府机构的用房；改革开放以来，政府机构逐渐迁至新址，原有建筑移交由所在地村委会管理。所有古建筑依旧保持原貌，至今保存相对完好。金崖古建筑及民居群较为全面地反映了西北地区丝路古镇所特有的地域文化。

（文/图：甘肃兰州市榆中县普查办）

三圣殿献殿木雕梁架
Wooden Carving of Sanshengdian

三圣殿戏楼
Opera Tower of
Sanshengdian

三圣殿献殿正面
Main Hall of Sanshengdian

第三次全国文物普查百大新发现

The Jinya Ancient Architectural Complex is located in Jinya Town, Yuzhong County, Lanzhou, Gansu Province, scattering along terraces on both sides of Yuanchuan River covering an area of 12 kilometers, the extant ancient achitecture was mostly built in the late Qing Dynasty, with 16 ancient buildings and 50 densely-distributed ancient residential dwellings. Jinya, as an on-land-dock which connected the west and the east on ancient Silk Road, gradually became the main producing area and distributing center of Lanzhou hookah as time went on. Jinya ancient architectural complex reflected the unique regional culture of a millennial ancient town, which is of significant value to the research of the inheritance and evolution of the local clan, commercial economy, folk culture, development of modern handicraft industry and architectural culture and so on.

水烟手工作坊
Tobacco Hand Workshop

第三次全国文物普查百大新发现

100 NEW DISCOVERIES OF THE THIRD NATIONWIDE SURVEYS OF CULTURAL HERITAGE

石窟寺及石刻

GROTTOES AND STONE INSCRIPTIONS

翻译：刘红艳（北京工商大学）

Translator: Liu Hongyan

石窟寺及石刻

——第三次全国文物普查百大新发现

第三次全国文物普查百大新发现评选出的100个项目，入选的石窟寺及石刻6处，虽然相对数量比较少，但是都具备典型性，也有一定的代表性，体现出"新"的概念。

辽宁葫芦岛市的香炉山岩画是东北地区首次发现，使该区域现存岩画扩大了分布的范围，它与内蒙古、宁夏、甘肃、云南等地的岩画形成了我国一个地域辽阔的岩画圈。

内蒙古准格尔旗的庙塔石窟寺，与开凿于崖壁上的石窟寺有很大的区别，它是用条石砌筑成洞窟的造型。集塔、洞窟、塑像、壁画为一体的石窟寺，这种组合形式比较新颖和独特，目前在全国其他地方还没有发现。

云南金沙江流域新发现的岩画，是目前云南境内已发现年代最早的一处岩画。它分布范围较广，保存下来的数量也比较多，内容丰富，表现形式独特，自成一个体系，是滇西北处于穴居和狩猎时期的先民们生产和生活的真实写照。

西藏定结县恰姆石窟寺的发现，影响也是比较大的。因为西藏境内保存至今的石窟寺数量不多，已知吐蕃时期石窟寺主要在拉萨及附近；后泓期（11~15世纪）石窟寺则主要集中在阿里地区的扎达县、普兰县和噶尔县；日喀则地区目前仅在基隆县、岗巴县发现两处石窟寺，恰姆石窟寺的发现丰富了该地区石窟寺的内容，为进一步研究西藏石窟寺的发展提供了实物资料。另外，恰姆石窟寺对于研究藏传佛教后泓初期的佛教复兴活动、藏传佛教密宗发展史、藏传佛教艺术史、西藏服饰史等方面均有重要意义。

四川省新发现的两处石窟寺，有两个显著的特点，一是保存状况比较"完好"；二是开凿年代记载也比较清楚。如：安岳县的灵游院石窟寺，现存碑刻就有"天成二年岁次丁亥二月"的记载，天成二年，即公元927年，这应当是该石窟寺最早开凿时间。还有明德四年（937年）和广政七年（944年）题记。此外，它题材比较丰富，雕刻手法具有地方特点，对四川石窟寺分期断代研究具有重要历史价值。而通江县的佛尔岩塆石窟寺，虽尚未发现准确纪年，但其形制、雕刻手法、造像特征等，与四川北部现存唐、宋时期石窟寺风格十分相似，应属这一时期。另外，在佛教石窟寺中加入一些道教造像的手法，这在川北地区是比较少见的。此窟造像数量虽不多，但造像布局严谨，构思奇巧，雕刻手法精致洗练，造像神形交融，面目表情富于变化，俨然一处世俗化的石刻画廊。

贺林

陕西省古建筑设计研究所副所长 研究员

The list of "100 New Discoveries of the Third Nationwide Surveys of Cultural Heritage" includes six grotto temples and stone inscriptions. In spite of the relatively small quantity, all of them possess typicality and certain representativeness which embody the "new" concept.

Xianglushan Mountain Petroglyphs, the firstly-discovered rock paintings in Northeast China, renders the existing petrogram a wider distribution range. By connecting with other rock paintings in Inner Mongolia, Ningxia, Gansu, Yunnan provinces and some other places, a vast rock painting zone comes into being, stretching all the way from northwest to northeast, which offers precious materials for researches into the national cultural heritage and is of great value for studying the life of ancient nomadic peoples.

The Grottoes of Qing Dynasty, the Tower Temple in Inner Mongolia differs significantly from those grotto temples excavated on the cliffs in that it was built with boulder strips, resembling a tower in appearance while cave-like inside. Such a grotto temple integrating caves, statues, murals and the temple tower is novel and unique and is said to be the only grotto of this style across the country.

As the oldest rock painting in Yunnan Province, the newly-discovered Petroglyphs in Jinsha River Valley enjoys a wide extent and a large quantity of rock pictures. Its abundant content and unique forms of expression establish its own system, making it a vivid portrayal of production and life of ancient people living in the era of cave dwelling and hunting in Northwest Yunnan.

The discovery of Chocim Cave Temple also has an immense influence since few Grotto Temples have survived in Tibet and the known Temples, built in the period of Tubo, were mainly distributed near Lhasa. Grotto Temples constructed in times of Houhong (11th-15th Century) were mainly located in Zhada County, Pulan County and Ge'er County in Ali region. As for the Jilong County and Gangba County in Shigatse region, two temples have been found. The discovery of the Chocim Cave Temple has

enriched the culture of Grotto Temples in this area, providing with material resources for the research of the development of Tibetan temples. Moreover, it is also significant for the study on Tibetan Buddhism's revival in the primary period of Houhong, the expansion history of Tantrism, the art history and the costume of Tibet, and so on.

There are two conspicuous features on the two newly-discovered grotto temples in Sichuan Province: first, the preservation condition is relatively intact; and second, the record of the excavated year is relatively clear. For instance, the inscriptions in Lingyouyuan Grotto Temple are found with words of "February, the second year under the reign of Emperor Tiancheng", namely 927 AD, which should be the earliest excavation time of the grotto temple. There are inscriptions like "the fourth year under the reign of Emperor Mingde (937 AD) and "the seventh year of under the reign of Emperor Guangzheng (944 AD) as well. Besides, owing to various themes and carving methods which are of regional characteristics, grotto temples are of great historical value for studying the dating stages of grotto temples in Sichuan Province. As for the Fo'eryanyuan Grotto Temple, whose accurate year of construction is unknown, yet it shares the similarity in style and shape, carving method, and features of statues with the existing grotto temples in the north of Sichuan during Tang and Song Dynasties, which draws the conclusion that there is no doubt that the Fo'eryanyuan Grotto Temple also belongs to this period. Moreover, it is rare in North Sichuan area to discover methods used for carving Taoist statues were added to buddhist grottoes. Although the number of statues in this grotto is small, they are Ingeniously devised, with a compact distribution and a concise carving method. The statues are lifelike in both figure and manner, just like a secularized time gallery.

He Lin

Research Fellow and Deputy Director of Ancient Architecture Design Institute in Shaanxi Province

庙塔石窟寺
Miaota Grottoes

　　庙塔石窟寺位于内蒙古自治区鄂尔多斯市准格尔旗薛家湾镇，东侧紧临黄河西岸，西侧为深沟，南、北两侧为天堑。在高台地上有一座石砌佛塔。塔座为长方形，塔基长5.3米、宽4.5米。塔身长5米、高4.5米、宽4.5米，由上、下两个佛龛组成，面朝东北。上面神龛高1.3米、宽1米，进深约1.5米；下面神龛高1.8米、宽1.05米，进深约2.3米。龛额顶端有一块眉石，上刻经文。塔尖高4.5米。佛塔东坡地上依山用石片砌筑了许多洞窟式建筑，鳞次栉比，别具特色，其中部分洞窟内有精美的壁画和彩绘雕塑。洞窟南侧有一条石阶小道，蜿蜒而下直达黄河边上。

　　庙塔石窟寺建筑年代稍晚，除有在自然岩石上开凿的石窟外，还有许多石砌窟。这种集石窟、壁画、佛塔于一体的石窟寺，在内蒙古地区喇嘛教寺庙中具有一定的代表性。

（文/图：内蒙古鄂尔多斯市准格尔旗普查办）

佛塔
Pagoda

石窟寺全景
A Full View of the Grottoes

133

第三次全国文物普查百大新发现

The Miaota Grottoes is located in Xuejiawan Town, Ordos, Inner Mongolia Autonomous Region, the Ziggurat Tower Temple can be dated back to Qing Dynasty. With a rectangle-shaped tower base which is 5.3 metres long and 4.5 metres wide, the tower body, with two shrines on top and bottom, is 5 metres in length, 4.5 metres in width and height respectively. Despite of grottoes chiseled on natural rocks, there are also many grottoes piled up with stones in which delicate murals with high artistic value are still preserved well. Such a grotto temple integrating grotto, mural and temple tower is the representative temple among lamaism temples in Inner Mongol region.

进入庙塔的古道
Ancient Road to the Grottoes

香炉山岩画
Xianglushan Mountain Petroglyphs

　　香炉山岩画位于辽宁省葫芦岛市南票区缸窑岭镇，海拔400多米的香炉山顶西南断崖石壁上。四幅岩画分布在断崖石壁上，距地面高度约1米，从东向西共30延长米。最大的一幅长0.9米、宽0.63米；最小的一幅长只有0.24米、宽0.2米。四幅岩画依次为：第一幅野牛图（长0.32米、宽0.21米），第二幅鸟形图等（长0.6米、宽0.5米），第三幅以鹿形为主的图案（共20只，长0.9米、宽0.63米），第四幅鸟形图（最小有3只，长0.24米、宽0.2米）。

　　香炉山岩画地处丘陵地带，四面环山，地势险峻。四幅岩画保存较好，图案完整清晰，只有局部石壁见有风化脱落现象。该岩画为东北地区首次发现，根据岩画的风格特点及附近有香炉山青铜文化遗址，初步认定为青铜时代岩画。该发现对研究东北地区的人文历史具有重要的历史价值。

（文：辽宁葫芦岛市普查办）

134

第三幅鹿形图案（摄影：曹阳）
Third Rock Painting

全景（摄影：孙建军）
A Full View of Xianglushan Mountain Petroglyphs

The Xianglushan Mountain Petroglyphs is located at the rock cliff on the southwest of the top of Xianglushan Mountain which is over 400 metres above sea level, Xianglushan Mountain Petroglyphs lies 2 kilometres east of Dadonggou of Wujiazi village, Gangyaoling Town, Nanpiao District, Huludao City of Liaoning Province. Scattered on steep rock cliffs, four rock paintings extend 30 meters from east to west with the longest one of 0.9 meters long and 0.63 meters wide while the smallest one is of 0.24 meters in length and 0.2 meters in width. According to the characteristics and style of the Petroglyphs and the Bronze cultural relics of Xianglushan Mountain nearby, these rock paintings are initially identified as the Bronze Age Petroglyphs, which were discovered for the first time in the northeast China.

第一幅四角麋鹿形图案（摄影：曹阳）
First Rock Painting

佛尔岩塬石窟寺
Foeryanyuan Grottoes

佛尔岩塬石窟寺位于四川省巴中市通江县杨柏乡。佛尔岩塬崖壁高约25米。石窟寺坐东向西，共有唐、宋造像4龛14尊，分南北两区，相距50米。1～3号龛分布在北区，造像11尊；4号龛分布在南区，造像3尊。龛外留有圆形、方形孔和沟槽，当为窟檐建筑遗迹。石窟造像有七尊、三尊、单尊三种。

佛尔岩塬石窟寺以佛教造像为主，兼有道教造像的特点，是川北其他石窟寺中不多见的。最具特色的1号佛教造像龛，造像为一佛、二弟子、二菩萨、二力士七身一铺组合，具有唐代风格，佛、弟子似道似佛的装束，在川北其他石窟中是少见的。3号道教造像龛中的神像，形象生动，极富有地方特色。2、4号龛中造像题材均为一观音、一善财、一龙女组合，造像刻工精美，形神兼备，两龛题材相同，但造型和风格表现却有差异。

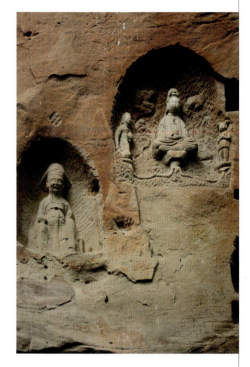

2～3号龛
Niche No.2-3

佛尔岩塬石窟寺所处位置较偏僻，整体保存状况较好，时代较早。在龛窟形制、造像式样、雕刻技法上，都具较为典型的唐宋风格。与川北地区其他唐宋石窟寺造像风格比较，也具有同一时期石窟寺造像的共同特点。数量虽不多，但龛窟造像布局严谨，构思奇巧，雕刻刀法洗练，风格富于变化，栩栩如生，具有较高的历史、艺术和宗教研究价值。

（文：四川巴中市通江县文物管理所　摄影：席凯）

136

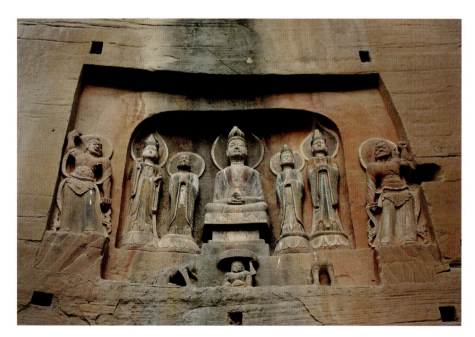

1号龛
Niche No.1

1～3号龛全景
A Full View of Niche No.1-3

The Foeryanyuan Grottoes is located on the 25-metre-high cliff of Foeryanyuan rock cliffs, Yangbai Town, Tongjiang County, Sichuan Province. Facing west, the Grottoes boasts of 4 stone niches and 14 statues originating from the Tang and Song Dynasty. These statues lie opposite on the South and North area, 50 meters apart. Niche No.1-No.3 are located in the north area, with 11 statues inside, while Niche No.4 Niche is in the south area, with 3 statues inside. Round and square-shaped holes and grooves outside the niches indicate these should be the remains of grotto architectures. There are 3 kinds of grotto sculptures: seven statues, three statues and one single statue.

In spite of the limited number of grotto sculptures, Foeryanyuan Grotto niche and sculpture are built with ingenious layout and design and skilled carving technique, with unique and lifelike style.

4号龛
Niche No.4

灵游院石窟寺

Lingyouyuan Grottoes

灵游院石窟寺位于四川省资阳市安岳县岳阳镇。开凿于五代，清代续凿。共有龛窟17个，造像913尊，碑刻题记20通。其中17号龛为空龛，13、14号和4、6号龛有不同程度的风化和毁坏，其余保存较好。

1号龛为一佛二弟子四菩萨龛，佛后壁左右各刻一飞天。2号龛为一佛二菩萨龛，共有造像10尊。3号龛为一佛二菩萨龛，共有造像4尊。5号龛为佛道合凿，共有造像25尊。7号龛为观无量寿经变龛，共有造像304尊。8号龛为罗汉龛，外龛龛内环壁刻罗汉501尊。10号龛为地藏龛，主尊为地藏，左壁刻一供养人。16号龛为观音龛，共有造像3尊。

灵游院石窟寺的龛窟多为方形双层平顶，具有较为典型的五代时期造像特点。在题记中，有后唐天成二年（927年）、后蜀明德四年（937年）、后蜀广政七年（944年）、明天启三年（1623年）和清道光五年（1825年）等。这批石窟寺的碑刻题记较多，开龛造像年代清楚，为四川石窟寺分期断代的研究提供了一定的参考价值。造像内容题材丰富，艺术风格具有四川地域特点，保存状况也较好，对于研究四川地区的历史文化、艺术宗教等方面具有一定的科学价值。

（文：四川资阳市安岳县文物局　摄影：付成全）

第8号龛
Niche No.8

第7号龛
Niche No.7

第5号龛
Niche No.5

第3号龛
Niche No.3

第三次全国文物普查百大新发现

The Lingyouyuan Grottoes is located on the north slope of Qi Zu Arhat Temple Hill at Chuanxing Village, Yueyang Town, Anyue County, Sichuan Province. The construction of the grotto temple started in the Five Dynasties and lasted until the Qing Dynasty. There are altogether 17 stone niches as well as 913 statues and 20 stone inscriptions. Most of the niches are built with two-storey square, flat roof which represents the typical characteristics of the sculpture of Five Dynasties. The stone sculpture mainly involves the content of observing the changes of Sutra of Contemplation on Buddha Amitayus, one Buddha with two Bodhisattvas, one Buddha and two followers as well as four Bodhisattvas, Arhat, Ksitigarbha, Kwan-yin and the combined niche of Buddhism and Taoism. With abundant themes and artistic style, the grotto temple is well preserved with the regional characteristics of Sichuan.

金沙江岩画
Petroglyphs in Jinsha River

金沙江岩画集中分布于云南省迪庆藏族自治州香格里拉县，丽江市玉龙县、古城区、宁蒗彝族自治县的金沙江两岸，属旧石器时代至新石器时代遗存。目前，在长约400千米、宽约60千米的范围内，已经实地调查采集信息资料的岩画有52处，约2970平方米。

岩画绝大多数绘在金沙江和金沙江支流两岸的崖壁上，离江面的直线距离在20米至2000米之间。岩画多绘画于岩厦的石壁上，内容有野牛、野羊、鹿、猴、人物、狩猎工具及一些符号和图案，其中野生动物占了很大的比例，而人物图像极少。岩画的技法主要有描绘和凿刻两种，描绘岩画占绝大多数，其颜色多为土红色。

金沙江岩画分布范围广，数量众多，内容多样，表现形式独特，构成一个完整的体系。专家认为金沙江岩画是云南境内目前发现的最为古老的岩画，它具有旧石器时代崖壁画动物种类及造型方法上的诸多一致性。也可能是迄今中国境内发现的年代较早岩画之一，它为中国乃至世界岩画的研究提供了新的范本，为云南原始艺术史和金沙江流域远古时期生态环境的研究提供了难得的实物资料。

（文：云南丽江市迪庆藏族自治州文物管理所）

丽江市树补丁岩画（摄影：和四奇）
Petroglyphs in Shubuding, Lijiang

迪庆州车轴关门山岩画（摄影：李钢）
Petroglyphs in Chezhouguanmenshan, Diqing

丽江市住古岩画（摄影：和四奇）
Petroglyphs in Zhugu, Lijiang

迪庆州德钦县羊拉里农岩画（摄影：斯那伦布）
Petroglyphs in Deqin County, Diqing

丽江市宝山达科鲁踏斜拉阔岩画（摄影：和四奇）
Petroglyphs in Lijiang

The Jinsha River Petroglyphs are centered around the following areas in Yunnan Province such as Shangri-la County, Diqing; Yulong County, Lijiang; and both sides of Jinsha River in Gucheng District and Ninglang County, which are the historical relics between the Paleolithic and Neolithic Ages. The petroglyphs are mainly painted on rock walls of the cliffs, including buffalo, wild goats, deer, monkeys, people, hunting tools, and some symbols and patterns. Drawing and Carving are two major types of techniques in rock paintings, among which drawing technique is applied into most rock paintings with the color soil red. Experts argue that it is the oldest petroglyph ever found in Yunnan, which offers precious object materials for the study of primitive art history in Yunnan and the eco-environment research in Jinsha River Valley in ancient times.

恰姆石窟寺
Chocim Caves

　　恰姆石窟寺位于西藏自治区日喀则地区定结县琼孜乡。石窟寺坐落在吉曲河西岸果美山半山腰上，高出地面约30米，崖面基本为南北走向，分布有3座洞窟。自南向北依次编号为K1、K2、K3，其中K1、K2朝向东，K3面朝东南。K1窟面阔5.73米、进深6.72米、高4米，窟内有泥塑佛像背光，残体泥塑镀金粉像。西侧有一高0.7米的圆形小背光，莲座下塑有一对背对着的泥塑残马，背光之间的空间里镶嵌有擦擦。窟顶平整，因遭香火熏黑，只能隐约看出一些壁画痕迹。正面窟壁（即西壁）共有7个泥塑佛像背光。北面窟壁西侧为双孔雀须弥座。东侧佛像背光下有似鸟的须弥座，北面窟壁佛像背光间有壁画，题材主要为人物、马、树等。K2洞窟为三间窟相通的"套间窟"，靠近第一间后面洞窟中央有用彩粉绘制坛城的长方形台座一个，面阔5.2米、进深10.3米，有4个供佛台和残佛像。K3洞窟，面阔5.37米、进深5.54米，窟顶壁画模糊不清，正面窟壁即西北壁前为供佛台座，四壁绘满清晰的壁画（可能是后期所绘）。

　　恰姆石窟寺是继岗巴县乃甲切木石窟寺之后，在日喀则地区发现的第二座石窟寺，它的发现进一步扩大了该地区石窟寺分布范围，也丰富了石窟寺内容，为研究石窟寺提供了实物资料。

（文：西藏自治区普查办　摄影：胡宏伟）

壁画
Murals

壁画
Murals

全景
A Full View of the Caves

The Chocim Caves which consists of three caves is located in Qiongzi Hsian, Dingjie county, Shigatse District in Tibet Autonomous Region. In cave 1, there is a clay Buddhist statue with background light, the remaining of which was gilded with gold powder. A rectangle pedestal, four buddha-offering platforms as well as a damaged Buddhist statue is placed in Cave 2 which is the suite cave in which three caves interlink with each other. On the ceiling of Cave 3, there are some obscure original murals, below which are murals clearly painted on four walls. Chocim Cave Temple is the second grotto temple ever discovered in Shigatse District.

壁画
Murals

壁画
Murals

第 三 次 全 国 文 物 普 查 百 大 新 发 现
100 NEW DISCOVERIES OF THE THIRD NATIONWIDE SURVEYS OF CULTURAL HERITAGE

近现代重要史迹及代表性建筑

IMPORTANT HISTORIC SITES AND REPRESENTATIVE BUILDINGS OF MODERN CHINA

翻译：聂江波
Translator:Nie Jiangbo

近现代重要史迹及代表性建筑

——第三次全国文物普查百大新发现

在此次"第三次全国文物普查百大新发现"评选中，近现代重要史迹及代表性建筑呈现出数量多、类型新和质量高的特点，从一个侧面反映了我国文物事业发展的快速稳健。

第一，申报参评项目的数量多、比例高。近现代部分参评项目有121处，除河南省外，全国（不含港澳台地区）30个省、自治区、直辖市均有参评。各地申报参评项目数量不等，最少的是河北省仅1处，最多的是上海市有9处，一般的均为4、5处。参评项目数量占全部参评项目305处的39.68%，远远高于其他类别。

第二，申报参评项目的新类型多。除了有部分项目是传统意义的"近现代重要史迹及代表性建筑"之外，有相当部分参评项目属于近20年来关注到的新类型，使近现代重要史迹及代表性建筑的内涵大大丰富，外延也大大扩展了。其中有工业遗产及附属物（老工业基地），还有道路、水上交通设施，交通海运设施，军事建筑及附属设施，文化教育建筑，乡土建筑或民族传统建筑，典型风格建筑及构筑物，名人故居（旧居），中华老字号等。这些新类型项目的名称虽不够规范，提法也不一致，如何界定尚需研究；但对新类型不可移动文物保护的重要性和紧迫性，已引起人们的重视。

第三，申报参评项目高质量的多。如吉林省辽源奉天俘虏收容所二分所旧址，是二战时期日军秘密设立专门关押美、英等盟国高级将领和官员的场所。浙江省玉环县的坎门验潮所旧址，1928年由著名天文与测地界专家曹谟先生主持选址、设计，1959年我国首次向世界公布了"坎门高程"精确数据。再如，海南省东方市的白查黎族船形屋，是中国最后一个黎族的村落建筑。

从入选的40处近现代重要史迹及代表性建筑来看，大致有以下几种类型：

第一，传统意义的"近现代重要史迹及代表性建筑"14处。有北京市建成于1918年的东方饭店早期建筑，江苏省起用于1928年的原国民政府中央广播电台发射台旧址，新疆维吾尔自治区建成于1973年具有时代和民族特色的农一师五团玉尔滚俱乐部，西藏自治区建成于1965年、见证西藏民主改革史的中央人民政府驻藏代表楼，四川省建于1965年的中国工程物理研究院旧址，广西壮族自治区创办于1951年、为越南培养干部的南宁育才学校旧址，福建省建于民国初年的陈塘红军医院旧址，湖南省见证1935年底途经新化转战贵州的红二军团长征司令部旧址，湖北省1938年初为表彰抗战阵亡将士建的武昌表烈祠、中华全国文艺界抗敌协会成立旧址，天津市的顺直水利委员会

旧址，重庆市的国民政府军委会旧址；还有上面提到的吉林省辽源奉天俘虏收容所二分所旧址和浙江省坎门验潮所旧址。它们从一个个侧面反映了与这一时期重要事件和历史人物有关的史迹、代表性的近现代建筑，其本体真实完整，尚有遗存。

第二，工业遗产(或老工业基地)14处。有吉林省奠定我国汽车制造工业基础的长春第一汽车制造厂厂址，山西省我国早期民族纺织工业遗产之一的大益成纺纱厂旧址，陕西省大华纱厂旧址，青海省英雄地中四井，重庆市我国核原料基地涪陵816工程遗址，上海市曾制造过一万二千吨水压式锻压机的上海重型机器厂，江西省有中国现代"红色官窑"之称的7501瓷生产基地，南昌新中国洪都机械厂八角亭车间旧址，贵州省清末以来保存完整酿造体系的茅台酒厂历史建筑群，广东省第一代机械化甘蔗制糖的顺德糖厂旧址；还有北京市首都钢铁厂旧址，天津市大港油田港五井，辽宁省本溪钢铁厂一铁厂旧址，上海市民生港码头等。这些项目从不同侧面反映了我国近代以来早期工业产生、发展的历史。

第三，交通设施4处。有河北省20世纪初修建的京张铁路张家口站，宁夏回族自治区建成于1950年代的宁夏第一座桥梁——青铜峡黄河铁桥，黑龙江省中东铁路西部第一座桥梁——哈尔滨中东铁路松花江大桥，重庆市见证了新中国成立后水利建设成就的南沱红星渡槽等。反映了近代以来我国交通设施某些方面的发展。

第四，交通海运设施2处。它们是浙江省浙东沿海近代灯塔群，山东省重要航标建筑青岛潮连岛灯塔等。

第五，典型风格建筑和乡土建筑3处。有内蒙古自治区见证近代中国被侵略屈辱历史的呼伦贝尔中东铁路建筑群，云南省至今保存最完整的少数民族传统村寨同乐傈僳族村寨，以及上面提过的海南省白查黎族船形屋等。

第六，还有3种新类型各1处。其一，近代军事建筑：黑龙江省的一座见证日军侵华战争期间发动空战罪行的西孟侵华日军飞机堡群；其二，名人故居（旧居）：上海市创作"三毛"艺术形象的漫画大师张乐平先生旧居；其三，中华老字号：青海省自清代以来保持着传统制盐工艺的多伦多盐场。这些新类型项目，都具有各自不同的特点和内涵。

夏燕月

原中国革命博物馆馆长 研究员

In selecting the "100 New Discoveries of the Third Nationwide Surveys of Cultural Heritage", important historic sites and representative buildings of modern China have gained much greater attention as a significant category, with a large number of nominations in diverse types and greater values submitted. This new trend, to some extent, reflects the fast and steady development of China's cultural heritage conservation.

First, more nominations have been submitted, accounting for a large proportion of all candidates. There are altogether 121 candidate sites and monuments from the period of modern China. Except Henan Province, all other 30 provinces, autonomous regions and municipalities directly under the central government (Hong Kong, Macao and Taiwan not included) have submitted nomination files. On average, each province has submitted 4 or 5 nominations, among which the largest contribution comes from Shanghai, with 9 nominations, while Hebei Province makes the least contribution, nominating only 1 candidate site. Candidate sites and monuments of modern China make up 39.68% of the total nominations, emerging as the largest category.

Second, more nominations in new types have been submitted. Quite a number of nomination files feature new types of sites and monuments were developed over the past two decades, significantly enriching the scope of cultural heritage of modern China. Among them, there are industrial heritage sites and their attachments like old industrial bases, roads, water transportation facilities, military buildings and their attachments, cultural and educational buildings, vernacular and ethnic buildings, buildings and structures in typical styles, former residences of celebrities, buildings of time-honored brands and more. While these new types of sites and monuments need further and more accurate definition, a consensus has been reached that they are important heritage types and require urgent protection.

Third, a great number of candidate sites and monuments with important values have been submitted. For example, the Japanese Senior Prisoner-of-war Camp in Liaoyuan, Jilin Province was used to house high-ranking general officers and senior civil officers of British and US troops during the Second World War. Yuhuan Tide Station, located in Zhejiang Province, was designed by Cao Mo, China's renowned astrologist and expert in geographic survey. In 1959, China released for the first time the accurate data of Kanmen Zero Datum of Yuhuan Tide Station. Baicha Village of Hainan Province, featuring boat-shaped houses, is known as China's last existing historic village preserving the lifestyle of Li ethnic group.

The 40 selected important historic sites and representative buildings of modern China can be classified into the following categories:

First, 14 are defined as typical examples of important historic sites and representative buildings of modern China. They include the early buildings of Beijing Dongfang Hotel built in 1918, the former site of the Transmitting Station of the National Government Central Radio put into use in 1928, Yu'ergun Club of Xinjiang Uighur Autonomous Region built in 1973, the office building for the Central People's Government Representatives to Tibet built in 1965, the former site of China Institute of Engineering Physics built in 1965, the former site of the Headquarters of Vietnam Central Cadre School founded in 1951, the former site of Chentang Red Army Hospital built in the early 20th century, the former site of the Headquarters of the Second Corps of the Red Army, the Martyrs' Shrine built in early 1938, the former site of the All-China Anti-Japanese Association of Literary and Arts Circles, the former site of Shunzhi Water Resources Commission, the former site of the Military Commission of the National Government, the Japanese Senior Prisoner-of-war Camp in Liaoyuan and Yuhuan Tide Station. These sites and monuments are associated with important incidents and historical figures in the history of modern China, whose authenticity and integrity as cultural heritage are well preserved.

Second, 14 are defined as industrial heritage sites or old industrial bases. They include the site of Changchun First Automobile Works, the former Site of Dayicheng Textile Factory, the former Site of Dahua Textile Factory, Central No. 4 Oil Well, the site of Project 816, Shanghai Heavy Machinery Plant, the production base of porcelain for the use by Chairman Mao, the former site of the workshop for new China's first aircraft, the historic building complex of Maotai Liquor Factory, Shunde Sugar Refinery, the former site of Capital Iron and Steel Works, No. 5 Oil Well, the former site of the First Iron Factory of Benxi Steel and Minsheng Wharf. These sites and monuments epitomize the history of China's early industrial development.

Third, 4 are defined as transportation facilities, including Zhangjiakou Railway Station, Qingtongxia Railway Bridge over the Yellow River, Songhua River Bridge of Chinese Eastern Railway and Red Star Aqueduct. They witnessed modern China's transportation development.

Fourth, 2 are defined as maritime transportation facilities, including the lighthouses along the coast of eastern Zhejiang and Chaolian Island lighthouse of Qingdao.

Fifth, 3 are defined as buildings in typical styles or vernacular buildings, including the historic monuments of Chinese Eastern Railway in Hulunbuir, Lisu People's vernacular building complex in Tongle and Li people's boat-shaped houses at Baicha Village.

Sixth, there are also three more new types of sites and monuments: Ximeng aircraft fort complex of invading Japanese army as a site of military constructions, the former residence of cartoonist Zhang Leping as a celebrity's former residence, and Duolunduo Salt Field as the site of a time-honored brand.

Xia Yanyue
Fellowship and Former Director of the Museum of Chinese Revolution

IMPORTANT HISTORIC SITES AND REPRESENTATIVE BUILDINGS OF MODERN CHINA | 100 NEW DISCOVERIES OF THE THIRD NATIONWIDE SURVEYS OF CULTURAL HERITAGE

147

东方饭店早期建筑
Early Buildings of Dongfang Hotel

　　东方饭店早期建筑位于北京市宣武区（现西城区）天桥街道。其初期建筑原由平面呈"口"字型的四幢三层楼房组成，现仅存1918年建设的西楼及1953年翻建的东南楼。平面呈不规则"L"型，砖混结构，西楼为三层，东南楼为四层，建筑风貌保护良好。

　　民国四年（1915年）在北京实施"香厂模范新市区"规划，以万明路和香厂路为中心的香厂新市区成为当时京城最新商埠、最新高档住宅区和最繁华热闹的娱乐场所。东方饭店为京城及江浙若干投资人在新市区开办的高档饭店，其地址系新市区最后一块旺地——中心广场西北、新世界对面万明寺的遗址。饭店占地约3300平方米，其建筑呈"U"字形，一半为两层（楼顶设有放映露天电影的屋顶花园），一半为三层（建有地下室，设锅炉间和库房），共约80间/套。1918年东方饭店落成开业后，与"新世界娱乐场"、"城南游艺园"一同成为新市区的地标性建筑。其客源一是军政要员，二是社会名流、洋行买办、巨商富贾、文艺名人和驻京记者等民间上层人士。每逢国会会议，南方诸省进京议员多在此下榻，一时与北京饭店、六国饭店两家外国高档饭店成鼎立之势，蜚声京城内外。

　　东方饭店建成并兴盛于民国初期；抗战期间被日本人占用；新中国成立后一直作为高级接待机构，至1986年恢复对外营业，留下了众多历史名人的足迹，见证了若干重大历史事件。

（文：北京市宣武区（现西城区）普查办）

客房内景（供图：东方饭店）
Interior of Room

建筑及庭院（摄影：杨建）
Buildings and Courtyard

第三次全国文物普查百大新发现

The Early Buildings of Dongfang Hotel is located at Tianqiao Street, Xuanwu District (present-day Xicheng District), Beijing, was initiated in 1917 and completed in 1918. It was occupied by Japanese invaders during the Second World War. After new China was founded in 1949, it was used as a high-end hotel accommodating VIP guests. In 1986, it began to open to the public.

Early buildings of Dongfang Hotel include four three-storey buildings which form a square layout. But only the West Wing built in 1918 and the Southeast Wing renovated in 1953 are still preserved today.

Dongfang Hotel is a landmark frequently visited by numerous celebrities and witnessing a number of major historical events in the first half of the 20th century. Thus, it is admired as a heritage monument with cultural and historical richness.

西楼大门，门楣可见 "1918" 字样（供图：东方饭店）
Gate of West Building

首都钢铁公司旧址
Former Site of Capital Iron and Steel Works

　　首钢主厂区位于北京市石景山区长安街最西端的石景山下，西南紧傍永定河，面积7.8平方千米。该厂始建于1919年，至今已有90年的历史。第一阶段（1919~1948年）在北洋日伪时期。1919年3月，北洋政府组建了官商合办的龙烟铁矿股份有限公司，选定石景山东麓为炼铁厂厂址，定名为"龙烟铁矿股份有限公司石景山炼厂"。1937年，该厂被日本侵占，改名"石景山制铁所"，并进行掠夺式开发生产。第二阶段（1949~1978年）新中国成立初期，恢复扩大生产。1958年结束了"有铁无钢"的历史，改名为"石景山钢铁厂"。1967年，改名为"首都钢铁公司"。第三阶段（1979~2008年）改革开放时期，具备了年产1000万吨钢的生产能力。北京奥运会前，国家决定搬迁首钢，开始了"一业多地"的生产新格局。

　　首钢不仅有高炉及配套设备设施、炼铁高炉、炼焦炉、烧结厂、动力厂、电力厂、三大炼钢厂、轧钢厂等工业遗产，还有龙烟别墅、日伪碉堡、红楼宾馆、群明湖等人文景观，展现了首钢丰富的历史、完整的钢铁冶炼生产工艺流程，反映了中国钢铁工业发展的历程。

（文：北京市石景山区普查办）

150

群名湖（摄影：马彦斌）
Qunming Lake

高炉全景（摄影：贾卫平）
A Full View of Blast Furnaces

The Former Site of Capital Iron and Steel Works is located at Shijingshan, the western end of Chang'an Avenue of Beijing. First built in 1919 and covering an area of 7.8 square kilometers, Capital Iron and Steel Works is known as one of the city's earliest large enterprises and preserves a great variety of industrial heritage sites and monuments of modern China.

Well-preserved technical flows for iron and steel smelting, factory buildings, equipment, technology and auxiliary facilities within the compound of Capital Iron and Steel Works present a comprehensive review of the development of China's iron and steel industries and major achievements of China's reform and opening up in the industrial sector.

3号高炉（摄影：马彦斌）
No.3 Blast Furnace

大港油田港5井
No. 5 Oil Well of Dagang Oil Field

　　大港油田港5井位于天津市滨海新区大港油田港东。面积900平方米，内有采油树一座，浮雕墙和简介碑各一座。

　　1964年1月25日，中共中央批准组织华北石油勘探会战，在津冀地区展开石油勘探。同年9月勘探人员在河北、天津相继打了20多口探井，仍然没有大的发现。港5井由于发大水，井场条件不具备，一直未动工。当时石油部副部长康世恩了解情况后，认为港5井不钻，功亏一篑。于是，勘探人员全力以赴钻探港5井。该井从1964年11月17日开钻，由3238钻井队承建，12月20日喜获高产工业油流。从此津冀地区的大规模油田建设展开，港5井成为华北平原及渤海湾储有石油的科学标志。2004年，大港油田40华诞之际，为了彰显港5井和第一代大港石油人为油田发展作出的贡献，大港油田集团公司、大港油田公司、大港石化公司共同建立了港5井纪念碑，并命名港5井为大港油田发现井。

　　港5井是华北地区的第一口发现井，是华北平原的第一口油井，也是新中国历史上的一口"功勋井"。它为中国石油史写下了辉煌的一笔。港5井的发掘是对我国著名地质学家李四光关于华北平原、渤海湾蕴藏石油学术观点的有力证明。

（文：天津市普查办　摄影：田继业）

港5井
No. 5 Oil Well

采油树
Christmas Tree

153

Covering an area of 900 square meters, No. 5 Oil Well is located in the eastern part of Dagang Oil Field in Binhai New Area, Tianjin City. Within the protected zone of No. 5 Oil Well are a Christmas tree, a commemorative relief wall and an inscribed monument. This oil well began to be built by Drilling Team 3238 on November 17, 1964 and produce high-yield industrial oil flow on December 20 of the same year. Large-scale oil field construction in the area of Tianjin and Hebei has proceeded ever since then.

No. 5 Oil Well was the first of its kind ever discovered and drilled in North China, contributing significantly to the development of new China's oil industry. It is recognized as an important landmark testifying to renowned Chinese geologist Li Siguang's viewpoint that there are great reserves of oil in North China Plain and Bohai Bay.

顺直水利委员会旧址

Former Site of Shunzhi Water Resources Commission

顺直水利委员会旧址位于天津市河北区光复道街道。1917年，海河流域暴发特大洪水。北洋政府委派前国务总理熊希龄负责水灾善后。1918年3月20日，由熊希龄主持的顺直水利委员会在意租界五马路11号成立（今自由道24号），负责海河、黄河流域的水利行政。顺直水利委员会成立之始，就在唐官屯、塘沽、通县、献县、大清河新镇、德州以及黄河陕县、泺口等地设立了水文站。1923年，顺直水利委员会又在引进国外技术基础上，建成了我国第一座大型钢筋混凝土水利枢纽工程——苏庄闸。1925年，编制了《顺直河道治本计划书》并主持海河、黄河流域的水利行政。1928年，民国政府建设委员会接收顺直水利委员会并改组为华北水利委员会。1949年1月天津解放后，被军管会水利接管处接管。

现旧址为砖木结构，两层带半地下室。平面呈"L"型，总建筑面积约2288.1平方米。建筑平顶出檐，上带露台，檐下水涡支撑。其入口处为三层塔楼，塔楼两侧各有一拱顶抱厦。一层阳台回廊以罗马柱支撑。整体建筑规模较大，造型典雅。旧址于2006年修复，保存较好。

1918年至1937年的20年时间里，顺直水利委员会和其改组后的华北水利委员会汇集了一大批知名中外水利专家，他们振兴华北水利，形成"大沽高程"，在多方面开中国水利发展之先河，在中国水利发展史上有着很高的地位，其旧址是中国水利发展史上的一处重要实物建筑。

（文：天津市普查办　摄影：常玉成　徐燕卿）

154

塔楼　Tower of the Site

门厅　Hall of the Site

全景
A Full View of the Site

The Former Site of Shunzhi Water Resources Commission is located at Guangfudao Street, Hebei District, Tianjin City, Shunzhi Water Resources Commission was founded by Xiong Xiling in the Italian Concession Territory during the period of the North Sea Warlord Government on March 20, 1918. This government agency was responsible for the administration of water resources of the valleys of Haihe River and Yellow River. Its former site is a compound of brick-and-wood structures, covering a total floor space of 2288.1 square meters.

In twenty years between 1918 and 1937, a great number of renowned Chinese and foreign experts in water conservancy worked for Shunzi Water Resources Commission (later renamed "North China Water Resources Commission"). They specified the location of Dagu Zero Datum, made great efforts to develop water conservancy projects in North China and launched quite many pioneering initiatives for the country's water resources development.

The former site of Shunzhi Water Resources Commission is an important heritage building in the Chinese history of water resources development.

回廊
Corridors of the Site

建筑内部
Interior of the Site

京张铁路张家口站
Zhangjiakou Railway Station

京张铁路张家口站位于河北省张家口市桥东区南站街道东安大街，于1909年9月24日运行，为京张铁路张家口起点站。站区占地面积约38.9万平方米。现存老建筑共5处，分别为建于1909年的候车厅、站台、办公用房和建于1930年代的日式运转楼和职工宿舍。

候车厅位于风雨棚南侧，车站办公地点北侧，青砖红瓦坡顶，南北约13米，东西约20米，现存建筑面积约260平方米。站台保存较好，靠北有风雨棚一排，棚顶为木制结构，前后坡顶，装饰花纹清晰可见。办公用房坐西朝东，南墙外刻有"张家口车站"字样，是张家口火车站现存的最早标志。日式运转楼为1930年代日本人所建，在唐山大地震后经过加固修缮，现仍为车站的中枢。现存的职工宿舍建于1930年代，位于运转楼北侧，为当时日军营建，青砖墙红铁皮顶，屋顶有烟囱。

张家口车站是中国近代史和中国铁路史上划时代的标志性建筑，不仅见证了张家口的百年发展历程，同时也是日本侵华的铁证。

（文：河北省普查办　摄影：刘小彦）

初期站舍东立面全景
A Full View of the East of the History Building

156

站台风雨棚（由南向北）
Platforms

火车站全景
A Full View of the Station

Zhangjiakou Railway Station is located at Dong'an Street, Qiaodong District, Zhangjiakou City, Hebei Province. Zhangjiakou Railway Station was a terminal of Beijing-Zhangjiakou Railway. It was put into use on September 24, 1909 and covered an area of 389,000 square kilometers. Five historic buildings are still preserved today, including the Station Hall, platforms and office buildings built in 1909 as well as the Japanese-style operation building and staff dormitories built in the 1930s.

Zhangjiakou Railway Station is a landmark monument in the railway history of modern China, witnessing the city's industrial development over the past century and serving as the ironclad evidence testifying to inhuman aggression by Japanese militarists.

候车厅
Station Hall

大益成纺纱厂旧址
Former Site of Dayicheng Textile Factory

大益成纺纱厂旧址位于山西省运城市新绛县古交镇山西新绛纺织有限责任公司生产区内。清光绪二十年（1894年）由新绛人李通创建。历经绛州纺纱厂、新绛工艺公司、新绛大益成纺织股份有限公司、新绛三林纺织厂、晋南纺织厂、新绛纺织厂等多次沿革，已有110余年的历史，是中国最早开办的民族纺织企业之一。

旧址坐南朝北，占地面积5万余平方米。现存主要遗存有大益成纺织股份有限公司办公旧址、纺织部旧址、材料库、晾水池、泵房、机电楼、锅炉房、水塔、八棱状烟囱、清花除尘楼等。

大益成纺纱厂旧址保存完整、遗存丰富、历史悠久，是我国现存最早的民族纺织工业遗产之一。大益成纺纱厂横跨三个世纪，涵盖了清末至新中国成立以后等不同的历史时期，至今仍是山西省重要的纺织基地，是研究中国纺织工业发展史之重要实例。

（文：山西省普查办）

水塔（摄影：王军）
Water Tower

全景（摄影：孙慧琴）
A Full View of the Site

机电楼、锅炉房（摄影：王军）
Mechanical Equipment Building and Boiler Room

The Former Site of Dayicheng Textile Factory is located in Gujiao Township, Xinjiang County, Yuncheng City, Shanxi Province. Dayicheng Textile Factory was founded by Xinjiang native Li Tong in 1894. It was one of the earliest textile enterprises invested and operated by Chinese. Covering an area of over 50,000 square meters, this industrial heritage site currently includes such historic structures as the office building, textile workshop, material warehouse, sunning water pool, pump room, mechanical equipment building, boiler room, water tower, octagonal-shaped chimney and cotton and dust cleaning building.

Dayicheng Textile Factory has witnessed different historical periods over the past century or so, including the late years of the Qing Dynasty, chaotic years of warlord battles, occupation by Japanese invaders, rule by local warlord Yan Xishan and early years of the People's Republic of China. Today, it still serves as an important textile base of Shanxi Province and provides many important references for studies of the Chinese history of textile industry.

八角形烟囱（摄影：王军）
Octagonal-shaped Chimney

清花除尘楼（摄影：王军）
Cotton and Dust Cleaning Building

第三次全国文物普查百大新发现

呼伦贝尔中东铁路建筑群
Historic Monuments of Chinese Eastern Railway in Hulunbuir

呼伦贝尔中东铁路建筑群位于内蒙古自治区呼伦贝尔市海拉尔区、满洲里市、牙克石市、扎赉诺尔矿区，建于20世纪初。

建筑群包括海拉尔牡丹小区俄式木刻楞、满洲里云杉社区二道街石头楼、博克图警署旧址、博克图日本宪兵队旧址、免渡河东正教教堂、免渡河铁道学校旧址、免渡河俄式木刻楞、免渡河中东铁路桥、牙克石沙俄护路军司令部旧址、伊列克得俄式木刻楞、牙克石蒸汽机车水塔、扎赉诺尔友谊社区俄式石头房、扎兰屯机车修理车间旧址等13处。

中东铁路于1897年8月开始动工兴建，1903年2月全线竣工通车。这条铁路的干线西起满洲里，经哈尔滨，东至绥芬河，支线则从哈尔滨起向南，经长春、沈阳直达旅顺口，全长近2500公里。中东铁路先后为俄罗斯、日本、前苏联占领、管理和使用，1952年中东铁路全部收归我国政府所有。

中东铁路既是近代中国屈辱历史的见证，也为新中国发展作出了重要的贡献。中东铁路沿线文化遗产种类丰富、数量众多，许多建筑设计精美，功能完善，不仅具有重要的历史价值，而且具有独特的艺术价值，古典主义、浪漫主义、巴洛克风格、俄式建筑、新艺术运动风格的建筑都不乏精品。

（文：内蒙古自治区普查办　图：牙克石市普查办　满洲里市普查办）

牙克石市免渡河东正教教堂
Orthodox Church in Mianduhe, Yakeshi City

满洲里市云杉社区二道街南石头楼
Stone Buildings in Erdao Street in Yunshan Community of Manzhouli

The Historic Monuments of Chinese Eastern Railway in Hulunbuir are scattered in Hailar District of Hulunbuir City, Manzhouli City, Yakeshi City and Jalainur Mine Area in Inner Mongolia Autonomous Region. Historic constructions preserved in these areas include Russian-style wooden houses called "mukeleng" in Mudan Community of Hailar, stone buildings in Erdao Street in Yunshan Community of Manzhouli, the former site of Bugt Police Bureau, the former site of Japanese Military Police Corps in Bugt, the Orthodox Church in Mianduhe, the former site of Mianduhe Railway School, "mukeleng" houses in Mianduhe, the Mianduhe Bridge of Chinese Eastern Railway, the former site of the Russian Command Headquarters for the Protection of Chinese Eastern Railway, the water tower for steam locomotives in Yakeshi, "mukeleng" houses in Yiliekede, Russian-style stone houses in the Friendship Community of Jalainur Mine Area and the former site of the locomotive repair workshop in Zhalantun.

While witnessing the humiliating period of modern China, these historic monuments along Chinese Eastern Railway are cherished as built heritage with cultural richness and architectural values.

Former Site of Bugt Police Bureau, Yakeshi City

牙克石市博克图警署旧址

牙克石市免渡河中东铁路桥
Mianduhe Bridge of Chinese Eastern Railway, Yakeshi City

本溪钢铁厂一铁厂旧址
Former Site of the First Iron Factory of Benxi Steel

本溪钢铁厂一铁厂旧址位于辽宁省本溪市溪湖区河沿街道。其中包括本钢一铁厂旧址、本溪湖"小红楼"和"大白楼"。目前，厂区内的主要设备仍然保留，是保存较好的工业遗产。

本钢一铁厂旧址为一处整体炼铁工业遗址，包括一条完整的炼铁生产线，其中1、2号高炉是中国现存最早的高炉，而本钢一铁厂则是中国现存最早的钢铁企业。现在，本钢一铁厂旧址处于关停阶段，除2号高炉拆毁外，厂区内仍保留着1号高炉、炼焦炉、洗煤楼、热风炉和除尘设备等一系列设施设备。

本溪湖"小红楼"和"大白楼"原是清末中日合资的本溪商办煤铁公司和伪满洲国本溪湖煤铁公司的办公大楼，均为砖瓦混凝土结构，外观基本保持原貌，两楼建筑面积2400平方米。

本钢一铁厂是中日第一家合办企业，也是日本帝国主义大肆掠夺本溪地区的煤铁资源的历史见证。本钢一铁厂也是新中国的重要钢铁企业，在20世纪五六十年代，1、2号高炉具有世界先进水平，为新中国的钢铁业发展作出了重要贡献，是中国钢铁工业史的重要物证。

（文：辽宁本溪市普查办）

注汽机车（摄影：于学成）
Locomotive

铁水罐车（摄影：于学成）
Tanker

1号高炉（摄影：于学成）
No. 1 Furnaces

第三次全国文物普查百大新发现

The Former Site of the First Iron Factory of Benxi Steel is located at Heyan Street,Xihu District,Benxi City, Liaoning Province, the First Iron Factory of Benxi Steel is a well-preserved industrial heritage site including a complete production line for iron smelting. It is China's earliest iron and steel works ever preserved and No. 1 and No. 2 furnaces within the factory compound are the earliest of their kind that survive until today. The Red Building and the White building around Benxi Lake, both of which are brick-and-concrete structures, were originally used as office buildings of Benxi Coal and Iron Company (a Chinese-Japanese joint venture) and Benxi Lake Coal and Iron Company respectively. Their original exteriors are basically retained today.

The First Factory of Benxi Steel was the first Chinese-Japanese joint venture, witnessing Japanese imperialists' ruthless looting of coal and iron reserves in Benxi.

2号高炉夜景
（摄影：周子栋）
No. 2 Furnaces

铁水奔流
（摄影：于学成）
Molten Iron

长春第一汽车制造厂厂址

The Site of Changchun First Automobile Works

长春第一汽车制造厂厂址包括长春第一汽车制造厂厂址生产区和长春第一汽车制造厂厂址生活区两大部分，是"一五"时期国家投资修建的第一汽车制造厂核心区域。

生产区位于吉林省长春市东风大街，建筑面积约38万平方米，内有各类工业建筑物20栋。生活区位于长春市创业大街以南，东风大街以北，日新路以西，长青路以东，以及迎春南路、迎春路两侧的范围内，建筑面积约32万平方米，内有各种居住、文教类建筑物94栋。区域内重要近现代史迹包括长春第一汽车制造厂奠基石（长春市文物保护单位）、江泽民同志居住址、李岚清同志居住址。2009年，长春第一汽车制造厂厂址被长春市政府公布为长春市文物保护单位。

长春第一汽车制造厂，可以说是新中国社会主义建设时期工业发展缩影的物质载体，是当时各项产业发展的基础。同时也是最具长春地域特色和个性的历史文化资源，也是长春城市文化遗产的重要组成部分。

长春第一汽车制造厂工业建筑物作为工业历史与文化的标志物，其变迁过程直接记录着企业的演变历史，对于企业文化建设和发挥社会影响具有重要作用。

（文/图：吉林省普查办 长春市普查办）

生活区"大屋檐"
Part of the Residential Zone

生活区"小屋檐"
Part of the Residential Zone

生产区1号门与奠基石
No.1 Gate of the
Production Zone

164

生产区全景
A Full View of the Production Zone

The Site of Changchun First Automobile Works is the core area of the First Automobile Works (FAW) invested and built by the state during the first Five-Year Plan period. It consists of the production zone and the residential zone. Covering an area of some 380,000 square meters, the production zone includes 20 industrial built structures in various types. The residential zone, with a floor space of 320,000 square meters, includes 94 buildings for living, educational and cultural purposes.

FAW is known as the birthplace of China's automobile industry, where the country's first generation of leaders and workers for the auto industry were trained and stood out. It epitomizes the industrial development in the early years of new China and witnesses the evolution of the country's auto industry.

生产区水塔
Water Tower in the Production Zone

辽源奉天俘虏收容所二分所旧址
Former Site of the Japanese Senior Prisoner-of-war Camp in Liaoyuan

辽源奉天俘虏收容所二分所旧址位于吉林省辽源市西安区北寿街道。二战期间日军设在中国境内的盟军战俘集中营很多，只有这里是专门集中关押盟军高级战俘，称为奉天俘虏收容所第二分所。二战时期日军在这里先后关押了美、英等国高级将领和高级文职官员总计34人。战俘营建在（原西安县）城北半坡之上，占地面积27954平方米，东高西低，周围围墙设有刺鬼，内有电网、铁丝网围着，铁丝网内区域周围都设有地下暗堡，地下修建有地道，暗堡与地道是相通的。正门在西面偏南处，大门口两边分别有一个子弹头式水泥岗楼。在大门口南侧，顺着大道有一趟南北走向的日式建筑平房，在东面山坡上共有3栋坐东面西的日式建筑平房。

地下室
Basement

辽源市文物管理所对该旧址进行了现场考察，对遗址的西面数百平方米的面积进行勘探。出土了5枚日式三八式步枪子弹壳、日本手雷；一些劳动工具和生活、医疗用品；另外，还发现折页、卡子、门栓、门叉、骨头等遗物。

日军辽源高级战俘营旧址是我国现存的唯一盟军高级战俘营，有着重要的教育意义。它可以告诫人们以史为鉴，反对战争、热爱和平、勿忘国耻、振兴中华。

（文：吉林省普查办 辽源市普查办 摄影：魏东）

166

地下通道
Underpass

现存平房
Bungalow

The Former Site of the Japanese Senior Prisoner-of-war Camp in Liaoyuan is located within the compound of the Command Sub-area of Liaoyuan in Beishou Street, Xi'an District ,Liaoyuan City, Jilin Province. It was used to house high-ranking general officers and senior civil officers of British and US troops. From December 1, 1944 to August 24, 1945, a total of 34 high-ranking generals and civil officers of Allied Forces were confined here.

Covering an area of 27,954 square meters, the camp is the only of its kind ever preserved in China, including such historic structures as Japanese-style houses, brick-and-concrete basements and tunnels made of red bricks.

出土日式手雷
Japanese Grenade

100 New Discoveries of the Third Nationwide Surveys of Cultural Heritage

第三次全国文物普查百大新发现

哈尔滨中东铁路松花江大桥
Songhua River Bridge of Chinese Eastern Railway

哈尔滨中东铁路松花江大桥位于黑龙江省哈尔滨市道里区斯大林街道。始建于1900年5月，1901年10月投入使用。是中东铁路西部线(滨洲线)的第一座桥梁，也是中东铁路沿线跨度最大的单线铁路桥，当年被称之为第一松花江大桥。该桥在俄罗斯桥梁专家、中东铁路工程局桥梁总工程师连多夫斯基亲自监督下，工程师阿列克谢罗夫负责施工。桥长949.185米，桥墩用花岗岩砌筑，十分坚固。1962年7月，由东北铁路工程局设计并进行该桥梁加固工程。

新中国成立后，松花江大桥不仅是滨州线的重要桥梁，担负着运输任务，也成为哈尔滨的一个著名景点。

这座大桥见证了中东铁路的通车，也见证了哈尔滨市由几个村镇迅速发展成为远东文化经济贸易中心的重要城市的过程，见证了哈尔滨市的城市发展历史。

（文：黑龙江哈尔滨市道里区文体局）

南岸西侧桥头堡（摄影：孙超）
Bridgehead

桥头堡（摄影：毕丛良）
Bridgehead

大桥（摄影：毕丛良）
The Bridge

The Songhua River Bridge of Chinese Eastern Railway is crosses over Songhua River at Daoli District, Harbin City, Heilongjiang Province. It started to be built in May 1900 and put into use in October 1901. with a total length of 949.185 meters, the bridge was constructed under the supervision of Russian engineers and bridge specialists. With piers made from solid granite, the bridge has survived attacks of several catastrophic floods. In July 1962, the bridge was reinforced by the Railway Engineering Bureau of Northeast China.

This railway bridge was the first in the western part (Binzhou section) of Chinese Eastern Railway and the longest and largest one-line bridge along the whole railway.

大桥全景（摄影：孙超）
A Full View of the Bridge

西孟侵华日军飞机堡群
Ximeng Aircraft Fort Complex of Invading Japanese Army

西孟侵华日军飞机堡群位于黑龙江省黑河市嫩江县海江镇。该建筑群建于1936年，由9个飞机堡和9个相同的附属设施组成，两个为一组，共9组。

飞机堡由南起向北成半圆形排列，建筑均为钢筋水泥结构，西侧有6个飞机堡，东侧有3个，飞机堡间为跑道。飞机堡呈半圆形，路西机堡均为北侧开门，路东为南开，机堡墙体分布有3个通风口，墙厚0.5米。飞机堡大门宽18.5米、高约5米，整体长28米，内径19.7米，每个可容纳一架战斗机。附属设施呈"T"形，门开于一端，均为两门，与对应机堡门对开，设施长8.7米，门高1米，门宽1.14米，附属设施内有地下通道，与其他附属设施相通。附设建筑用于存放配件和油料。

西孟侵华日军飞机堡群充分见证了日本发动侵华战争的罪恶行径。其具有面积大、范围广、保存好、防御性能强等特点，为"二战"历史和军事科学研究提供依据。

（文：黑龙江黑河市嫩江县文物管理所　摄影：仲建华）

飞机堡单体
Aircraft Fort

飞机堡与附属设施
Aircraft Forts and
Auxiliary Facilities

飞机堡群
Aircraft Fort Complex

The Ximeng Aircraft Fort Complex of Invading Japanese Army is located in Haijiang Township, Nenjiang County, Heilongjiang Province. Built in 1936, it consists of nine aircraft forts and auxiliary facilities.

The nine aircraft forts are laid out from south to north, forming a half circle. Between forts are runways. All the constructions are reinforced concrete structures. In a semi-circle shape, each fort is 28 meters long with an inner diameter of 19.7 meters, capable of housing one single fighter. Connected by tunnels, auxiliary facilities were used for storing spare parts of aircrafts and gasoline.

This aircraft fort complex is highly valuable for studies of invading Japanese Army's military presence in this region.

飞机堡背部
Back of Aircraft Fort

上海重型机器厂旧址
Former Site of Shanghai Heavy Machinery Plant

上海重型机器厂旧址位于上海市闵行区江川路街道，现名"上海重型机器厂有限公司"。占地面积93万平方米，建筑面积33万平方米。

工厂前身始建于1934年，1953年被更名为"上海矿山机器厂"；1958年在现址建立新厂；1962年被正式命名为"上海重型机器厂"，隶属于上海第一机电工业局。1993年起成为上海电气（集团）总公司的成员企业之一。2004年3月，上海重型机器厂更名为上海重型机器厂有限公司，由工厂制改制为公司制企业。

1961年闻名全国的万吨水压机在该厂诞生，它是我国首台自行设计和制造的一万二千吨水压式锻压机，达到了当时的世界一流水平。之后，该厂开始制造军工产品（飞机、坦克、潜艇的零部件），为我国的机电工业和国防事业作出了巨大的贡献。

上海重型机器厂是新中国建立之初的国有机械重工支柱企业，曾是万人大厂，为我国的机电和军事工业作出过重大贡献，历史上被誉为上海闵行机电工业基地的"四大金刚"之一，而今仍发挥着主力军的作用。

该厂至今仍保留着一定数量的20世纪五六十年代建设的厂房建筑和设备。其中最有代表性的是第二水压机车间，制造于1961年的一万二千吨水压式锻压机就矗立于其中，它是新中国机械工业发展的里程碑。

（文/图：上海市闵行区普查办）

172

水压机车间
Hydraulic Plant

大门
Gate of the Former Site

173

万吨锻压车间
1200-ton Hydraulic Forging Shop

The Former Site of Shanghai Heavy Machinery Plant, currently named "Shanghai Heavy Machinery Company Ltd.", is located in Jiangchuan Road, covering an area of 930,000 square meters and a floor space of 330,000 square meters. It was built in 1934 and renamed "Shanghai Mining Machinery Factory" in 1953. A new factory was built on the current site in 1958 and again renamed "Shanghai Heavy Machinery Plant" in 1962. China's first 1200-ton hydraulic forging press designed by Chinese engineers was produced in this factory. Today, a number of factory buildings and facilities built in the 1950s and 60s are still preserved.

Shanghai Heavy Machinery Plant was a pillar state-owned enterprise founded in the early years of the People's Republic of China and has made remarkable contribution to the country's electromechanical industry and national defense industry.

民生港码头
Minsheng Wharf

　　民生港码头位于上海市浦东新区洋泾街道。其前身为英商"蓝烟囱"码头，于清宣统二年(1910年)建成。一期工程有两个万吨级泊位，后又于1924年完成二期工程两个万吨级泊位，成为当时远东设施最先进的码头。上海解放后，民生港码头划归港务局经营，属第二装卸作业区。现存历史建筑包括厂房、仓库、别墅、办公室等多种类型，共11栋，建筑规模群宏大。

　　民生港码头虽然厂区本身面积并不大，但是历史建筑极为密集，每栋建筑本身又各具特色，很能反映当时历史条件下工业建筑的特点，加之厂区内还存有早期兴建的别墅类建筑，就使得整个厂区内建筑空间形式丰富多样。民生港内其他附属载体，如广场上因长期受压而产生自然裂缝的方形混凝土铺底，巍峨耸立的大型设备，都因承载了丰富的历史信息而有其值得珍视之处。

　　民生港码头至今百年之间，历经变换，是上海市浦江沿岸码头历史发展的见证。

(文/图：上海市浦东新区普查办)

174

粮仓
Granary

原高级职工住宅
Senior Staff Housing

原货运仓库
Cargo Warehouse

原办公及调度室
Office Buildings

Minsheng Wharf is located at Yangjin Community, Pudong New Area, Shanghai City. Minsheng Wharf is an industrial heritage site where 11 historic structures are preserved today, including factory buildings, warehouses, villas and office buildings. Its predecessor, Blue Chimney Wharf built by British merchants, was completed in 1910, which was celebrated as the most advanced wharf in Far East. After new China was founded in 1949, Minsheng Wharf began to be managed and operated by Shanghai Port Authority. In 1986, it was renamed "Minsheng Stevedoring Company" which operates Minsheng, Yangjing and Zhujiamen wharfs.

The factory area of Minsheng Wharf is not large but has a concentration of historic buildings with diverse architectural forms. These built heritages reflect characteristics of industrial buildings of the time and witness the development of wharfs along Huangpu River in Shanghai.

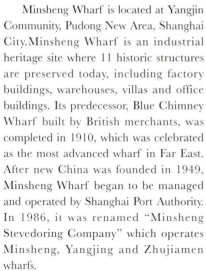

原仓库
Warehouses

五原路近代建筑群
Historic Building Complex at Wuyuan Street

　　五原路近代建筑群位于上海市徐汇区湖南街道五原路。五原路上有分量的名人故居"密度"较高，沿线西班牙式、法国文艺复兴式等风格的建筑极富特色。其中五原路288弄3号是张乐平故居，建筑占地面积192平方米，为近代独立式花园住宅，砖混结构两层。我国著名漫画家张乐平曾于1950年6月～1992年9月在此居住，二楼西房摆设仍保持张先生生前工作室原状，现为其子女居住。

　　张乐平（1910～1992年），浙江海盐人，毕生从事漫画创作，画笔生涯达60个春秋，是中国儿童连环漫画的开创者，中国当代杰出的漫画家之一。他塑造的"三毛"这一家喻户晓的漫画人物，在中国美术史上留下了不可磨灭的印记。

　　五原路近代建筑群是上海历史文化结点的集中体现，反映了上海城市发展的轨迹和文化沉淀。

（文/图：上海市徐汇区普查办）

五原路建筑
Historic Buildings at Wuyuan Street

张乐平故居
The Former Residence of Zhang Leping

176

张乐平书房
Zhang Leping's Studio

The Historic Building Complex at Wuyuan Street is located at Wuyuan Street, Hunan Community, Xuhui District, Shanghai. There are many Former residences of celebrities at the street. The former residence of Zhang Leping is located at 3, Alley 288, Wuyuan Street. Renowned cartoonist Zhang Leping lived here from June 1950 to September 1992. Today, his children still live here. The residence covers an area of 261 square meters, with a floor space of 192 square meters. It is an independent garden house with a two-storey brick-and-concrete building. The west room on the second floor still keeps the original state as Zhang's studio. Proclaimed as a key heritage monument under the protection of Xuhui District during the Third Nationwide Survey of Cultural Heritage, this residence has been used for patriotic education for community residents.

五原路建筑
Historic Buildings at Wuyuan Street

国民政府中央广播电台发射台旧址
Former Site of the Transmitting Station of the National Government Central Radio

国民政府中央广播电台发射台旧址位于江苏省南京市鼓楼区江东门北街。1931年开工，1932年5月竣工。建成后的发射台，是当年东南亚地区发送功率最大的发射台。同年11月12日孙中山66周年诞辰纪念日，新广播电台开播，频率为660千赫，被称为"东亚第一、世界第三"，电波遍及海内外。

新发射台机房为一幢白色建筑，坐北朝南，钢混结构，建筑面积约1800平方米。机房大门为西式拱券式，外墙为紫沙色面砖，高约为两层楼。现屋内保存着发射台使用过的各种仪器、设备、电缆等物。发射台院内目前还保留有配电房、警卫营房、碉堡各一、发射铁塔两座、宿舍数幢，其建筑基本完好。两座发射铁塔表面刷着红白相间的油漆，70多年过去，依然如新。两塔相距250米，高度同是125米，如今仍在使用。在配电房的外墙上还嵌着一块白色的小碑，上刻有"上海华中营业公司承建，中华民国二十年十二月"字。发射台由江苏省广播电台使用至今。

1927年4月，国民政府定都南京后，深感"主义急于灌输，宣传刻不容缓"。1928年2月，陈果夫等人提议设立广播电台，获得通过。1928年8月1日开始播音，是国民党主要宣传工具之一。

国民政府中央广播电台发射台是民国时期重要机构旧址，对南京民国文化的研究具有重要意义。

（文：江苏省普查办　图：南京市鼓楼区普查办）

发射塔
Transmitting Towers

配电房
Distributing Substation

178

建造碑
Construction of the Monument

发射机房
Transmitting Station's Machinery Room

The Former Site of the Transmitting Station of the National Government Central Radio is located at Jiangdongmen North Street, Gulou District, Nanjing City, Jiangsu Province, the National Government Central Radio was officially launched on August 1, 1928. The Central Radio's transmitting station was originally set at Dingjiaqiao. In 1930, the new radio station was built at Beihekou, outside Jiangdong Gate of Nanjing and equipped with a complete set of wireless radio devices purchased from Germany-based Telefunken Company. The new transmitting station, completed in 1932, had the largest transmission power output in Southeast Asia.

The new transmitting station's machinery room is a reinforced concrete structure, with a total floor space of 1800 square meters. Old apparatuses, equipment and cables used for signal transmission are still preserved in the transmitting station today. Within the station compound, there are a number of historic structures, including the distributing substation, barracks for security guards, the fort, two iron transmitting towers and several dormitory buildings. The transmitting station is still used by Jiangsu Provincial Radio today.

浙东沿海近代灯塔群
Lighthouses along the Coast of Eastern Zhejiang

浙东沿海灯塔群位于浙江省宁波市舟山市，由分布于东海洋面的舟山群岛的嵊泗列岛白节山、半洋礁、唐脑山、鱼腥脑、洛伽山、大菜花山、七里屿，象山石浦海域的东门岛及渔山列岛北渔山等各岛屿的13座近现代灯塔所组成。最早可以追溯到始建于1865年的宁波镇海口的七里屿（峙）灯塔。

灯塔一般由一座主灯塔和周边的附属控制、生活等设施组成。主塔为独立塔身，主体建筑一般采用定形石块垒砌，筑成圆锥形状或八角形的塔身，塔顶置镜机。

灯塔基座多由成形石砌筑成园形或覆盆形；塔身呈椎形，外多刷黑色油漆或沥青，也有通体漆成白色或白红相间横纹的外观；塔顶为钟形玻璃圆罩的灯笼，笼壁下部多为铁质桶形圆柱体，笼上部一般设八扇玻璃窗，塔身顶部外为圆环形带铁栏杆的回廊，笼顶与笼身呈穹顶状，顶正中设风向标与避雷针等；灯器设备放置于灯笼内的灯台中央基座上。灯器多为四等镜机，闪白光，周期3秒，射程10～20海里。另在灯塔周边建有附属设施与守塔人员的生活用房，以及发电房、蓄水池等。

灯塔自晚清至民国建立后均由海关管理。1949年新中国成立后，归属交通部管理，并大都改为电光源，现改为太阳能光源。1969年移交海军航保部管理。1980年浙江沿海航运灯塔归上海航道局管理，现多数由上海海事局宁波航标处、温州航标处管理。

浙东沿海灯塔，是中国开埠通商的重要见证之一，是中西文化交流与海上交通运输的重要标志，是近现代海洋文化与海事科技发展的见证，是中国近现代海上交通避险保航的重要保障设施。

（文：浙江宁波市文物保护管理所　图：宁波市江北区文管所　宁波市航标处　宁波市文管所）

180

太平山灯塔　Lighthouse in Taiping Hill

大菜花山灯塔
Lighthouse in Dacaihua Hill

The 13 Lighthouses along the Coast of Eastern Zhejiang built in the 19th and 20th centuries are scattered in islands of East Sea within the territory of Ningbo City, Zhejiang Province, including Baijie Hill, Banyang Reef, Tangnao Hill, Yuxingnao, Luojia Hill, Dacaihua Hill, Qili Islet, Dongmen Island and Beiyu Hill. The earliest lighthouse is the one at Qili Islet which was built in 1865. Generally, each lighthouse is composed of one main lighthouse and surrounding auxiliary control devices and facilities for living purposes.

These lighthouses along the coast of eastern Zhejiang were managed and operated by the customs from the second half of the 19th century to the first half of the 20th century. They were put under the administration of the Ministry of Communication after new China was founded. In 1980, they were transferred to Shanghai Waterway Bureau. These lighthouses are the country's earliest lighthouses in modern sense and the important witness of China's opening to the outside world for business and trade.

洛伽灯塔
Lighthouse in Luojia

坎门验潮所旧址
Former Site of Kanmen Tide Station

坎门验潮所旧址位于浙江省台州市玉环县坎门街道。鸦片战争后，帝国主义列强在我国沿海陆续设立验潮机构，建立高程测量基准面，服务其资源掠夺和殖民统治。为了建立中国自己的高程测量基准面，1928年由我国著名的天文与测地界专家曹谟先生主持选址、设计，1929年6月11日由中华民国政府陆地测量总局始建中国历史上第一座自己的验潮机构——坎门验潮所。1930年5月正式验取潮汐资料，经多年观测，确定了"坎门零点"。1936年1月，"坎门高程"正式启用，并引测到浙江、江苏、北京等17个省市，应用于军事测图等。1948年8月，当时的国民政府国防部测量局曾准备将"坎门零点"作为全国大地测量的法定起算面，但因国民党败逃台湾，未能实现。1959年我国首次向世界公布了"坎门高程"的精确数据。"坎门高程"在国内外具有相当高的知名度。坎门验潮所目前仍是国际海洋水文气象资料交换站。

坎门验潮所作为历史上中国人自行选址、设计、建造的第一座验潮所，记录了中国人民为维护国家主权和领土尊严的风雨历程，其观测资料被直接广泛应用，为近代测绘事业和科学研究作出了重大的贡献。

（文/图：浙江台州市玉环县历史文化遗产保护管理委员会办公室）

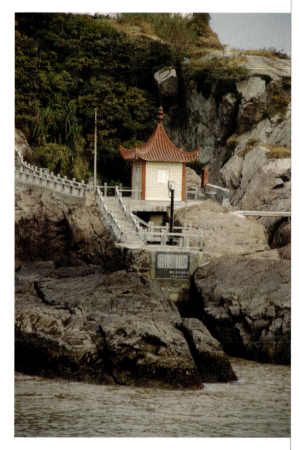

验潮所近景
A Close View of the Station

二五二号一等水准点
Kanmen Zero Point

回澜闸
Huilan Brake

验潮所全景
A Full View of the Station

验潮井
Tide Well

Yuhuan Tide Station, known as China's first tide station, is located at Changyuao, Lighthouse Community, Kanmen, Yuhuan District, Zhejiang Province. Its location was chosen and its constructions designed by Mr. Cao Mo, China's renowned astrologist and expert in geographic survey. On June 11, 1929, Yuhuan Tide Station began to be built under the supervision of the General Administration of Land Survey and Mapping of the National Government. In May 1930, tide data began to be officially acquired through this tide station. Over years of observation, Kanmen Zero Point was determined. In January 1936, Kanmen Zero Datum was officially put into use. It was later used in surveys conducted in 17 provinces and municipalities including Zhejiang, Jiangsu and Beijing and for military surveying and mapping as well. In 1959, China released for the first time the accurate data of Kanmen Zero Datum. Yuhuan Tide Station is still a station for exchanging international information about atmospheric and oceanographic data.

陈塘红军医院旧址
Former Site of the Chentang Red Army Hospital

陈塘红军医院旧址位于福建省三明市宁化县石壁镇。1933年春，原设于江西瑞金的红军第四医院随军进驻石壁陈塘村，收治在东线战斗中的伤病员。医院按职能分为住院部、后勤部、行政管理部等几个部门，另有操演场及红军墓地等革命遗迹。住院部设于陈塘村"下新屋"（张氏祖屋），后勤部设在"新厝里"（今陈塘村10号），行政管理部的位置在"修齐堂"，红军墓地共70余座。

整座建筑坐北朝南，占地约850平方米，平面呈长方形，由门楼、下厅、天井、正厅、后厅、东西两侧过雨亭、户厝等组成。在"下新屋"内，正厅楼道、阁楼壁板、横屋檐廊壁板上，共存有红军标语20余条，宣传与卫生、医疗有关的漫画13幅，并有马灯、茶钵、等当时医院使用的器具。"新厝里"内现存有石质药碾、储药罐等物品。"上新屋"内张姓人家，仍藏有当年红军医院照价赔偿给他家的一口水缸。

陈塘红军医院旧址是当年红军在闽西浴血奋战的历史见证，其建筑组群规模较大，主要建筑保存完整。"下新屋"红军医院内保存有大量的红军标语及红军漫画，内容丰富，各处与卫生医疗相关之漫画虽用笔简单却形神皆备，成为当年红军战地医院的生动写照。

（文：福建三明市宁化县博物馆　摄影：张标发）

住院部宣传漫画
The Red Army's Propaganda Cartoons in Inpatient Department

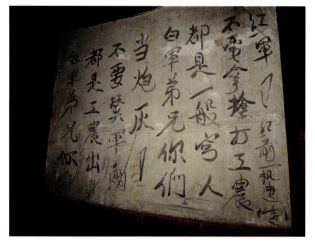

住院部宣传标语
The Red Army's Slogan in Inpatient Department

住院部全景
A Full View of Inpatient Department

The Chentang Red Army Hospital, also known as the 4th Red Army Field Hospital, is located in Shibi Township, Ninghua County, Fujian Province. Covering an area of 850 square meters, it is a rectangular structure composed of the gate tower, the lower hall, the courtyard, the principal hall, the back hall and the rain shelter pavilion. In the spring of 1933, the 4th Red Army Field Hospital was moved to Chentang to accept and treat injured and sick soldiers fighting in battlefields of the east line. The hospital consists of several functional departments, including the inpatient department, the logistics department and the administrative department as well as the drill ground and the cemetery. This hospital site is a historical witness of the Red Army's struggle in western Fujian.

住院部宣传漫画
The Red Army's Propaganda Cartoons in Inpatient Department

7501瓷生产基地
Production Base of 7501 Porcelain

7501瓷生产基地位于江西省景德镇市珠山区新厂街道的中国轻工业陶瓷研究所院内。总面积为9.6万平方米。该生产基地由指挥部（现行政楼）、艺术楼、成型车间（含原料与球磨两个车间）、琢器车间、窑房、窑炉、烟囱（两根）、白瓷仓库等8处文物建筑构成。它们始建于1950年代，均为青砖墙体，人字梁木构架，屋顶铺以红色琉璃瓦，规模宏大，布局科学，形成了7501瓷研制、成型、彩绘及烧造等一整套专门的生产体系，主要生产有"水点桃花"和"水点梅花"的文具、餐具和茶具等装饰产品，是闻名遐迩的中国现代"红色官窑"所在地。

7501瓷是1975年初中共中央办公厅指示中国轻工业部陶瓷研究所为毛主席设计、烧制的一套专用瓷器。其胎质细致，造型端庄，釉色温润，纹饰精美，集中地代表了中国现代制瓷工艺的最高水平。

（文：江西景德镇市普查办 摄影：何身德）

窑房侧面
Left of the Kiln

7501瓷制品餐具系列
7501 Porcelain

基地大门
Gate of the Production Base

窑房正面
Kiln

The Production Base of 7501 Porcelain is located in the Ceramic Institute of China Light Industry at Xinchang Street,Zhushan District, Jingdezhen City, Jiangxi Province. It consists of eight historic buildings, including the command department (currently the administrative building), the art creation building, the molding workshops (material processing and grinding workshops), the carving workshop, the kiln, the furnace, two chimneys and the white porcelain warehouse. First built in the 1950s, all these historic structures feature grey-brick walls and collar-beam roof paved with red glazed tiles. This magnificent production base with reasonably designed layouts has developed a complete production system including research, design, molding, color painting and firing.

窑炉
Furnace

洪都机械厂八角亭车间旧址
Former Site of the Octagonal Pavilion Workshop of Hongdu Machinery Factory

　　洪都机械厂八角亭车间旧址位于江西省南昌市青云谱区洪都街道，现为洪都集团公司二车间。八角亭是由意大利工程师设计的，于1936年建成，当时名为"中央南昌飞机制造厂"，新中国成立后收归国有，更名为洪都机械厂。1954年，在该车间生产的第一架国产飞机"雅克18"初级教练机秘密试飞成功。

　　该车间保存完好，主体结构为钢筋混凝砖木混合结构，平面呈正八边形，总占地面积5876平方米，上下两层，底层八边形的每边长34米，左右六面墙上开8个四开木窗，南、北墙面开大门出入。底层内空高达4.3米，以八边形中心为中点，呈放射状排列五根立柱支撑钢筋混凝土梁，形成通透空间。底层中间用砖隔砌出一中空小八边形，为二层基础。另在底层上部以八边形中心为中点，呈放射状盖有8条长形采光透窗。有楼梯可上至二层。二层原为全通透的观察监视室，八面均有监视窗可直视底层。在第二层上部还有一小层八角形采光顶。

　　洪都机械厂八角亭车间旧址的车间建筑、机器设备及周边空间是中国代表性的航空工业史迹，体现了中国人自力更生和奋发图强的民族自尊。

　　　　　　　　（文：江西南昌市普查办　摄影：周颖）

顶部的八角天窗
Octagonal Skylight on the Top

二层技术组
Technology Group on the Second Floor

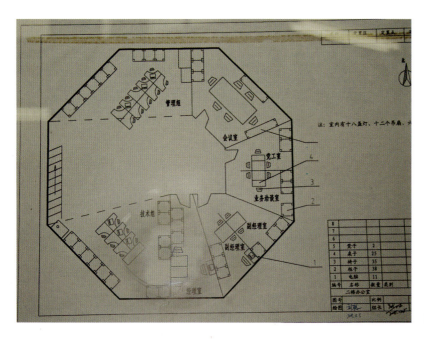

二层平面图
Plan of the Second Floor

八角亭
Octagonal Pavilion Workshop

The Former Site of the Octagonal Pavilion Workshop of Hongdu Machinery Factory is located in the current second workshop of Hongdu Group in Nanchang, Jiangxi Province. Designed by Italian engineers, it was completed in 1936. Then named "Central Nanchang Aircraft Factory", it was renamed "Hongdu Machinery Factory" after new China was founded. In 1954, the country's first homemade aircraft, Yak-18 primary training aircraft, was produced in this workshop and succeeded in test flight.

This well-preserved aircraft workshop covers an area of 5876 square meters. Its main structure is a octagonal-shaped brick-and-wood reinforced concrete structure with two stories. It is China's first aircraft workshop built on its own, witnessing the development of the country's aviation industry.

一层生产车间
Workshop on the First Floor

青岛潮连岛灯塔
Chaolian Island Lighthouse of Qingdao

青岛潮连岛灯塔位于山东省青岛市崂山区沙子口街道潮连岛。建于1899年，是德国海军在青岛海域建造的规模最大的灯塔。

潮连岛灯塔采用的是少有的建筑与灯塔连为一体的建筑形式，建筑面积约为300平方米。建筑平面呈"工"字形，南北四面石砌山墙呈"人"字形。建筑在南侧、西侧各有一个入口，西入口颇具德国建筑特色，附设九级台阶直达一层入口平台，平台下部为镂空形式，中部四根方形立柱，顶部为拱卷，与建筑其他部分形成虚实对比。整栋建筑厚重、坚固，在潮连岛的最高点上，虽体量不大，却给人以气势恢宏之感。建造时就地取材，建筑材料主要为花岗石。依地势而建，地上一层，有半地下室，红瓦坡屋顶。灯塔地上二层，为八角形石塔，塔高12.8米，灯质闪白10秒，射程24海里。

这座灯塔虽历经百年，但直到今天仍在发挥作用。潮连岛距青岛市区约55公里，周围多陡峭礁石，该灯塔的主要作用是对从青岛去上海、日本的船舶以及到青岛的船舶提供助航及定位作用。

青岛潮连岛灯塔是黄海海域最早的航标建筑之一，融合了中西方建筑艺术的特色，对于研究航标历史等有着重要作用。

（文：山东青岛市普查办）

灯塔内景（摄影：汤臻）
Interior of the Lighthouse

雾号（摄影：李静）
Fog Signal

灯塔（摄影：李静）
The Lighthouse

190

灯塔全景（摄影：汤臻）
A Full View of the Lighthouse

The Chaolian Island Lighthouse of Qingdao is located at Chaolian Island, Laoshan District, Qingdao City, Shandong Province, this lighthouse was built in 1899. It is the largest lighthouse that the German Navy has ever built in the sea area of Qingdao and still in use today. With a floor space of 300 square meters, the lighthouse is integrated with other supportive constructions, featuring an I-shaped structure. The lighthouse's built structure, against the island's sloping terrace, consists a ground floor and a semi-basement, with a red tile-covered roof. The lighthouse is a two-storey octagonal-shaped stone tower, with a height of 12.8 meters and a light radiation of 24 miles. This lighthouse is a highly artistic and practical building, providing important values for studies of the navigation history.

灯塔西立面（摄影：汤臻）
West Facade of the Lighthouse

武昌表烈祠
The Wuchang Martyrs' Shrine

武昌表烈祠位于湖北省武汉市武昌区首义路街道。地处蛇山南麓，坐北朝南，中轴线上依次为牌楼、神道、主楼。牌楼为砖混结构，四柱三门式，绿琉璃瓦顶；神道依山就势修筑，逐级抬升，采用条石砌筑，分左右两路，中间以"陛"隔开，直抵主楼月台；主楼平面成"凸"字形，砖混仿木结构，重檐歇山绿琉璃瓦顶，整座建筑给人肃穆庄严之感。该祠是在充分吸收西方先进技术的基础上，采用中国古典式建筑形制和布局建成，整个建筑实现了中西建筑元素的完美结合。

抗战初期，由于武器装备落后，单兵素质相对较低等客观原因，中国军队伤亡极大。为了鼓舞士气，祭奠为国捐躯的烈士，1938年初，国民政府军事委员会命令18军工程营，在其驻地左侧的蛇山南坡，建成了这座表彰先烈、供奉阵亡将士的祠堂——表烈祠。由于战事惨烈，祠堂落成后，几乎每天都有前方阵亡将士的灵位入祀。其中包括在忻口会战中牺牲的郝梦龄、刘家祺等知名抗战将领，武汉保卫战的空战英雄李桂丹、陈怀民等。

该祠作为武汉会战的重要遗存，为目前已知规模最大，保存最完整的抗战烈士纪念建筑之一，是中国人民抵御外辱，争取民族独立和国家主权的重要见证。

(文/图：湖北省普查办)

牌楼
Archway

主楼及神道
The Divine Path

主楼远景
A Distant View of the Main Building

The Wuchang Martyrs'Shrine is located at Shouyilu Street in Wuchang District, Wuhan City, Hubei Province. It was built in early 1938 by the engineer battalion of the 18th Army of the National Government in commemoration of soldiers who died in the anti-Japanese war. Facing the south, the Martyrs'Shrine is composed of such structures as the Archway, the Divine Path and the Main Building, all of which are set on the axis line. It is widely recognized as an outstanding example of memorial buildings of modern China. While using advanced technology of the Western world, all its built structures feature a Chinese classical style. As one of the best-preserved anti-Japanese martyrs'memorials and an important historic monument in commemoration of the Battle of Wuhan, the Martyrs'Shrine witnessed the Chinese people's heroic struggle against foreign aggression and for national independence and territorial integrity.

主楼
The Main Building

中华全国文艺界抗敌协会成立旧址

Former Site of the All-China Anti-Japanese Association of Literary and Arts Circles

副楼
Part of the Building

中华全国文艺界抗敌协会成立旧址位于湖北省武汉市江汉区水塔街道中山大道。1938年3月27日，在周恩来领导下，由著名作家老舍发起并筹建的文艺界抗日民族统一战线组织——中华全国文艺界抗敌协会在此召开成立大会，通过了《告世界文艺家书》《致日本被迫害作家书》《向抗敌将士致敬书》《宣言》和《简章》，推举郭沫若、矛盾、老舍、巴金等45人为理事。

旧址原为汉口市商会大礼堂，1920年由商会主席万泽生筹资兴建，建成于1921年，占地面积约400平方米，汉协盛营造厂设计、施工，是一栋现代风格的古典主义建筑。砖混结构，平面呈矩形，共4层，面阔七间，中段五开间向外凸出，正中入口处有两根爱奥尼式立柱支撑的门斗，门斗上方的三角形与二层上的宽檐相连，三角檐上有"汉口总商会"5个金字。一、二层的每个开间均有一根方形柱，与门斗两根圆柱并列。建筑底部采用花岗岩砌筑，外墙为假麻石贴面。1922年，汉口总商会在此承办了第四届全国商会联合会代表大会。

该旧址是抗战初期武汉作为全国文化中心的重要见证。抗日战争全面爆发后，在国民政府各军政机关迁驻武汉的同时，各地文化界人士及其机构、团体也纷纷迁移武汉。中华全国文艺界抗敌协会的成立将他们凝聚成为一个主体，凸显了武汉作为全国文化中心的重要历史地位。

(文/图：湖北省普查办)

外门楼
Outside the Building

一楼大厅
Lobby

大楼正面
Facade of the Building

第三次全国文物普查百大新发现

The Former Site of the All-China Anti-Japanese Association of Literary and Arts Circles is located at Zhongshan Street, Jianghan District, Wuhan City, Hubei Province. Covering an area of some 400 square meters, it is a classicalist building with modern elements. Featuring a brick-and-concrete structure, it is a four-storey building in a rectangular layout. Built in 1921, this historic building was originally used as the auditorium of the Chamber of Commerce of Hankou City. The 4th National Congress for the All-China Federation of Chambers of Commerce was convened here in 1922. On March 27, 1938, the All-China Anti-Japanese Association of Literary and Arts Circles was founded here. As a landmark of Wuhan's highly-developed commerce, this monument witnessed the revolutionary past of Hankou General Chamber of Commerce and the glorious period of Wuhan as a national cultural center in the early years of the Chinese People's Anti-Japanese War.

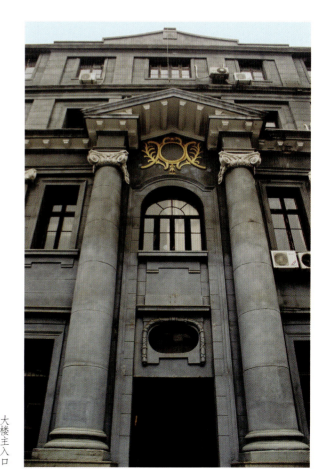

大楼主入口
The Main Entrance of the Building

红二军团长征司令部旧址
Former Site of the Headquarters of the Second Corps of the Red Army

　　红二军团长征司令部旧址位于湖南省娄底市新化县奉家镇。1935年中国工农红军第二军团为策应中央红军战略转移，于12月12日进入新化县上团乡进行休整，将当地大地主奉仕卿大宅院（竹园）作为临时司令部所在地。

　　宅院始建于清末，是一座保存完整具有浓郁地方特色的四合院，抬梁式砖木架构，共有房屋近80余间。占地面积约7000平方米，建筑面积5680平方米。建筑布局自南而北为大门、前厅、院坪、正房、两侧厢房。大门为牌头形制，由青砖券拱而成，粉白灰；拱门上方有"毛主席万岁"5个浮雕大字。前厅为单层砖木结构。正屋、厢房均为上下二层，平面呈"凹"字型，外出廊柱，每根廊柱均垫有不同图案的浮雕石鼓。两侧厢房正面呈阁楼式，二楼均设通廊互通。整个房屋均为一进二间，大都采取门窗对应，以利通风采光。房屋前后及四周砌有条石排水沟。院内前、后原设有碉楼（已毁）用于看家护院。目前整个建筑墙体上多处保留了非常清晰的毛主席语录和大跃进时期的绘画。

　　旧址反映了中国工农红军第二军团在长征途中从事"反围剿"斗争，由湘西挥师湘南、途径新化转战贵州建立红色革命根据地中的一段珍贵历史，反映了红军在长征途中散播"红色火种、扩充革命力量"的艰难历程。

（文/图：湖南娄底市新化县普查办）

手雷
Grenades

红军袋
The Red Army's Bags

院内
Courtyard

二层回廊
Corridors of the Second Floor

旧址俯瞰
A Panoramic View of the Former Site

The Former Site of the Headquarters of the Second Corps of the Red Army is located in Fengjia Township, Xinhua County, Loudi City, Hunan Province. Built in the late Qin Dynasty, this large courtyard house is a brick-and-wood structure with a post-and-lintel frame, with its roofs covered by small black tiles. Facing the south, it covers an area of 7000 square meters or so. Slogans from "Chairman Mao's Quotations" and drawings made during the period of the Great Leap Forward Movement in the late 1950s are still available on its walls. This headquarters of command witnessed the history of the Second Corps of the Red Army when it launched campaigns against KMT troops' anti-besiegement attempts and tried to found a revolutionary base in western Hunan during the Long March. This well-preserved historic house with distinctive indigenous characters is a physical carrier of the history of both Chinese people's revolutionary struggle in the 1930s but also the Cultural Revolution taking place from 1966 to 1976.

行军灯
Light

标语
Slogans

大门
Gate

顺德糖厂旧址
Former Site of Shunde Sugar Refinery

顺德糖厂旧址位于广东省佛山市顺德区大良街道。为1934年陈济棠兴办地方实业时，投资330万元建成。捷克斯可达工厂连工包料承建，制糖设备来自捷克，压榨能力为1千吨/24小时。1949年后，顺德糖厂先后隶属中央轻工业部、广东省轻工业厅、广东省糖业公司和佛山市糖纸公司，1985年1月由顺德糖酒工业公司管理。1993年11月，顺德糖厂转换经营机制，实行租赁经营。

糖厂现尚存制糖车间、压榨车间和两间成品糖仓库等早期厂房，以及助晶箱、桔水罐等早期设施。钢框架结构，大跨度钢桁架上盖铁皮顶，空心红砖墙。砖身有"永业砖窑""永""河南小港"等铭文。

作为我国第一批现代化甘蔗糖厂，顺德糖厂是见证广东近现代工业发展史的珍贵实物。

（文/图：广东佛山市顺德区普查办）

旧成品糖仓库空心红砖砌墙
Red Hollow Bricks of Finished Product Sugar

制糖车间内景
Interior of Sugar-refining Workshop

运输糖料的渡口
Transporting Sougar Crossing

制糖车间外景
Outside of Sugar-refining Workshop

The Former Site of Shunde Sugar Refinery is located at Daliang Community, Shunde District, Foshan City, Guangdong Province. It was built in 1934 by Czech-based Skoda Factory, with all sugar-refining equipment imported from Czech. Early-period buildings still preserved today include the sugar-refining workshop, the sugar-extracting workshop and two storehouses of finished product sugar as well as other auxiliary facilities like steel framework structures, long-span steel frames covered by iron roofs and walls of red hollow bricks. Inscriptions are carved on these old bricks.

Shunde Sugar Refinery was one of the earliest sugarcane refineries of modern China, witnessing the history of both China's sugar refining industry and Guangdong's modern industrial development.

制糖车间内景
Interior of Sugar-refining Workshop

南宁育才学校旧址
Former Site of Yucai School,Nanning

南宁育才学校旧址位于广西壮族自治区南宁市西乡塘区心圩街道。该址原为黄氏宗祠，建于清道光十九年（1839年），坐西北向东南，占地面积340平方米，建筑面积255.4平方米。整个建筑为硬山顶砖木结构，青砖青瓦清水墙，地面青砖铺砌，建筑呈两进两廊中座拜亭的围合布局。

越南中央学舍区（广西南宁育才学校）总部创办于1951年7月，它是毛泽东主席应越南主席胡志明的要求，专门为越南培养干部人才而成立的一所学校。先后设高等基础科学学校、华语学校、社会科学中级师范学校、自然科学中级师范学校、高级师范学校、初级师范学校、普通学校(中小学)和幼儿园等8所学校，在校师生3000多人。毕业回国的学子大多数成为越南各条战线上的英才，还有不少成长为越南党和国家领导人。

该旧址是在特殊的历史条件下设立的，不仅是越南革命干部的摇篮，也是培植中越两国人民友谊的园地，有着极其特殊的历史意义。

（文：广西南宁市普查办　摄影：莆晓东）

200

一进建筑
First Row of the Building

拜亭
Pavilion

二进建筑
Second Row of the Building

The Former Site of Yucai School, Nanning, is located at Xinyu Street, Xixiangtang District, Nanning City, Guangxi Zhuang Autonomous Region. Built in 1839, it originally functioned as the ancestral temple of Huang Family. Facing the southeast, it covers an area of 340 square meters, with a total floor space of 255.4 square meters. This courtyard house features brick-and-wood structures with flush garble roofs, paved with black bricks and covered by black tiles. The whole construction consists of two rows of courtyard connected by two corridors, with a pavilion in the center.

Founded in July 1951, the Headquarters of Vietnam Central Cadre School was known as a cradle for training Vietnamese revolutionary cadres, witnessing the traditional friendship between Chinese and Vietnamese people.

旧址全景
A Full View of the Site

白查黎族船形屋
Li People's Boat-shaped Houses at Baicha Village

　　白查黎族船形屋位于海南省东方市江边乡。白查村坐落在山坳里的一块面积16万平方米的平地上，群山环抱，椰林摇曳，槟榔婆娑，是中国最后的一个黎族古村落，被誉为"黎族最后的精神家园"。村内至今保存着81间黎族船形屋。

　　船形屋是黎族千年来的建筑结晶，取材简单，却融入不少建筑智慧。船形屋用藤条、树枝、木棍扎制屋架，用茅草覆顶，屋檐接地，檐墙合一，远看像船底，因而被称为船形屋。屋形长而阔，茅檐低矮，有利于防风防雨。房子分为前后两节，门向两端开，船形屋的中间立三根高大的柱子，黎语叫"戈额"，象征男人；两边立6根矮的柱子，黎语叫"戈定"，象征女人，其寓意着一个家是由男人和女人共同组成。屋内为泥地，这些泥是村民从外面挖回的黏土，把地面铺平，浇上水后用脚踩平，晒干或晾干地面，使之平坦坚硬。

　　根据黎族的传说，他们的祖先原本生活在海上，以船为家，后迁入陆地，为怀念祖先的船家，遂在陆地上盖起了船形屋。千百年来，船形屋记录着黎族生存与发展的轨迹，记录着黎族历史与文明传承的脉络。

（文／图：海南东方市普查办）

船形屋
Boat-shaped House

船形屋近景
A Close View of the Boat-shaped House

船形屋局部
Part of the Boat-shaped House

船形屋屋顶
Roof of the Boat-shaped House

Li People's Boat-shaped Houses at Baicha Village is located in Jiangbian Township, Dongfang City, Hainan Province. 81 boat-shaped houses with traditional characteristics of Li ethnic group are still preserved today in the village.

A boat-shaped house features structures made from rattan and tree branches and wood bricks and thatch-covered roofs. Its eaves extend down to the ground, looking like boat bottoms. Baicha Village is Li people's last historic village, known as the "last spiritual homeland of Li ethnic group". This historic village is an important heritage site for studies of architectural traditions and lifestyles of China's ethnic minorities.

重庆国民政府军事委员会旧址

Former Site of the Military Commission
of the National Government in Chongqing

重庆国民政府军事委员会旧址位于重庆市渝中区南纪门街道解放西路，建于1935年底。当时国民政府颁定"军事委员会委员长重庆行营"，辖区包括川、康、黔、藏在内的整个大西南。1937年，"卢沟桥事变"数月之后，国民政府迁都重庆，国民政府军事委员会即设在此处。作为国民政府正面战场指挥中心，国民政府军事委员会在此制定战略决策、筹谋作战方针、颁布作战命令、直接指挥正面战场的抗战。1941年12月2日军事委员会外事局在此办公，主持对外军事联络。作为国民政府军事委员会委员长，蒋介石最初的官邸就设在此处。

旧址为三幢两楼一底的砖木结构建筑群，坐东南朝西北，建筑面积1991.14平方米，建筑占地面积806.41平方米，分布面积840.78平方米。外墙为小青砖勾缝，建筑屋顶为歇山与悬山两种，周围有封火墙，属于民国时期典型的中西合璧的建筑。内设壁炉、砖柱台灯、地下室、哨台、雕花扇门等，至今保存完好。

国民政府军事委员会旧址是第二次世界大战时期，中国最高权力统驭机构的驻地，也是重庆首次发现的抗战时期国民政府军事委员会委员长蒋介石最早的城区官邸，对于研究当时的历史有着重要的意义。

（文/图：重庆市文物局）

旧址全景
A Full View of the Site

旧址内部
Inside of the Site

The Former Site of the Military Commission of the National Government in Chongqing is located at Jiefang West Road, Yuzhong District, Chongqing Municipality. Built in the end of 1935, it is a brick-and-wood building complex consisting of three buildings. Facing southeast, the compound has a floor space of 1991.14 square meters. Its exterior walls are made of small black bricks, supporting saddled and garbled roofs. The buildings are encompassed by fireproof walls. Inside the buildings are fireplaces, lamps on brick pillars, basements, watch-posts and screen doors with carved patterns, all of which are well preserved today.

The former site of the Military Commission of the National Government is an important heritage monument witnessing the history of Chongqing as China's war capital during the anti-Japanese war and Chinese people's heroic struggle against Japanese invaders.

旧址外部
Outside of the Site

涪陵816工程遗址
The Site of Project 816 in Fuling

涪陵816工程遗址位于重庆市涪陵区白涛街道。

816工程遗址是由周恩来总理亲自批准修建的中国第二个核原料工业基地。从1966年9月开始修建，经过17年建设，整个洞体总建筑面积10.4万平方米，洞内建成大型洞18个。1984年2月，随着国际形势的变化和国民经济战略调整的需要，根据中央军委的指示，816工程全面停工。816工程体系庞大复杂，完全隐藏在一处毫不起眼的山体内部。洞体内厂房进洞深度400米左右，顶部覆盖层最厚达200米，核心部位厂房的覆盖层厚度均在150米以上。据专家评估，816工程乃世界第一大人工洞体。洞体可以承受100万吨氢弹空中爆炸冲击，还能抵抗8级地震的破坏，是一处理想的战备工程。816工厂原职工队伍通过军转民，改建化肥厂。

816工程遗址是新中国成立后我国建设的一项重要的军事工程，是研究1960年代毛泽东同志提出的"深挖洞，广积粮，不称霸"的战略方针和全面三线建设、国防战备特殊时期重要的实物资料。

(文/图：重庆市文物局)

洞体通道
Channel in the Cave

控制室
Control Room

遗址近景
A Close View of the Site

遗址全景
A Full View of the Site

The Site of Project 816 is located in Baitao Community, Fuling District, Chongqing Municipality. Beginning from September 1966, its construction lasted for 17 years. The whole cave structure has a total floor space of 104,000 square meters, including 18 large caves. Factory buildings are set 400 meters deep from the cave entrance and 200 meters underneath the mountain top. This cave structure can resist air attacks by 100 million-ton h-bombs and 8.0-magnitude earthquakes. It is truly a successful wartime project.

The site of Project 816 provides important physical references for studies of Chairman Mao's strategic guideline of "digging deep tunnels, piling up stores of grain and never seeking hegemony" and China's third-front national defense construction campaigns launched in the 1960s.

烈士墓群
Martyrs Graves

100 New Discoveries of the Third Nationwide Surveys of Cultural Heritage

第三次全国文物普查百大新发现

南沱红星渡槽
Red Star Aqueduct in Nantuo

南沱红星渡槽位于重庆市涪陵区南沱乡，建于20世纪50年代至70年代。渡槽西北东南走向，长达9000余米，占地面积3.15万平方米，横跨连丰、关东、焦岩、南沱、沿坪、石佛6个村。高架槽基础宽3.5米。渡槽单拱最大跨度49米，最高处约20余米，内为三合泥地坪，内宽1米，内空高0.88米，槽沿0.3米。渡槽侧立面阴刻有："念念不忘高举毛泽东思想伟大红旗，念念不忘突出政治，念念不忘无产阶级专政，伟大的导师，伟大的领袖，伟大的统帅，伟大的舵手毛主席万岁"、"人民，只有人民才是创造世界历史的动力"等16段文革时期标语和语录题刻。因所跨区域不同，红星渡槽又称作连丰渡槽、五星渡槽。

整座渡槽气势磅礴，宏伟壮观，是新中国成立后农村水利工程建设的取得巨大成就的见证和重要标识。对于研究新中国成立后工农业生产的发展状况、国家对农村生产发展的规划与农村水利工程建造技术等具有重要的参考价值。

（文/图：重庆市文物局）

墩柱上的语录题刻
Quotations Engraved on the Bridge Pier

渡槽局部
Part of the Aqueduct

208

渡槽
The Aqueduct

第三次全国文物普查百大新发现

Built between 1950s and 1970s, the Red Star Aqueduct in Nantuo is located in Nantuo Township, Fuling District, Chongqing Municipality. The aqueduct stretches six administrative villages from northwest to southeast, including Lianfeng, Guandong, Jiaoyan, Nantuo, Yanping and Shifou. Totaling 9000 meters, it covers an area of 31500 square meters. The aqueduct's foundation is 3.5 meters wide, with the largest single arch spanning for 49 meters and the highest point reaching up to 20 meters. The aqueduct' has an inner width of 1 meter and an inner height of 0.88 meter, with brims as wide as 0.3 meter.

Red Star Aqueduct is an important heritage monument for studies of the agricultural and industrial production, national planning for rural production and technologies for rural water conservancy projects in the early years of new China.

墩柱
The Bridge Pier

中国工程物理研究院旧址
Former Site of China Institute of Engineering Physics

中国工程物理研究院旧址位于四川省绵阳市梓潼县长卿镇。中国工程物理研究院，前身是1958年成立的第三机械工业部九局211研究基地和中国科学院九所，研究基地在青海省海晏县金银滩。1969年基地迁至四川梓潼和广元，总部设在梓潼县长卿镇白家湾。1983年迁至绵阳近郊。1985年更名为中国工程物理研究院。

迁至绵阳科学城后，原"九院"院址移交梓潼县政府管理。占地面积581，418平方米，有砖混建筑163栋和防空洞1处。原院部内的办公楼、大礼堂、图书室、档案室、情报室、通讯站、模型厂、邮局、防空洞、诊所、中小学、邓稼先旧居，以及其他科学家居住的别墅区、家属宿舍、招待所基本保持原状。目前大部分建筑已对外开放，并辟有"九院院史展览"，部分区域被规划为绵阳市红色教育旅游基地。

"九院"在我国核科技和计算机发展史上具有极其重要的地位，先后有"两弹元勋"邓稼先、"中子弹之父"王淦昌以及朱光亚、胡仁宇、陈能宽等16位国家科学院院士和大批科研知识分子在此，攻克了氢弹的核心技术；在计算机研发和应用上取得多项技术先进的成果。"九院"旧址是我国尖端科学技术发展的历史见证。

（文：四川绵阳市梓潼县文物管理所　摄影：张兴发）

大门
Gate

防空洞
Air-raid Shelter

邓稼先故居
The Former Residence of Deng Jiaxian

旧址远景
A Distant View of the Former Site

The former site of China Institute of Engineering Physics is located in Changqing Village, Changqing Township, Zitong County, Mianyang City, Sichuan Province. Built between 1965 and 1993, it covers an area of 581,418 square meters and includes 163 brick-and-concrete buildings and one air-raid shelter. All the buildings are basically preserved in their original states, such as the office building, the auditorium, the library, the archives, the information service, the telecommunication station, the model factory, the post office, the air-raid shelter, the clinic, the elementary and middle schools, the former residence of Deng Jiaxian, scientists' villas, dormitories and the guest house. Thirteen slogans on the office building's walls painted during the Cultural Revolution (1966-1976) are still preserved today, such as "United to Achieve Greater Victory!"

The former site of China Institute of Engineering Physics is a historical witness of the development of state-of-art science and technology in new China.

院部办公楼
Office Building

茅台酒厂历史建筑群
Historic Building Complex of Maotai Liquor Factory

茅台酒厂历史建筑群位于贵州省遵义仁怀市茅台镇。建于明代，因战乱几次被毁，清同治元年(1862年)在被毁的旧址上恢复重建，分别建有粮仓、曲药房、窖池、烤酒房等基础设施，加上后来国营茅台酒厂时期修建的各类酿酒厂房共计10处遗址群，包括茅台酒厂的前身——成义烧房旧址、恒兴烧坊旧址、荣和烧坊旧址及其踩曲仓旧址和干曲仓旧址、二片区制曲石磨坊旧址、干曲仓旧址、踩曲仓旧址、发酵仓旧址、一片区发酵仓旧址、下酒库第八栋和第五栋酒库，占地面积约1.3万余平方米，完整保存了自清末迄今的酿造工艺。

茅台酒是享誉世界的三大著名蒸馏酒之一，茅台酒厂历史建筑群是茅台酒悠久的传统酿造工艺的实物载体，是清代以来中国民族工业从艰难前行一直到不断发展壮大、创造辉煌的历史见证。

(文/图：贵州仁怀市普查办)

成义烧房旧址
Former Sites of Chengyi Liquor-making Workshop

212

生产车间
Workshop

酒库
Liquor Storehouses

第三次全国文物普查百大新发现

The Historic Building Complex of Maotai Liquor Factory is located in Maotai Township, Zunyi City, Guizhou Province. First built in the Ming Dynasty (1368-1644), the liquor factory was rebuilt in 1862 and expanded after new China was founded. Altogether, the whole complex covers an area of 13,333 square meters and consists of 10 historic buildings, including former sites of Chengyi liquor-making workshop, Hengxing liquor-making workshop, Ronghe liquor-making workshop, yeast distilling workshops and liquor storehouses.

The historic building complex of Maotai Liquor Factory witnessed China's earliest liquor-making system since the Han Dynasty (202 BC – 220 AD) and is widely recognized as a highly valuable heritage site for studies of China's liquor-making history and technology.

成义烧库房
Storehouse of Chengyi Liquor-making Workshop

酒窖
Wine Cellar

同乐傈僳族村寨
Lisu People's Village in Tongle

同乐傈僳族村寨位于云南省迪庆藏族自治州维西傈僳族自治县叶枝镇。是云南傈僳族乡土建筑群中保存最完好的村寨，充分体现了傈僳族依山、临水、就林的建村理念，完整地保留了傈僳族居住、生产生活、社会活动设施的传统风貌。

同乐村建于一片北南向山坡上，建筑均为井干式结构板房，以木楞为墙、木板为瓦，层层叠叠，一栋连一栋。此外，各家还在远离村寨的田边和牧点建有二三处庄房，山上建有"火房"。村民春秋收种季节下到河谷住"庄房"，上山采集、打猎时住"火房"。村寨下方的山箐上建有10多座水磨房。村里历史最久的民居已有190多年，但大多数民居为三四十年前所建。村尾有叶枝王氏土司的避暑山庄。

同乐村的傈僳族文化底蕴深厚。村民信仰原始宗教，主要节日有阔时节等，保留有傈僳族音节文字、天文历法、祭天古歌和"木刮"丧歌，善麦秆编制、蔴料纺织，有射弩、斗牛等传统体育活动，是"阿尺木刮"歌舞的发源地。

2006年同乐傈僳族村寨被云南省政府列为第一批省级傈僳族传统文化保护区。同乐傈僳族村寨是傈僳族物质文化和非物质文化的重要载体，有重要的历史文化价值和文化人类学价值。

(文：云南维西傈僳族自治县文物管理所)

同乐村秋景（摄影：李钢）
Autumn of the Village

同乐村全景（摄影：郑良）
A Full View of the Village

The Lisu People's Village in Tongle is located in Yezhi Township, Weixi Lisu People's Autonomous County, Yunnan Province. All these historic buildings are wooden houses of log cabin construction, with walls piled up by logs and roofs paved by wooden planks. These wooden houses are connected with one another, forming a complicated building complex. The village's oldest house can date back more than 190 years, but most of these vernacular houses were built 30 or 40 years ago. The vernacular buildings in Tongle Village are known as the best-preserved folk houses of Lisu people in Yunnan Province. They fully reflect Lisu people's architectural concept of building houses near mountains, rivers and forests and integrally preserve Lisu people's traditional lifestyles, production scenes and facilities for social activities.

板房（摄影：刘建辉）
Wooden Houses of Log Cabin Construction

"阿尺木刮"歌舞（摄影：和琼辉）
Achimugua Dance

中央人民政府驻藏代表楼

Office Building for the Central People's Government Representatives to Tibet

中央人民政府驻藏代表楼位于西藏自治区拉萨市城关区功德林街道。1964年由中央人民政府拨专款修建，1965年建成使用，是西藏革命历史的重要见证。

代表楼建于根培山南坡半山腰上，坐北向南，占地20万平方米。整个建筑群体现了我国早期现代建筑风格，砖石结构，东西对称分布。内部房间紧凑，设施齐备，均铺有木质地板。东南侧为工委会议室，设计独特，酷似贝壳，内部宽敞明亮。此外会议室东侧还有四座工委领导的住所，错落分布在绿树与灌木丛中，均为独立小院，砖石结构，略带欧式风格。

（文：西藏自治区普查办　摄影：索朗达瓦）

办公楼内景
Interior of the Office Building

办公楼正面
Focade of the Office Building

The Office Building for the Central People's Government Representatives to Tibet is located at Gongdelin street, Chengguan District, Lhasa City, Tibet Autonomous Region. Its construction began in 1964, with the special fund earmarked by the Central People's Government of China. The building complex was completed in 1965. The whole building complex is a brick-and-stone structure, symmetrically laid out from east and west. Featuring an early modern style, this monument consists of compactly-designed rooms and well-equipped facilities. It is an important witness of Tibet's revolutionary history, involving many historical events and figures.

办公楼侧面
Aspect of the Office Building

大华纱厂旧址
Former Site of Dahua Textile Factory

大华纱厂旧址位于陕西省西安市新城区太华南路。大华纱厂创办于1935年，是中国西北地区首家机械纺织企业和近现代工业基地，为陕西及其周边地区的工业近代化作出了很大贡献。新中国成立后，大华纱厂成为西安重要的工业基地和骨干企业，为国民经济恢复和发展作出了重要贡献。

大华纱厂作为一个拥有着80余年历史的老企业，各个历史时期都在这里留下了具有时代烙印的建筑。这些建筑既有生产车间、仓储库房等工业建筑，也有民宅似的管理用房；既有民国时期的青砖小院，也有新中国成立后的红砖建筑，还有改革开放以来的钢筋混凝土车间。

旧址现存民国时期的厂房、南门门楼、办公用房、库房等工业建筑遗存。其中最有价值的是纺织车间厂房，它由原上海象新公司包建，采用了当时最先进的建筑材料、结构、设备，为西北现存最早、规模最大、最具有代表性的单体钢结构工业建筑。该厂房一直作为纺织车间使用，虽经数次地震仍很坚固。厂房内现有民国时期以及上世纪五六十年代的机器设备、工具器具；反映大华纱厂各方面情况的档案、图片、文章等史料。

（文：陕西西安市普查办 摄影：赵晶）

纺织厂房顶部结构及内部梁架
Textile Workshop Built during the Period of the Republic of China

原厂房内使用的美国进口机器（20世纪初产）
Machine Made in America in Old Workshop

老南门
Old South Door

生产车间
Production Workshops

The Former Site of Dahua Textile Factory is located in Xincheng District, Xi'an City, Shaanxi Province. Built in 1935, Dahua Textile Factory was the first textile factory and modern industrial base in northwest China. Currently-preserved buildings within the factory are involved with different historical periods of modern China, including production workshops, storehouses, office buildings, black-brick courtyards from the period of the Republic of China, red-brick buildings of new China and reinforced concrete workshops built after 1978. The most valuable building is the textile workshop built during the period of the Republic of China. It is a single steel structure built by Shanghai Xiangxin Company.

民国时期办公用楼
Office Buildings during the Period of the Republic of China

多伦多盐场
Duolunduo Salt Field

多伦多盐场位于青海省玉树藏族自治州囊谦县娘拉乡。地处囊谦县的东南部，南接西藏自治区，气候温和湿润。盐场坐北朝南，东南依多兰山，西邻察卡村，北靠察卡山，整个盐场南北长281米，东西宽235米，总面积达66975平方米。盐泉来自北山的山腰上，盐田北高南低，按地形走势分割成1000多个区块，一条条、一块块，错落有致。远远望去，白色的盐田和山腰上红色的藏式民居，浑然一派自然而古朴的田园式美景。制盐技术至今依然保持着原始的以人工集体作业方式：即定期召集当地村民，将盐水从山上的盐泉引入事先整理好的山脚处台地盐池，让水分自然蒸发，将剩下的颗粒盐收集，再利用马匹把盐从盐田运往附近的仓库后销往各地。

20世纪六七十年代多伦多盐矿是青藏川交汇地带唯一的盐产地，年生产量在3500吨左右，产品颇受藏族农牧民的欢迎。近年来，由于交通运输的发展，在四面八方运来的精制食盐的冲击下，多伦多盐场似乎失去了往日兴旺的景象，但所产食盐因不受任何污染，依然深受西藏昌都、四川西部和云南西北部边远藏区群众的青睐。

多伦多盐场是一座古老的保持传统制盐工艺的民族作坊，对探索玉树地区古老制盐产业，研究、开发和利用玉树地区盐业资源有着重要的意义。

(文：青海玉树藏族自治州普查办 摄影：索南旦周)

盐库
Salt Gallery

盐场近景
A Close View of the Salt Field

盐场远景
A Distant View of the Salt Field

采盐场景
Salt Mining

The Duolunduo Salt Field is located in Niangla Township, Nangqian County, Yushu Tibetan Autonomous Prefecture, Qinghai Province. The whole field covers an area of 66,975 square meters. Its salt spring is located half way up the North Hill. The salt field slopes from north to south and is divided into more than 1000 segments in accordance with landforms. Duolunduo Salt Field is an old workshop producing salt with traditional techniques. Today, the primitive way of handmade collective work is still used to produce salt here. There is a quiet village near the salt field, all of its dwellers are Tibetan. The salt industry is an important industry for local villagers. This salt field is a highly valuable site for studies of the salt production in Yushu.

运盐场景
Transport of Salt

英雄地中四井
Central No. 4 Oil Well

英雄地中四井位于青海省海西蒙古族藏族自治州冷湖行政委员会，是柴达木盆地冷湖油田第一口油井。

英雄地中四井西为冷湖五号构造一高点，东为冷湖油田五号老基地，西和南均为高原荒漠，北面约15千米处为冷湖行政委员会所在地冷湖镇。1958年8月21日，青海石油局派出石油勘探大队1219钻井队开始在该地区钻探寻找石油资源，1958年9月13日，由1219钻井队钻至650米后发生井涌，继而出现井喷，喷势异常猛烈，原油连续畅喷3天3夜，油井附近成为一片油海，日喷原油高达800吨左右，从此冷湖油田第一口油井诞生。地中四油井喷油标志着全国"四大油田"的冷湖油田正式诞生，展示了柴达木盆地石油工业发展的广阔前景。地中四井喷油，引起了石油工业部高度重视，部领导亲临冷湖探区部署指导，调整方案，作出了暂时收缩茫崖、马海地区，将人力、物力集中起来，加快冷湖勘探步伐的决定，冷湖石油大会战的大幕正式拉开。在不到半年的时间内，相继探明了冷湖五号、四号、三号油田。与此同时，开发工作也紧锣密鼓、轰轰烈烈地开展起来，1960年，冷湖油田年产原油30多万吨，成为当时全国四大油田之一。

英雄地中四井为研究新中国石油开发史提供了十分宝贵的实物资料，是青海柴达木地区石油早期开发活动遗迹的直观反映。

（文：青海海西蒙古族藏族自治州普查办　摄影：宋耀春）

纪念碑
Monument

全景
A Full View of the Oil Well

The Central No. 4 Oil Well is located at No. 5 Field of Lenghu Administrative Committee, Haixi Mongolian and Tibetan Autonomous Region, Qinghai Province. On August 21, 1958, No. 1219 Drilling Taskforce from the Oil Survey Team of Qinghai Petroleum Bureau was sent to search oil resources in this area. On September 13, 1958 when the driller reached 650 meters beneath the ground, blowout happened vigorously and continued for three days and three nights. The area near this well became a sea of oil. It is the first oil well of Lenghu Oil Field, producing up to 800 tons of oil.

抽油机
Pumping

青铜峡黄河铁桥

Qingtongxia Railway Bridge over the Yellow River

青铜峡黄河铁桥位于宁夏回族自治区吴忠市青铜峡市青铜峡镇。1959年7月1日正式竣工通车。主要是为青铜峡水利枢纽工程及黄河两岸运输物资而建，目前已不再使用。2010年12月，宁夏回族自治区人民政府将该铁桥公布为自治区级文物保护单位。

青铜峡铁桥是一座综合利用的桥，桥面可走火车、汽车、架子车和行人，是包兰线青铜峡车站至余桥12千米专用线之间的咽喉。该桥为半永久性桥梁，桥长292.3米，单车道桥身由七孔折穿式花梁和折装式桥梁等组成，桥墩采用木桩及铁丝笼片石结构，桥两端边跨采用美国卡耐基钢铁公司、伯利恒钢铁公司、加拿大阿尔哥玛公司制造钢桁架，每组长49米，自重185吨。中跨采用5组英国多门朗公司制造的ESTB军用钢梁。每组长35米，自重110吨。钢梁安装使用了35000个铆钉。

标注英文的钢梁
Beams Engraved English

桥两端边跨钢梁上标注有钢材的产地以及1944至1947制造年份的铭牌。铁桥在1964年，1980年曾大修过。目前铁桥多处生锈，桥墩有不同程度的沉陷下移，桥面出现不同程度的裂缝，钢架结构腐蚀情况严重，仅通行摩托车、自行车。

青铜峡黄河铁桥是宁夏第一座黄河桥梁，为加速青铜峡水利枢纽工程建设、促进宁夏经济发展作出了贡献。

（文：宁夏青铜峡市文物管理所　摄影：李鹏）

铁桥中跨
Mid Span

铁桥全景
A Full View of the Bridge

The Qingtongxia Railway Bridge over the Yellow River is located in Qingtongxia Township, Wuzhong City, Ningxia Hui Autonomous Region. As the first bridge over the Yellow River in Ningxia, it was completed and put into use on July 1, 1959. This railway bridge was built primarily for transporting materials for Qingtongxia Water Control Project as well as between both banks of the Yellow River. It is a semi-permanent bridge standing at a strategic position of the 12-kilometer-long special railway line between Qingtongxia and Yuqiao. 292.3 meters long, it is composed of seven-arch folded rail beams and dismountable beams. The bridge piers are made of wooden pegs and iron wire-covered stone.

铁桥边跨
Side Span

农一师五团玉尔滚俱乐部
Yu'ergun Club of the 5th Regiment of the 1st Agricultural Division

农一师五团玉尔滚俱乐部位于新疆维吾尔自治区阿拉尔市五团民族分场。1971年11月始建，1973年10月竣工，为当时阿克苏地区最大的俱乐部。

建筑坐东朝西，占地约1140平方米，呈"工"字形，土木结构，为苏式建筑。中间为礼堂，东、西两侧为办公室。正面门额上有"农一师五团玉尔滚俱乐部"字样，下为"1973.10.1"，南墙西侧上部有俄文。建筑四面墙体上部均有标语，有"百花齐放""推陈出新""高举毛泽东思想伟大红旗奋勇前进""愚公移山改造中国""厉行节约勤俭建国""人民公社好"等多条标语，有正门、侧门，门扇上均有五星图案。礼堂内有舞台、座椅。该俱乐部曾是当地居民的重要娱乐活动场所，现礼堂已成危房，两侧办公室由民族分场场部等单位办公使用。

农一师五团玉尔滚俱乐部反映了1970年代开垦边疆、建设新疆的时代风貌。

（文：新疆阿拉尔市普查队　摄影：刘维玉）

正面门额
Top of the Facade

侧门
Side Entrance

礼堂
Auditorium

全景
A Full View of the Club

第三次全国文物普查百大新发现

The Yu'ergun Club of the 5th Regiment of the 1st Agricultural Division is located in Ala'er City, Xinjiang Uighur Autonomous Region. It began to be built in November 1971 and completed in October 1973, known as the then largest club of Akesu Region. Facing the west, the club covers an area of 1140 square meters. It is an I-shape, earth-and-wood structure in a Soviet style. The auditorium is set in the middle, surrounded by offices in the east and west sides. On top of the fa?ade are inscribed characters which read, "Yu'ergun Club of the 5th Regiment of the 1st Agricultural Division, October 1, 1973." There are Russian words on the upper part of the western section of the south wall. Slogans are visible in all the walls of the four sides. The auditorium has become a structure in danger now. This club reflects the history of pioneering and constructing Xinjiang in the early years of new China.

俱乐部正面
Facade of the Club

第 三 次 全 国 文 物 普 查 百 大 新 发 现
100 NEW DISCOVERIES OF THE THIRD NATIONWIDE SURVEYS OF CULTURAL HERITAGE

其他
OTHERS

翻译：刘红艳（北京工商大学）
Translator: Liu Hongyan

其他类的参评项目共有8个省（区）11处，其中农业与水文化遗产项目占绝对多数。而且多是由自然与人文因素紧密结合的"文物复合体"，是"动态或活体的文物"，更兼具物质文化与非物质文化的特性。其他类参评项目包含的"文物"空间范围非常大，时间也更接近当代，更接近普通百姓的生产生活。它们与当地居民有着天然的历史、文化和情感联系，这种联系已经成为"文物"不可分割的组成部分。

农田水利、茶文化、栽培种植等与普通民众的生活密切相关，尽管它们不是那么富丽堂皇、雍容华贵，但是在人们的生产生活中，它们却有着其他文物不可替代的重要作用，甚至在推动当地社会生产力发展的历史进程中起到过独特的作用，有些可以说是先进思想文化和先进生产力的代表。这些属于平民化、大众化的"文物"，具有鲜明的民族性、地域性特征，也是不可多得的人类文化多样性的重要表现形式。

其他类参评项目有5个项目入选"第三次全国文物普查百大新发现"。

农田水利在中华民族的发展史上占据突出地位。2011年中央1号文件《中共中央国务院关于加快水利改革发展的决定》开宗明义提出："水是生命之源、生产之要、生态之基。兴水利、除水害，事关人类生存、经济发展、社会进步，历来是治国安邦的大事"。中华五千年发展史，某种意义上讲是人类与洪水抗争奋斗的历史，在此过程中，留下了诸多弥足珍贵的水文化遗产，它们凝聚着中华民族的辉煌创造，镌刻着中华民族的伟大精神，是水文化传承的重要载体，也是中华民族的文化瑰宝。从巍峨的黄河大堤到誉满全球的成都都江堰和广西灵渠，从春秋战国时代的陕西郑国渠到秦汉时代宁夏的秦渠和汉渠，古代水文化遗产无不闪耀着中华民族的聪明智慧和卓越创造。广西全州县的贡陂堰和甘肃迭部县的多儿水磨坊群是"第三次全国文物普查"发现的水文化遗产的代表。贡陂堰是始

自南宋至今还在使用的一处农业水利灌溉设施，主要由堰堤、引水沟、渠道三大主体工程组成，设计科学巧妙，是研究我国古代水利设施发展的一处珍贵的实物资料。甘肃迭部县的多儿水磨坊群建于清代，使用至今，与其周边自然环境和谐统一，是甘南藏区保存至今具有成片规模的水磨坊群，具有鲜明的地域文化特点，其建筑形制、水磨制作工艺、机械原理和古朴风貌，体现了藏区传统的生产生活方式。

茶文化在我国有着悠久的历史，不仅与民众生活息息相连，更是作为中华民族的文化载体远播海内外。湖南安化素有"茶乡"之称，产茶制茶历史悠久，明清时期安化黑茶远销西北诸省。绵延在湖南省安化县崇山峻岭和山涧溪流之间的运茶古道，是这一地区繁华经贸活动的缩影。沿线至今仍完整保存着大量反映安化黑茶悠久历史文化和独特制作工艺的历史遗存，包括古茶园、古道（风雨桥、茶亭）、黑茶加工作坊、古街古集市、船码头等。安化古道独特的文化长廊等与沿线优美的环境组成了文化内涵与自然因素有机结合的文物景观。

按照《中华人民文物保护法》和相关法规，"具有科学价值的古脊椎动物化石和古人类化石同文物一样受国家的保护"。甘肃会宁县的泉坪猛犸象化石点项目是在第三次文物普查中发现的，经中国科学院古脊椎动物与古人类研究所金昌柱等专家初步鉴定，发现的象头骨和下颌骨化石为早期猛犸象类，距今约300万年，这是国内发现的第一具完整的早期猛犸象头骨化石，世所罕见。特别是为研究猛犸象类群在欧亚大陆的起源和演化提供了珍贵的的实物资料。

王建平

黄河博物馆馆长　研究员

There are eleven other eligible projects across eight provinces, the majority of which are heritages on agriculture and water culture. What's more, most of them are "heritage complex" with the combination of natural and humanistic factors. They are also products of dynamic and living objects, characterized by both material culture and nonmaterial culture. Other categories are wider in spatial dimension, closer to modern times and more intimate to the production and ordinary people's lives. They have natural attachment to the history, culture and emotion of local inhabitants, which has become an indispensible component of cultural relics.

Irrigation and water conservancy, tea culture and cultivation are closely related to ordinary people's lives. They play an important role in production and people's lives which other cultural or historical relics can not substitute, although they don't seem so magnificent or elegant. With unique prominent influence on promoting local productive forces, irrigation and water conservancy, tea culture and cultivation might even be regarded as the representatives of advanced ideology and productive forces. Those cultural relics belonging to the popular and mass culture with distinctive ethnic and regional characteristics also serve as a rare but important form of cultural diversity for human beings.

There are four items among eligible projects of other categories nominated for "One Hundred New Great Discoveries in the Third National Culture Relic General Survey", according to the evaluation rules and requirements. The main characteristics of these projects are as follows:

First and foremost, the irrigation and water-conservancy project in argriculture displays a prominent role in the history of development of Chinese nation. According to No. 1 Document of 2011 entitled " A Decision on Accelerating Reform and Development of Water Conservancy systems issued by "the CPC Central Committee and State Council" and State Council, it announced its purpose at the outset, "Water is the source of life, essential to production and ecology. Only by making use of water conservancy projects and getting rid of water disasters can we guarantte the survival of mankind, economic development and social progress, which is of paramount importance for the stability and prosperity of the country." Five thousand years of development of Chinese nation are, in a sense, a history of mankind struggling to combat floods, during which course, a multitude of precious water culture heritages had been left. These heritages, congealing splendid creation and engraving great spirit of Chinese nation, are significant carriers for inheritance of water culture and the gem of Chinese culture as well. Stretching from the lofty Huanghe River Dike to the world-renowned Dujiang Weir of Chengdu and Lingqu Canal of Guangxi Province, ranging from Zhenguo Canal of Shaanxi constructed in Spring and Autumn and Warring States Period to Lingqu Canal and Hanqu Canal of Ningxia Province which was built in Qin and Han dynasties, none of these water culture heritages are not sparkled with brilliant wisdom and transcendent creativity of Chinese nation. Gongpo Weir in Guangxi Province and Duo Er Watermill Group in Gansu Province are also representatives of the precious water cultural heritage in the Third National Cultural Relic General Survey. Gongpo Weir, an agricultural water irrigation conservancy facility, has been used since the Southern Song Dynasty up to now. It was composed of three major parts: the embankment,

feed ditch and channel. The scientific and ingenious design of the weir makes it a precious material for the study of the development of China's ancient water conservancy facilities. The Duo Er Watermill Group in Gansu province, which is perfectly blended with the surrounding environment, was constructed in the Qing Dynasty, and is still in use now. The watermill group, with distinct regional regional and cultural characteristics, is preserved on a grand scale in Gannan Tibetan area. The traditional modes of life and production in Tibetan area are presented through its architectural structure, watermill processing technology, mechanical principles and primitive beauty.

Secondly, with a long history, Chinese tea culture not only has been connected with people's life, but also has been well known as a symbol of Chinese culture both at home and abroad. Anhua County of Hunan Province has enjoyed the name of "the Homeland of Tea" for its long history of growing and producing tea. During the Ming and Qing Dynasties, the Black Tea of Anhua County was sold all the way to Northwest China. Stretching along the steep mountains and wild waters, the ancient road for tea transporting provides us with a miniature of the properouse economy. Along the road, considerable historical remains have been preseved, reflectng a long history of Anhua Black Tea culture and its unique production process. Historical sites include Ancient Tea Garden, Ancient Track (Wind-Rain Bridge, Tea Pavilion), the Processing Workshop of dark tea, Ancient Street and Bazaar, Dock and so on. The combination of distinctive culture of the Ancient Tea Road in Anhua and the wonderful scenery alongside has provided a cultural landscape with both cultural and natural context.

Thirdly, according to the Law of the People's Republic of China on Protection of Cultural Relics and some relevant laws and regulations, "Fossils of paleovertebrates and paleoanthropoids of scientific value shall be protected by the State in the same way as cultural relics." The project of "The Site of Woolly Mammoth Fossils in Quanping" of Gansu Province was discovered in the Third National Cultural Relic General Survey. Through the preliminary identification made by the Chairman of Stratigraphic Council of International Union for Quaternary Research in the Asia-Pacific Region and Professor Jin Changzhu from the Institute of Vertebrate Paleontology and Paleoanthropology, Chinese Academy of Science, the fossil of skull and lower jaw show that the animal belongs to the early woolly mammoths, possibly from the Pliocene Epoch of 3 million years ago. It is learned that this is the very first complete fossil of early woolly mammoth ever discovered in China, which is also rare in the world for its significant value in scientific research, especially for its role as the most valuable material for the study on the origin and evolution of woolly mammoth groups in Asia-Europe Continent. Owing to its unparalleled value, it has also been inscribed into the list of "One Hundred New Great Discoveries in the Third National Cultural Relic General Survey".

Wang Jianping
Research Fellow and Curator of the Yellow River Museum

安化古道
The Anhua Ancient Route

　　安化古道位于湖南省益阳市安化县东坪镇、江南镇、田庄乡。安化县素有茶乡之称，早在唐代便有"渠江薄片其色如铁"的记载。明万历年间朝廷颁布《安化黑茶章程》，正式定安化黑茶为运销西北的官茶。明末清初，晋陕甘鄂湘等地茶商纷纷到安化设庄开行收茶制茶，资江沿线茶庄、茶行鳞次栉比，形成了黄沙坪、唐家观、江南、小淹等诸多茶叶集市，茶叶年产销达15万担。安化黑茶从最初的茶马交易，继而发展成生产、制作、运输、销售一条龙的经营链，源源不断地销往我国西北地区和周边国家。

　　安化茶马古道分两条线路：一条是从田庄乡至东坪镇的黄沙坪至江南镇经桃江、益阳从资江水路通往境外；另一条是从田庄乡至东坪镇的黄沙坪至江南镇的洞市经新化从陆路通往境外。沿线现存大量的清代、民国时期的古镇、老街、老商铺、老作坊以及古道路等文化遗迹。其中保存比较好的有高马二溪古茶园、万善桥、思贤桥、永锡桥、东长亭、永兴茶亭、裕通永茶行、良佐茶栈、德和茶行、黄沙坪老街、唐家观古镇、洞市老街、五富宫码头、江南大码头、梁家码头等，反映了安化黑茶悠久历史和独特制作工艺。安化茶马古道是我国明清时期南方山区繁华经贸活动的缩影，也是演绎古梅山地区民俗风情的文化长廊。

　　（文：湖南益阳市安化县普查办　摄影：欧阳红焰 周德淑）

五富宫码头
Wufugong Dock

永兴茶亭
Yongxing Tea Pavilion

德和茶行
Dehe Processing
Workshop of Dark Tea

232

高马二溪古茶园
Gaoma Erxi Tea Plantation

第三次全国文物普查百大新发现

The Anhua Ancient Route is located at Anhua country, traversing through Dongping town, Jiangnan town and Tianzhuang township, Hunan province.the Ancient Route is is not only a remained testimony for dark tea production, transportation and sales at AnHua in Ming and Qing Dynasty, but also an epitome of the whole culture of Dark Tea. Numerous cultural relics, which are closely related to Dark Tea culture, are well preserved along the extant AnHua Ancient Tea Route such as Ancient Tea Garden, Ancient Track (Wind-Rain Bridge, Tea Pavilion), the Processing Workshop of dark tea, Ancient Street and Bazaar, Dock and so on. As a crucial material carrier of AnHua Dark Tea culture, AnHua Ancient Tea Route is also an epitome of flourishing trade in Southern mountain areas back in Ming and Qing Dynasty.

永锡桥
Yongxi Bridge

洞市老街运茶马帮
Train of Horses Carrying Tea in Dongshi Ancient Street

贡陂堰
Gongpo Weir

贡陂堰位于广西壮族自治区桂林市全州县龙水镇，为广西唯一的至今保存完好的宋代农业水利灌溉设施。据清康熙版《全州志》卷七记载：南宋绍兴年间，万乡（今龙水）人刘霆捐资倡修贡陂堰，距今已有八百多年的历史，一直发挥着防洪灌溉作用。贡陂堰原为土堰，清嘉庆年间改筑为石堰。

贡陂堰所在的地区属于丘陵间平地地貌。该堰利用流经该区的山川河地势高、万乡河地势低的地理条件，在山川河段斜向修筑堰堤，拦截河水顺地势经引水沟流入万乡河，形成蓄水量深的堰潭。它主要由堰堤、引水沟、渠道三大主体工程组成。堰堤自山川河段至万乡河段全长1公里，用宽约55厘米、厚约50厘米的条石砌筑。石堤设计成拱形，利用力学原理，分散洪水冲击力；做成台阶状，上窄下宽，逐级内收，当水量大时，以缓和下泄水流的冲击力。同时借鉴灵渠筑坝原理，石堤下用松木纵向排列铺垫，大大增强抵抗洪水冲击的能力。在堰堤上部还设置了大小不一的泄水天平13个，使水量较少时有效地拦截河水用以灌溉农田，在洪水来临时又可及时分流洪水。并且在堰堤下方河滩种植大量柳树，缓解洪水对堰堤的反冲力。1965年，因山川河段水位变低，引水沟引水量小，已不能满足灌溉需求，所以在山川河段老堰上方约30米处，重新用混凝土修筑了滚水坝蓄水，并开挖了引水沟分流，以满足现在的灌溉需求。灌溉渠道共7条，新中国成立后进行了维修加固。

（文：广西全州县普查办　摄影：廖文丽）

清代堰堤
Dike Built in Qing Dynasty

堰堤上的泄水天平
Sluice Balances

234

1965年重修的滚水坝
Dam Rebuilt in 1965

The Gongpo Weir is located on the Wanhe River, Longshui town of Quanzhou County, Guangxi Zhuang Autonomous Region, the Gongpo Weir was built in step-shape with plagioclases. The gradual transition of wide in bottom and narrow at top can smooth the fast speed of watercurrent release as well as ensure the safety of the dike. Under the plagioclases was paved by pines longitudinally so as to make sure of the solidity of the weir, which greatly increased its capacity against floods. The weir was constructed in an arch shape with many different sizes of sluice balances settled on the top and a great number of willows were planted on the shoals below the wier to prevent floods. Gongpo Weir has received effective maintenance and management ever since Southern Song Dynasty and has been serving an important role in irrigation and flood prevention until today.

1965年重修的引水沟
Ditch Rebuilt in 1965

流经河口里村的主渠道
Main Drains in Hekouli Village

峨蔓古盐田
Eman Ancient Salt Pans

　　峨蔓古盐田位于海南省儋州市峨蔓镇细沙、盐丁、灵返、小迪4个自然村，其中最大的为有130多户人家的盐丁村盐田。

　　盐丁村盐田面积约16.5万平方米。盐田由晒盐田、卤水池、石盐槽和盐房组成。卤水池在晒盐田中间，上面铺着稻草或竹片和盐泥，用于过滤；盐田中共有5000多个形态各异的砚式石盐槽，大的直径3米，小的直径0.5米，都是不规则的圆形或椭圆形，均以黑色的火山石依其自然形状凿刻而成，每个盐槽普遍有1～2厘米的沿边，用以防止卤水流出；26间石砌盐房坐落在盐田中央，用以存放工具和储蓄盐粒。据考证，盐丁村祖先李行中自宋代迁徙至此，并开始土法制盐，世代沿袭至今。

　　灵返村盐田面积约8万平方米，168块晒盐田，有1500多个形态各异的砚式石盐槽，盐田里有9间石砌盐房。细沙村盐田面积约4.8平方米，没有盐房，有1000多个砚式石盐槽。

　　盐丁、灵返和细沙村的盐田，虽然面积及砚式石槽大小各不相同，但是制盐的方法都是一样的，完整保留了海南省先民们土法制盐的传统技艺和大量的古法生产器具、生产工地遗存。

　　　　　　　　　　　　　　　　　　　　（文/图：海南儋州市普查办）

236

盐田
Ancient Salt Pans

盐田—砚式石盐槽
Shallow Sinks Made of Black Volcanic Rocks

The Eman Ancient Salt Pans in the Xisha, Yanding, Lingfan and Xiaodi Villages, Eman Township, Zhanzhou City, Hainan Province. The pan in the Yanding Village which is about 16.5 ha in area, is the largest. It consists of more than 5000 shallow sinks made of black volcanic rocks. The sinks are various in shapes and sizes, with the diameters from 0.5 m to 3 m. Each sink has a 1 cm to 2 cm wide rim. There are 26 stone houses in the middle of the pans for storage.

The salt pans in Yanding, Lingfan and Xisha are different in sizes, yet the process of salt making is the same. These ancient salt pans in the Eman area completely preserve the traditional methods and tools of salt making in the Hainan Province.

盐丁村砚式盐槽之一
Shallow Sinks Made of Black Volcanic Rocks in the Yanding Village

泉坪猛犸象化石点
The Site of Woolly Mammoth Fossils in Quanping

泉坪猛犸象化石点位于甘肃省白银市会宁县新庄乡，在一条季节性小河的河床断崖处，距河床垂直高度约为2.5米。河谷两岸陡峭，巨石林立，部分断崖裸露红色、桔红色砂岩，质地坚硬，含有多次沉积旋回，化石地层为夹砾石条带的第四纪黄土地层。发掘出土的象化石为头骨和下颌骨，及部分肋骨、肢骨残片。象头骨长135厘米、最宽处90厘米，下颌骨长87厘米、最宽处65厘米。两门齿残缺仅留存根部，上下四颗臼齿保存完好。

2008年5月会宁县第三次文物普查队接到群众反映赶赴现场勘察认定为大象化石，并采取了有效的保护措施。随后对化石进行了挖掘工作，运回县博物馆收藏。2010年8月，经中国科学院古脊椎动物与古人类研究所金昌柱教授和王元博士的初步鉴定：该象头骨和下颌骨化石为早期猛犸象类，时代可能为上新世，距今约300万年。据悉，这是国内发现的第一具完整的早期猛犸象头骨化石，在世界也很罕见，具有非常重要的科学研究价值，特别是为研究猛犸象类群在欧亚大陆的起源和演化提供了最好的材料。

（文/图：甘肃白银市会宁县普查办）

修复展出
Display of Fossils after Protection

化石出土
Woolly Mammoth Fossils

猛犸象化石点全貌
A Full View of the Site

The Site of Woolly Mammoth Fossils in Quanping is recently discovered at the cliff of the riverbed in Hougou Hamlet, Xinzhuang Country, Huining Country, Baiyin City, Gansu Province. The newly unearthed fossils include bones of the head, the lower jaw, and some ribs as well as limb fragments. The skull is 135 cm long, with the width of 90 cm at most; the lower jaw 87 cm long, with the width of 65 cm. Neither of the incisors is complete and only remains of the root can be seen. Both the upper and lower molars are preserved quite well. The fossil of skull and lower jaw show that the animal belongs to the early woolly mammoths, possibly from the Pliocene Epoch of 3 million years ago. It is learned that this is the very first complete fossil of early woolly mammoth ever discovered in China, which is also rare in the world for its significant value in scientific research, especially for its role as the best material to study the origin and evolution of woolly mammoth groups in Asia-Europe Continent.

专家鉴定
Fossil Appraisal

多儿水磨坊群
Duoer Watermill Group

多儿水磨坊群位于甘肃省甘南藏族自治州迭部县多儿乡。建于清代，沿用至今，具有鲜明的地域文化特点。11个独立的水磨坊，集中分布在长不过150米、坡度陡降约15%的多儿河之上。每个磨坊长约7.5米，宽约5.6米不等，高约6~7米，主体木结构，外层部分由泥石构筑，"人"字型顶建筑。水磨坊大部分位于河岸上，仅少部分延伸出河面上，下有木立柱支撑，以便安装水磨的水轮及联动木轴，将水引至磨坊底部的方形木轮上，利用水的冲力带动连着木轮的木轴及磨坊内部的石磨旋转，来达到磨制青稞、小麦等农作物的目的。

多儿水磨坊群的建筑形制、水磨制作工艺、机械原理都保留了比较传统的风格，体现了甘南藏区传统的生产生活方式与其周边自然环境的和谐统一。

（文/图：甘肃甘南藏族自治州迭部县普查办）

水磨坊内部结构
Main Structure of Watermill

单体水磨坊俯视
A Panoramic View of A Single Watermill

磨坊群全景
A Full View of the Watermill Group

The Duoer Watermill Group Located beneath the bluff of Duoer River, Duoer Town, Diebu County, Gansu Province, Duoer watermill group was built in Qing Dynasty and has been remaining function until today. 11 water mills are centered on Duoer River which is less than 150 m long with the sudden drop slope of about 15%. With 7.5 m in length, 5.6 m in width and 6 to 7 m in height, the mill was built with the herringbone-shaped dome and timber as the material for main structure, cement stone for its outer-layer. Duoer Watermill Group, as a centered watermill group with a large-scale, has been preserved well until today at GanNan Tibetan Areas. With distinct characteristics of regional cultures, the watermill group reflects harmony and unity between traditional ways of production and living in Tibetan areas and its surrounding environments.

水磨坊底部水轮
Herringbone-shaped Dome

第 三 次 全 国 文 物 普 查 百 大 新 发 现
100 NEW DISCOVERIES OF THE THIRD NATIONWIDE SURVEYS OF CULTURAL HERITAGE

附录（参评项目）
APPENDIX

西山古道

    位于北京市门头沟区，是京西山区通往京师的重要交通干线，历经金、元、明、清、民国，长达800多年。特别是明代以来经过修建，古驿道成为联系山西、内蒙古草原的主要道路。

    西山古道按功用分为：商旅通行道路，如玉河古道；军用道，如西奚古道；进香道，如卢潭古道、庞潭古道。

    西山古道与北京的历史和社会发展也有着很多关联，门头沟地区在其基础上也逐渐发展形成了多条重要的交通干线和枢纽。此外，古道上还有众多文物古迹，蕴含着丰富的文化内涵。

玉河遗址

    位于东城区交道口街道，是元代连通海子与通惠河的主要河段。现遗址范围内已发掘出玉河河道及堤岸。河道遗存以石质为主，保存较完好，有明清两代遗迹的叠加，但整个遗迹分布呈片段状，局部遗留有完整条石及墙体。

    玉河是北京皇城水系的重要组成部分。发掘出的元明清时期的河道泊岸及东不压桥遗存是北京中心城区唯一的古河道遗址，是研究北京历史水系规模、流向变迁的实证。

弘曕府遗存

    位于西城区什刹海街道。总面积为1172.5平方米。弘曕(1712~1750年)，字思敬，别号思敬主人，一号石琴道人。清康熙帝之孙，理密亲王允礽第六子，曾任右宗丞。雍正六年(1728年)三月封奉恩辅国公。现存四栋清代建筑，正房五间，东西厢房各三间，穿堂三间。

    此处为弘曕在京唯一一处府邸遗存，建筑虽已翻修但也是基于原址上重建，清《乾隆京师全图》上仍可见其位置。

清太医院旧址

    位于东城区交道口街道。原为千祥寺，始建于元泰定年间（1324~1327年），明正统三年（1438年）赐名吉祥寺。

    明、清中央级的衙署是皇都文化的重要组成部分，但至今没有遗留下一处完整的遗存。太医院作为当时全国医药行政主管机构，保存了清朝的中央官衙制度，其中的先医庙和药王庙（铜人庙）保存了中国古代的医药文化。

清末自来水厂旧址

    位于东城区东直门街道。原名"京师自来水公司"，筹办于清光绪三十四年三月（1908年4月）。当时鉴于北京城内浅井水质不好及救火无水，以国有股270万元筹建京师自来水公司。1908年4月在东直门外香河园动工建厂，1910年1月竣工并开始分段供水，自此北京正式有了自来水供应。

    清末自来水厂是清朝政府自筹资金建设的现代化设施，是民族工业的萌芽，反映了北京城市化建设的进程。

第三次全国文物普查百大新发现

贝满女中建筑遗存

位于东城区东华门街道。由美国基督教公理会于1864年创建，亦称"贝满女子学堂"，该校是美国人Eliza Jane Bridgman夫人捐款建立，故以其姓氏来为学校命名。初期由美国传教士任教，学生全是教徒。现为北京二十五中学。

贝满女中是基督教新教教会在北京最早建立的西式学校，也是北京最早的女子专校。它见证了近代中国教育机制改革、学堂取代传统私塾、西学在中国传播的历史进程。

京奉铁路正阳门东车站信号所

位于崇文区（现东城区）东花市街道。与京奉铁路正阳门东车站旧址同为英国铁路工程师金达于1901年设计建造，是原京奉铁路从正阳门至东便门路段间东便门车站的一个信号房，距今有百余年的历史。

京奉铁路（北京—辽宁）与我国第一条铁路唐胥铁路相连通，而正阳门东车站是中国第一条实用铁路的终点站，其信号所作为京奉铁路的附属性建筑具有特殊的历史意义和较高保留价值。

东方饭店早期建筑

位于宣武区（现西城区）天桥街道。建于1918年；抗战期间被日本人占用；解放后一直作为高级接待机构，至1986年恢复对外营业。其早期建筑原由平面呈"口"字型的四幢三层楼房组成，现仅存1918年建设的西楼及1953年翻建的东南楼。

东方饭店诞生并兴盛于民国初期，留下了众多历史名人的足迹，见证了若干重大历史事件，有着深厚的历史文化积淀。

《没有共产党就没有新中国》歌词创作地旧址

位于房山区霞云岭乡。1943年10月，晋察冀边区抗日宣传小分队19岁的曹火星同志借用当地民间流行的"霸王鞭"民歌形式在该地谱写了《没有共产党就没有新中国》这首脍炙人口的不朽歌曲。1950年，毛泽东同志又亲自在这首歌"中国"前加了一个"新"字。半个多世纪来，《没有共产党就没有新中国》唱遍了大江南北。

首都钢铁公司旧址

首钢主厂区位于石景山区长安街最西端的石景山下，西南紧傍永定河。始建于1919年，面积7.8平方公里。是北京市最早的近现代大型工业企业之一，保留着比较丰富的近现代工业遗产。

首钢厂区内丰富的可移动及不可移动文物，再现了完整的钢铁冶炼生产工艺流程。其厂房、设备、技术及配套设施反映了中国钢铁工业发展的历程和改革开放的重大成果。

南塘遗址

位于天津市滨海新区。遗址坐落在约有300平方米面积的高台上，现有石碑一通，碑体长2.4米、宽0.9米、厚0.27米，碑边沿有纹饰，两面均有文字。石碑东侧有莲花石座一个，石座上雕有莲花（仰莲纹）、麒麟浮雕、双兽浮雕和花卉纹等浮雕。高台四周散落大量汉、唐、宋、金、元、明等时期的碎瓦片、碎砖和瓷片。为唐代遗存。

亚细亚火油公司塘沽油库旧址

位于塘沽区三槐路街道。1915年亚细亚火油公司修建储存量为2.2万吨的油库和码头。此后的20余年，天津一直是亚细亚火油公司在华北地区运输和销售的枢纽。1954年，亚细亚火油公司关闭。

旧址现保存有1915年建造的办公楼一座、油罐两座，使用至今。亚细亚火油公司塘沽油库旧址至今已有近百年历史，是近代西方列强对中国进行经济渗透和掳掠的历史见证。

顺直水利委员会旧址

位于河北区光复道街道。1918年3月20日，由北洋政府时期熊希龄主持的顺直水利委员会在意租界成立，负责海河、黄河流域的水利行政。现旧址为砖木结构，总建筑面积约2288.1平方米。

1918年至1937年的20年时间里，顺直水利委员会和其改组后的华北水利委员会汇集了一大批知名中外水利专家，他们振兴华北水利，形成大沽高程，在众多方面开中国水利发展之先河，在中国水利发展史上有着很高的地位，其旧址是中国水利发展史上的一处重要实物建筑。

独流木桥

位于静海县独流镇。该桥为木质结构，始建于1936年，圆木做桥墩，上铺横木，面上铺厚木板，是当时独流镇水旱交通运输的主要桥梁。1952年重修。是京杭大运河静海段内唯一保存较好的木质桥梁。对研究当时桥梁建筑特点和城镇发展等具有重要意义。

海河防潮闸

位于塘沽区渤海湾天津港航道外端、海河干流入海口处，北距新港船闸13.3海里。海河防潮闸建于1958年。闸体结构为开敞式，共8孔闸门，两岸控制楼为仿古建筑，气势宏伟，占地近1.3万平方米。

海河防潮闸是新中国成立后国务院批准的首批重点水利工程，旨在实现"清浊分流"、"咸淡分家、根治海河"的目标。它是一座泄洪、挡潮、蓄淡综合利用的大型河道水闸，是治理海河历史上的一座丰碑，是"塘沽三闸"之一。

大港油田港5井

位于滨海新区古林街道大港油田港东。面积为900平方米。该井从1964年11月17日开钻，由3238钻井队承建，12月20日获高产工业油流。津冀地区的大规模油田建设从此展开，港5井成为华北平原及渤海湾储有石油的科学标志。现港5井保护区内有采油树一座，浮雕墙和简介碑各一座。

港5井是华北地区的第一口发现井，也是新中国历史上的一口"功勋井"。它的开采是对我国著名地质学家李四光关于华北平原、渤海湾蕴藏石油学术观点的有力证明。

大水沟遗址

位于河北省张家口市崇礼县高家营镇。分布面积约52万平方米。遗址处暴露有文化层、灰坑、石器、陶器等遗物。属新石器时代晚期的龙山文化。

遗址地处中原文化与北方文化相互交错的燕山西延余脉，它的发现对研究当地龙山文化的特征及南北文化的交流有重要意义。

田村遗址

位于邢台市隆尧县尹村镇。遗址东西长400米，南北宽300米，面积约12万平方米。遗址处暴露有文化层和丰富的遗物，文化层顶部距地表约0.3米，本身厚0.5～0.6米。遗物以陶片为主，另有少量磨制石器。陶片有泥质红陶、夹砂红陶、泥质灰黑陶，部分器物（红顶钵）口沿处有橙色条带，可辨器形有钵、壶、碗、罐、盆等。属新石器时代的后冈一期文化。

太子务遗址

位于廊坊市文安县孙氏镇。在约2万平方米的范围内暴露有文化层和丰富的遗物。文化层顶部距地表约0.1米，本身厚约0.3米。遗物以陶器为主，另外还发现有鹿角器。陶器质地有泥质、夹砂、夹蚌三类。可辨器形有钵、壶、盆、碗、罐、釜（鼎）、豆、鬲等。根据遗物可知，遗址属新石器时期仰韶文化和商代两个时期，以前者为主体。

太子务南台子遗址的发现，填补了新石器时代仰韶文化在该区域内的空白。

下元遗址

位于邢台市沙河市白塔镇。面积约3万平方米。台地西北部断面处距地表1.5米以下暴露有厚约2米的文化层。遗址遗物丰富，以陶器为主，另有少量石器。一类陶器，可辨器形有红顶钵、鼎、盆、罐等，属新石器时代仰韶文化的后冈一期文化；另一类陶器以夹砂黑褐陶、泥质灰陶为主，纹饰以绳纹为主，可辨器形有鬲、罐等，属商代。

下元遗址的发现对深入研究冀中地区太行山东麓新石器时代的文化面貌提供了重要资料。

西辽城村遗址

位于邯郸市涉县辽城乡。面积约5万平方米。遗址所在地暴露有文化层和丰富的遗物，文化层顶部距地表约0.5米，厚1～2米不等，内含烧土、陶片、残骨和蚌。遗物以陶器为主，可辨器形有红顶钵、碗、鬲、盆、罐等。属新石器时代仰韶文化、龙山文化和商周时期等。

西辽城遗址面积大、堆积厚、遗物丰富、延续时间长，它的发现对深入研究冀南太行山东麓史前文化面貌，完善清漳河流域考古学文化序列有重要意义。

248

蔚县关帝庙

位于张家口市蔚县西合营镇。现存一进四合院，格局为前殿、东西厢房、正殿。关帝庙建于清康熙五十三年(1714年)，重修于清光绪年间，庙内保存的清代"百工图"，真实反映了清代市井生活的状况，表现了64种社会行业的从业情况，是研究清代社会、政治、经济、人文、民俗、宗教、信仰等方面的珍贵资料。

大梁江村古村落

位于石家庄市井陉县南障城镇。建筑风格以清代为主。古村落保存完整，占地约4.2万平方米。有保存完好的明清古民居院落162座，以及古街道、古建筑、古碑刻、古井、石臼、石磨、石碾、石槽等。

大梁江古村落是一组规模宏大、布局完整的乡土建筑群体，村内基本保持了明清时期的路网格局。其建筑形式和建筑细部的装饰图案，对于研究建筑史、民俗史学等有着重要意义。

石洞村古村落

位于邯郸市武安市石洞乡。古村落较好地保存了清至民国不同时期的建筑。现存院落78座、古阁3座、宗庙2座。村内街道保存较完整，共有胡同13条，为鹅卵石与毛石铺墁。

石洞村蕴含着丰富的文化内涵和具有鲜明的地区文化特征，是冀南地区保存比较完整的一处古村落。

同会村古民居群

位于武安市北安庄乡。该民居群以四合院式的单体院落为主，也有较为复杂的复式院落。均为一层平顶或硬山顶，个别二层。几乎所有的传统民居都保存有门楼、雕饰、匾额。这些传统民居大部分仍在使用，有许多群组布局别致、工艺精湛、保存相对完好。

同会村古民居群集中保存了一批晚清至民国时期民居建筑，吸收了当时的流行元素，并结合当地的生活和传统习惯，形成冀南地区民居地方特色。

京张铁路张家口站

位于张家口市桥东区东安大街。1909年9月24日运行，为京张铁路张家口起点站。站区占地面积约38.9万平方米。现存旧建筑共5处，分别为建于1909年的候车厅、站台、办公用房和建于1930年代的日式运转楼和职工宿舍。

张家口车站是中国近代史和中国铁路史上划时代的标志性建筑，不仅见证了张家口的百年发展历程，同时也是日本侵华的铁证。

独堆遗址

位于山西省临汾市汾西县永安镇。东、西、南三面环沟，分布面积约10万平方米，遗存属西周时期和汉代。西部断崖上暴露文化层，厚0.5~1米，采集有西周时期的泥质灰陶罐、人面形陶器和汉代泥质灰陶罐等残片。

该遗址分布面积较大，遗物丰富，特别是西周早期文化遗存为研究晋南地区汾河两岸西周早期文化面貌提供了实物资料，所发现的人面形陶器为此前山西地区所仅见。

大河口墓群

位于临汾市翼城县隆化镇。分布面积约10万平方米，是一处西周至东周的族墓群。

墓葬为土坑竖穴，有车马坑。地面采集有东周时期泥质灰陶绳纹盆残片。出土了大批青铜器、玉石器、漆木器和陶瓷器等。其中，墓区中央一座大墓，在其墓壁四周，共有11个壁龛，里面放置着漆器、原始瓷器、陶器等。墓主人可能为侯伯级身份。此墓群对研究西周时期晋南地区的封国及其与晋国的关系具有非常重要的价值。

西顿济渎庙

位于晋城市泽州县高都镇。坐北朝南，一进院落，占地面积1294平方米。据檐柱题记及碑文记载，始建于宋宣和四年（1122年），金大定二十八年(1188年)、清乾隆四十三年(1778年)重修。现存建筑正殿为宋、金遗构。

济渎庙为祭祀中国"四渎"之一——济水之神的庙宇。西顿济渎庙是国内现存济渎庙中建筑年代最久者。是研究中国早期木构建筑的重要标本，也为研究济神崇拜的分布范围和传神形态提供了重要资料。

北池稷王庙

位于运城市新绛县阳王镇。始建年代不详，据庙内梁脊板及现存碑刻载，明弘治、万历及清康熙、道光、光绪年间均有重修和扩建，现存建筑为明清遗构。坐北向南，占地面积1241平方米。四合院布局保存完整，中轴线存戏台、正殿，两侧有东西耳殿、配殿、土地庙及门楼。

北池稷王庙为研究明清时期稷王庙的建制和道教诸神的源流提供了丰富的实物资料。

大益成纺纱厂旧址

位于运城市新绛县古交镇。清光绪二十年（1894年）由新绛人李通创办。历经多次变革，是中国最早开办的民族纺织企业之一。占地面积5万余平方米。现存办公旧址、纺织部旧址、材料库、晾水池、泵房、机电楼、锅炉房、水塔、八棱状烟囱、清花除尘楼等。

大益成纺纱厂历经110多年，经历了不同的历史时期，至今仍是山西省重要的纺织基地，是研究中国纺织工业发展史的重要实例。

250

阳泉火车站旧址

位于阳泉市城区上站街道。清光绪三十二年（1906年）由法国银行公司承办修筑，次年正式通车。阳泉建火车站后，山西保晋公司在这里办铁厂，建煤矿，阳泉从此逐渐由荒滩变成商贸中心集镇，进而发展成为晋东工业重地、煤炭基地、交通枢纽和政治、经济、文化中心。

阳泉火车站为现存中国最早的火车站之一，见证了山西能源重化工基地的产生和发展。

晋华纺织厂旧址

位于晋中市榆次区晋华街。总占地面积11.4万平方米。1919年，榆次商业资本家贾俊臣等人集资150万元，创建晋华纺织股份公司，1924年投产后改为现名。该厂在第一次国内战争时期就成立了山西较早的共产党支部。2006年破产。现存有东门、南门、办公楼、车间、水塔、库房及大部分生产设备、设施，厂区布局完整。

晋华纺织厂是近代山西规模最大的民族纺织企业，见证了中国近现代工业发展的历史。

槐荫两级学校

位于忻州市五台县东冶镇。1934年，由时任阎锡山晋绥军骑兵总司令的槐荫村人赵承绶为改善村民办学条件而创办。占地面积10714.7平方米。

槐荫两级学校建制齐全，规模宏大，建筑雄伟，保存完整，是研究民国时期学校建制、教育体制和民国时期建筑的重要实例。槐荫两级学校培养了大量优秀人才，为研究山西近代革命史、教育史提供了重要资料。

大寨村

位于晋中市昔阳县大寨镇。1960年代起，大寨村人民在陈永贵的带领下，发扬自力更生、艰苦奋斗的精神，创造了水利、梯田、民居等重要物质建设成就。

大寨人因地制宜大力推广的梯田式农作方式，以及相配套的水利灌溉设施和水土保持办法，广泛推广于当时的中国大部分山区农村。在20世纪六七十年代的中国，学大寨运动对于推动全国农村开展农田基本建设起到了很大的积极作用。

锡崖沟挂壁公路

位于晋城市陵川县城东南部晋豫两省交界处。锡崖沟四面奇峰壁立，地势险要。锡崖沟人为了冲破闭塞、走出大山，从1960年代开始，前后历时30年，终于在悬崖峭壁上凿出一条"之"字形的挂壁公路，公路全长7.5公里，1991年6月正式通车。

锡崖沟人是在一无资金、二无设备、三无技术的困难条件下，经过前后30年艰苦奋斗创造了中国农民筑路史上的奇迹。

魏家窝铺遗址

位于内蒙古自治区赤峰市红山区文钟镇。总面积约9.3万平方米，是一处保存较好、规模较大的红山文化早、中期聚落址。

该遗址发现较多的房址和丰富的遗物，对研究红山文化时期的生活方式、经济方式及聚落分布等提供了较为重要的实物资料，且对深入探讨红山文化的社会结构、组织方式、文明程度以及与周边文化的关系等方面提供更为可靠的资料。

采石沟聚落址与墓群

位于赤峰市克什克腾旗经棚镇。分布于采石沟的南、北两侧。沟北坡为居住区，分布面积约3000平方米。地表暴露多处灰土层，文化层厚1～3米，属于夏家店上层文化早期遗存。沟南坡为墓葬区，面积约5000平方米。地表采集有陶纺轮、石纺轮、角器、骨匕等遗物。

该遗址的发现，为研究西拉木伦河以北的夏家店上层文化遗存提供了宝贵的资料。采石沟聚落址及墓葬群中的畜牧业文化因素浓厚，对于研究游牧业的起源有着重要意义。

黑矾沟瓷窑址群

位于呼和浩特市清水河县窑沟乡。依坡而筑，结构分为单座、双座或多座等形式。建造特点为圆形圆顶状（俗称馒头窑），高矮粗细不一，最高者在12～13米，低者在6～8米。窑身为上、下结构，各有窑口，下部有出灰口。该窑址群是一处保存完好的明清时期烧造瓷器的民窑作坊遗址。

黑矾沟瓷窑址群的发现，将内蒙古中南部地区烧制瓷器的历史推前到明代中后期。

八里罕沟墓群

位于通辽市奈曼旗青龙山镇。东西长500米，南北宽300米，分布面积15万平方米。地表部分墓葬遭盗掘破坏，可见墓葬形制有砖室墓和石室墓等，排列有序，清理出土一座柏木棺床小帐，追缴回一批辽代的瓷器，有青瓷葵口碗、温碗、白瓷壶、白瓷盘等。墓群地表散布大量辽代的砖瓦残片。该墓群内被盗墓葬出土遗物较为丰富，应为辽代贵族墓葬区。

宝日陶勒盖墓葬

位于锡林郭勒盟正镶白旗伊和淖苏木。墓葬形制为土坑竖穴偏洞室墓，共出土文物200余件，主要有陶器、金银器、铜器、玻璃器以及镶宝石首饰等。该墓葬的年代大致相当于北魏太和初年至迁洛以前（496年），应为北方民族的贵族墓葬。出土北方草原且随葬品如此丰富的北魏墓葬，该处是仅见的，对于研究北魏时期北方草原地带的部族分布有着重要意义。

敖伦布拉格岩画

位于阿拉善盟阿拉善左旗敖伦布拉格镇巴彦哈日嘎查乌日图乌兰山南侧一带。岩画分布在东西长500米、南北宽300米的范围内，共发现岩画133幅。画面多凿刻而成，主要题材有羊、马、骆驼、骑者、符号、藏文、蒙文等。年代不详。该处岩画幅面多，题材广泛，对于研究古代北方民族艺术有着重要价值。

敖伦敖包岩画

位于包头市达尔罕茂明安联合旗满都拉镇巴音塔拉嘎查一带。岩画分布在山丘的山脊上，面积约5平方公里，有岩画400余幅。岩画内容以马、羊、鹿、狼、骑者、车、蒙古包等为主要题材，画面凿刻清晰，形象生动。画面之间有明显的叠压打破关系，应包含不同时期的北方民族作品。年代不详。

岩画幅面多，题材丰富，刻画艺术水平较高。如双鹿图等，栩栩如生，为北方民族岩画中的精品。

庙塔石窟寺

位于鄂尔多斯市准格尔旗薛家湾镇，属清代遗存。塔座为长方形，塔基长5.3米，宽4.5米。塔身长5米，高4.5米，宽4.5米，由上、下两个佛龛组成。塔尖高4.5米。除有在自然岩石上开凿的石窟外，还有许多石砌之窟。窟内至今保存有精美的壁画，具有较高的艺术价值。如此集石窟、壁画、佛塔于一体的石窟寺，在内蒙古地区喇嘛教寺庙中具有一定的代表性。

呼伦贝尔中东铁路建筑群

位于呼伦贝尔市海拉尔区、满洲里市、牙克石市、扎赉诺尔矿区。包括：海拉尔牡丹小区俄式木刻楞、满洲里云杉社区二道街石头楼、博克图警署旧址、博克图日本宪兵队旧址、免渡河东正教教堂、免渡河铁道学校旧址、免渡河俄式木刻楞、免渡河中东铁路桥、牙克石沙俄护路军司令部旧址、伊列克得俄式木刻楞、牙克石蒸汽机车水塔、扎赉诺尔友谊社区俄式石头房、扎兰屯机车修理车间旧址。中东铁路是近代中国屈辱历史的见证，沿线文化遗产种类丰富、数量众多，许多建筑设计精美，功能完善。

内蒙古东部区侵华日军东北军事要塞旧址群

位于呼伦贝尔市海拉尔区、新巴尔虎左旗；兴安盟阿尔山市、科尔沁右翼前旗、科尔沁右翼中旗。包括：阿尔山市苗圃后沟阵地旧址、海拉尔区日伪铁路桥头堡、小靠山屯日军碉堡、吐列毛杜日军工事掩体和甘珠尔庙日军工事。

侵华日军要塞不但是侵略的历史见证，也是罪恶的见证，提醒今人勿忘历史、勿忘国耻，有着深刻的爱国主义教育意义。

孤山子山城

位于辽宁省铁岭市开原市松山乡。城址整个形制如马蹄形，东西长130米、南北宽100米，四周墙迹清晰可见，现残高1米左右。山城采集标本以夹砂红褐陶为主，有鬲裆、四棱锥形和圆锥形鼎足等，属青铜时期遗址。

孤山子山城在铁岭柴河流域的发现，极大地拓宽了人们对青铜时期城址的视野，对研究青铜时期考古学文化的时代、性质及文化内涵，以及与周边文化的关系，提供了重要的考古学信息。

青山沟小城子山城

位于丹东市宽甸县青山沟乡。属高句丽时期遗存。南北长约400米，东西宽约200米，东侧、北侧均为悬崖峭壁，西侧、南侧皆以高句丽特有的楔形块石筑墙。西面城墙长约400米，底部存宽约4米，顶部存宽约2米，残高1.5~6米。山城的东南角和西北角各设一座城门。

该山城的发现对研究早期高句丽民族的山城结构和文化内涵，以及辽东地区高句丽诸山城间的布局及内在联系具有重要的价值。

车杖子积石冢群

位于朝阳县东大道乡，由马莲桥积石冢和老山洼积石冢两部分组成。马莲桥积石冢是一处红山文化墓址，现发现积石冢8个，所有较小的积石冢都围绕着中间较大的积石冢呈放射状分布。老山洼积石冢是一处新石器时代红山文化遗存，现发现积石冢13座。

该处积石冢群是牛梁河遗址以外规模最大的红山文化积石冢群。它的发现对研究红山文化在朝阳的分布、特别是红山文化在大凌河两岸的分布具有重要的意义。

香炉山岩画

位于葫芦岛市南票区香炉山缸窑岭镇。四幅岩画分布在断崖石壁上，从东向西共30延长米。最大的一幅长0.9米，宽0.63米；最小的一幅长只有0.24米，宽0.2米。根据岩画的风格特点及附近香炉山青铜文化遗址初步认定为青铜时代岩画。该岩画为东北地区首次发现。

鞍山"石窝"形岩刻群

位于鞍山市千山区、海城、铁东区，共发现49处"石窝"形岩刻。它们相互组合，形成梅花、日月星辰、方格、十字等图案，而且多刻在龟形石上。普查队共普查"石窝"形岩刻图案共114组，疑似这种"石窝"形岩刻为青铜时代，其准确时代有待于进一步论证。

鸦户嘴堡垒

位于大连市旅顺口区铁山街道。清朝末年为清军所建，沙俄统治时期扩建。日俄战争期间，日军称其为"鸦户嘴堡垒"。堡垒总计建筑面积1800平方米，建有指挥堡垒、作战堡垒、重炮堡垒、双面堡垒，双向暗堡、单向暗堡、暗道等。

现存鸦户嘴堡垒以日俄战争遗迹为主，是目前旅顺所存日俄战争遗址中保存最完整、规模最大、功能最全的工事建筑群。

烟台街近代建筑群

位于大连市西岗区。由胜利街、烟台街、团结街等街道的围合区域内狭窄的街巷两边分布的28幢近代欧式建筑组成。这些建筑均为砖木结构，多为二层，始建于19世纪末20世纪初，是沙俄统治时期规划建设的达里尼行政市街重要组成部分之一。

该建筑群是大连市最早的城市住宅区，是大连市以港兴市的历史见证，是研究大连地区地方近代史、城市发展史以及铁路发展史和建筑史等的实物资料。

抚顺炭矿事务所、矿长住宅及西露天矿

位于抚顺市新抚区。抚顺炭矿事务所旧址始建于1925年3月，建筑平面呈"X"形，建筑主体中间为3层，四翼2层，内设地下室。矿长住宅旧址始建于1930年代，为两层砖混结构日式建筑。西露天矿开采于1901年，1905年3月被"日俄战争"中获胜的日军非法占据。

抚顺炭矿事务所、矿长住宅及西露天矿是日本侵略者掠夺抚顺煤炭资源、对抚顺进行殖民统治的历史见证，是研究日本帝国主义侵华历史的重要实物资料。

255

鞍山制铁所1号高炉旧址

位于鞍山市鞍钢集团厂，占地约300平方米。1917年由中日合办的振兴铁矿无限公司开始兴建，1919年4月29日竣工投产，是仿照日本八幡制铁所制造的同样容积的高炉。

鞍山制铁所1号高炉旧址是鞍钢百年历史的见证，是日本帝国主义侵略鞍山、掠夺鞍山钢铁资源的重要实证。

本溪钢铁厂一铁厂旧址

位于本溪市溪湖区河沿街道。本钢一铁厂是中国现存最早的钢铁企业，是保存完整的炼铁工业遗址。现留存有一条完整的炼铁生产线，其中1、2号高炉是中国现存最早的高炉，而本溪湖小红楼和大白楼原是清末中日合资的本溪商办煤铁公司和伪满洲国本溪湖煤铁公司的办公大楼，均为砖瓦混凝土结构，外观基本保持原貌。

本钢一铁厂是中日第一家合办企业，也是日本帝国主义大肆掠夺本溪地区的煤铁资源的历史见证。

五台山遗址

位于吉林省农安县永安乡。遗址面积9141.205平方米。地表散布有夹细砂灰褐陶陶片，纹饰主要有单线划纹、双线划纹、双曲划纹、斜格划纹等；采集到小型石斧一件。

五台山遗址是一处地表遗物较多、文化堆积较丰富、保存现状较好的新石器时代遗址。地表采集的小型石斧，夹砂灰褐陶陶器残片等应与巴吉垒元宝沟遗址属于同一种文化类型。该遗址的发现，为进一步研究吉林省中部地区新石器时代文化类型提供了新的资料。

辽春捺钵遗址群

位于乾安县赞字乡、余字乡。遗址群由成片的土台基构成，共有四区，共发现了1540余处人工堆筑的圆形、长方形台基，台基剖面和地表发现辽代陶、瓷、石、铁器残片、兽骨、灶台、北宋铜钱等，以及广泛分布的红烧土，且台基高低错落，分布有序，符合辽代春捺钵的临时营地、毡帐式居住、野炊等基本要素，结合地理历史研究成果，可以认定为春捺钵遗址。

四时捺钵是辽代独有的政治制度，春捺钵不仅是契丹族的风俗，也是其笼络女真、稳定后方的重大政治活动，辽代帝王曾前后29次到此。该遗址群的发现，再现了这一盛景。

纸坊沟城址

位于磐石市宝山乡。山城建在小锅盔山两条山脊之间的峪口里，城墙横贯峪口，墙体是用山上的砂石土叠筑而成，墙身均向两侧沿山坡直至山脊，依墙为屏，依脊为障。城围近5千米，地势险要，易守难攻。

城内有大小平台数十块，最小者25平方米，最大一块面积达3000平方米，当地群众称其为"点将台"。2009年普查队在复查过程中还发现了古城内遗留的十余处房址地基，并在城内发现若干段城墙，遗址面积增加至60万平方米。初步判断该山城应为高句丽时期建立的防御性军事城堡。

后太平墓群

位于双辽市东明镇。面积3万平方米，发掘了37座墓葬，出土有罐、壶、杯、钵、碗、壶形鼎、白石管、黑石管、玛瑙珠、绿松石、玉管饰件及骨镞、铜镞、铜扣、铜饰件、动物骨骼、人骨等遗物。有的陶器纹饰繁缛，有的陶器素面。

后太平墓群位于东辽河流域、松辽平原与科尔沁沙地交界地带，是由13处遗址构成的吉林省境内规模最大的青铜时代聚落——后太平遗址群的核心。该遗址群以商至战国的青铜文化为主要内涵，同时含有新石器时代及辽金时期遗存，年代跨度之长，遗存内容之丰富都是东北地区所罕见的。

夹皮沟金矿

位于桦甸市长白山西北麓金银壁岭下。矿区面积800平方公里。整个矿区为太古界鞍山群地层，砂金、脉金矿床分布广泛，具有埋藏浅、储量大、易开采的特点。据记载，夹皮沟有组织大规模开采黄金从清嘉庆末年开始，延续至今。分布有大大小小各个时期的矿井300多个，仅清代矿井就有85个。其间经历了沙俄和日伪时期日本人疯狂的掠夺。新中国成立以来，夹皮沟金矿先后开采了东山青、立山线、下戏台、二道沟、红旗坑等坑口，累计开采黄金70多吨，成为国家大型金矿基地。

中东铁路南满支线四平段机车修理库

位于哈大铁路吉林省四平火车站北约1.5千米处，占地面积约2万平方米，主体建筑面积约6000平方米，现由主楼、车间组成，砖混结构，屋顶由铅皮铺设。

四平街是20世纪初"中东铁路南满洲支线"的四大编组站之一。1925年11月，"满铁"在四平街车站以北修建了能容纳24台机车的扇形机车库。机车库共12间，西北侧等距分布着12扇门，分别与12组（每组2条）呈放射状分布的铁轨相接。该建筑现今保存完好，仍在正常使用。是中东铁路南满支线现存的唯一保存完好的机车修理库。

辽源奉天俘虏收容所二分所旧址

位于辽源市（原西安县）西安区北寿街道，是二战时期日军秘密设立的专门用来关押美、英等盟军高级将领和高级文职官员的场所。1944年12月1日到1945年8月24日，这里关押了盟军高级将领、高级文职官员总计34人。

收容所旧址占地面积27954平方米，现存有日式建筑平房、砖砌水泥勾缝的地下室、红砖砌成的地道。是我国现存的唯——所高级盟军战俘营遗址。

锦江木屋村

位于抚松县漫江镇。木屋始建于1937年，在民国初期由来自辽宁省凤凰城一带的游民建造，沿用至今，被当地人称为"木嗑楞"，意为用圆木凿刻垒垛造屋，好像上下牙齿咬合在一起，可经百年风霜而不朽。木屋所在的锦江村属于长白山满族木文化遗存，是满族的发祥地。这些木屋是长白山满族先人所创造的木文化积淀，具有浓厚的民族风情和地方特色。

伪满洲国国民勤劳部旧址

位于长春市人民大街，修建于1932年7月至1941年4月，又曰"第三厅舍"。始建时归属伪财政部使用，后被伪营缮需品局、建筑局等部门相继使用，1945年划归伪满洲国国民勤劳部使用。建筑为钢筋混凝土框架结构，建筑元素中有日式的平直屋顶和构件，有中式的兽饰。建筑原地上二层，中间局部三层，新中国成立后有加筑，现建筑面积5310平方米。2010年使用单位上海浦发银行对旧址进行保护修复。是目前长春市遗留的伪满重要官厅建筑之一。

长春第一汽车制造厂厂址

位于长春市汽车产业开发区。包括长春第一汽车制造厂生产区和生活区两部分，是"一五"时期国家投资修建的第一汽车制造厂核心区域。生产区建筑面积约38万平方米，内有各类工业建筑物20栋；生活区建筑面积约32万平方米，内有各种居住、文教类建筑物94栋。长春第一汽车制造厂作为中国汽车工业的摇篮造就了中国汽车工业的第一代领导人和产业工人，是新中国社会主义建设时期工业发展缩影的物质载体，其变迁过程直接记录着企业的演变历史。

常兴遗址

位于黑龙江省伊春市嘉荫县。遗址面积约3万平方米。普查时采集到42件石制品，有大尖状器、砍砸器、刮削器、斧形器、石片、石叶等。打片和第二步加工均使用锤击法。随后的复查和试掘，在砾石层中共出土石制品80余件。根据出土的石器标本特征和地层对比分析，该遗址属于旧石器时代晚期，时代距今约2～3万年。该遗址的发现填补了黑龙江省东北部没有发现旧石器遗址的空白。

大板城址

位于双鸭山市饶河县八五九农场。遗址完全被林木覆盖，西端被采石场破坏，现存面积约23万平方米。发现基本呈圆形的地表坑110个；修整平直掘筑而成的土台（部分为石砌）；疑是积石冢的石堆44处；人工修整的土台环绕山的主峰，疑是祭坛；疑是早期通道的大面积裸露石块。采集的标本有夹砂红陶、红衣灰褐陶、黑陶，纹饰有旋纹、手指纹、指甲纹等。遗存年代大体为新石器时代至汉魏时期。由于受地域、民族、交通、环境等诸多因素影响，其文化特征同中原地区同时期的考古学文化有很大的差异。

海西东水陆城站

主要分布在佳木斯市、汤原县、桦川县、富锦市、同江市、抚远县。海西东水陆城站始建于奴儿干都司创设之年，即明永乐七年（1409年），全长2500公里，为明代东北地区六条驿道中最长的一条。其水路从吉林市松花江段出发，顺江而下，直抵奴儿干都司；陆路从海西底失卜站（今黑龙江省双城市石家崴古城）出发，沿松花江、黑龙江下游两岸45个驿站东北而行，到亨滚河口北岸的终点——满泾站（在奴儿干都司城附近）。共经10城与45站，合为55城站。

目前大多数城站都已遭到破坏，位于佳木斯辖区内的6城多为后世所沿用，保存较好。

东明嘎墓葬群

位于泰来县泰来镇。遗址分布面积约3万平方米，地表分布有陶片、石器及人骨。普查时发现较浅的取土坑内有暴露的墓葬，普查人员对两座墓葬进行了抢救性清理。均为土坑竖穴墓，清理出玉璧6件，石器7件。遗物特征属昂昂溪文化范畴。为研究嫩江流域新石器时代遗址的分布、特征及葬式、葬俗提供了重要信息。

哈尔滨中东铁路松花江大桥

位于哈尔滨市道里区斯大林街道。始建于1900年5月，1901年10月投入使用。该桥在俄罗斯桥梁专家、中东铁路工程局桥梁总工程师连多夫斯基亲自监督下，工程师阿列克谢罗夫负责施工。桥长949.185米，桥墩用花岗岩砌筑，十分坚固。历经几次特大洪水冲刷而安然无恙。1962年7月，由东北铁路工程局设计并进行桥梁加固工程。

该桥是中东铁路西部线(滨洲线)的第一座桥梁，也是中东铁路沿线跨度最大最长的单线铁路桥。

老黑山侵华日军工事

位于牡丹江市西安区温春镇。依次排列有6座碉堡，总占地面积643.5平方米，分布面积约为4万平方米。碉堡为半地下式，钢筋混凝土结构，形制相同，平面呈圆形，地下深2米，地上高3.6米，壁厚1.43米，直径11米，内有圆孔、正方形射击孔、二斜孔及一个烟囱状圆柱。

老黑山侵华日军工事是东宁、绥芬河、虎林等边境要塞的梯次配置，是侵华日军为防御苏军及进攻苏联而实施边境"筑城计划"的一部分。

侵华日军水利设施

包括位于鹤岗市小鹤立河流域中上游的一处侵华日军修建的水库、水塔、大坝底部通向水塔的廊道，水库坝外修建的泵房、锅炉房、变电所、家属住宅等附属设施，以及鹤岗市区修建的北山配水池和西山净水场等供水配套设施。

侵华日军水利设施建于日伪时期，1939年在小鹤立河中下游建立水源井及输水管路；1943年此项工程竣工。在伪满洲国时期，隶属于满炭株式会社鹤岗炭矿工作课水道系。据走访调查，修建此处水利设施导致大批劳工的伤亡。

西孟侵华日军飞机堡群

位于黑河市嫩江县海江镇，建于1936年，由9个飞机堡及附属设施组成。

飞机堡由南起向北呈半圆形排列，堡间为跑道。建筑均为钢筋水泥结构。单体飞机堡呈半圆形，整体长28米，内径19.7米，每个机堡可容纳一架战斗机。附属设施内有地下通道，与其他附属设施相通，用于存放配件和油料。此机堡群对研究侵华日军在该地的军事情况有着重要的历史价值。

向阳半截河要塞

位于鸡西市鸡东县向阳镇。南起青狐岭庙，北至蜂密山，正面宽120千米，纵深11千米。分布于完达山脉丘陵地带。1934年6月开始施工，1937年12月主体工程完工。修建永久性阵地3处、野战阵地6个，同时建有军用仓库、医院、军舍、营房，并在平阳镇正北建有飞机场，成为侵华日军的野战阵地核心。

互为一体的半截河、庙岭要塞，是日军两个重要的军事指挥防御重地，1945年8月9日遭到苏联远东军全面进攻而失守。要塞部分主体现保存完整。

总机厂

全称"大庆石油管理局总机械修理厂"，是大庆油田会战初期第一座机械修理厂。位于大庆市萨尔图区，占地面积7.4万平方米，有4座厂房，均为砖混结构，黑色漆脊屋顶，长120米、宽60米、高8米，建于1960年。

当时大庆油田会战领导小组决定成立钻井、采油、油建和水机电等8个指挥部，总机厂主要负责当年钻井的钻头等前线关键设备维修工作，此外还担负着拖拉机、柴油机等设备的维修及一些配件的生产工作。是大庆油田研发和生产机械的重要基地，也是大庆油田开发的见证。

北水关遗址

位于上海市嘉定区嘉定镇。经抢救性考古发掘确认，北水关始建于明嘉靖年间，为嘉定故城四座水关之一。遗址曾遭多次破坏，下部结构较完整，南北长14米，东西现宽9.3米，残高1.5米左右。

北水关遗址不仅是水利设施，同时还具有军事防御功能，历史上曾为抵御倭寇侵入等发挥过重要作用，对研究嘉定人文历史、水利城防设施等具有重要价值。

宋嘉树旧居

位于东余杭路530号、526弄17号、23~31号。1887年宋嘉树与倪桂珍结婚后，买下虹口朱家木桥（今东余杭路）空地造房居住，并在这里养育了宋庆龄等六名子女。宋嘉树在住所自办印刷所，承印《万国公报》和其他西文书刊以及孙中山领导的兴中会、同盟会的大量宣传品。原建筑已改建，现为居民住宅。见证了宋耀如、孙中山早期从事革命活动以及宋庆龄革命思想的启蒙。

周恩来同志在沪早期革命活动旧址

位于虹口区永安里。1927~1931年期间，周恩来、邓颖超夫妇在上海党中央机关工作，北四川路永安里44号的居所成为不为人知但在危急时刻可以随即启用的最佳掩护场所。直至1931年周恩来离开上海前往瑞金。

永安里44号建筑现为民居，保存完好。该建筑是上海已发现的革命旧址遗迹中存在时间最长的，增补了周恩来同志早年在上海从事革命活动时期的一段重要史料。

丰田纱厂铁工部旧址

位于长宁区中山西路，占地面积16226平方米。1921年由日本丰田企业集团的创始人丰田佐吉创办。1942年改名丰田机械制作社，后独立成为丰田机械制造厂。1945年工厂由国民党中国纺织建设公司接管；1950年，工厂经改造后，在现址成立国营上海第一纺织机械厂。

现存原建筑有：恒温车间烟囱，高35米，为上海早期使用钢筋混凝土材料的建筑之一；办公楼；食堂；大课堂；织造车间，建筑结构采用纺织行业专用北透光形式锯齿型屋顶；配电间，钢筋混凝土结构，四周建有隔热墙；另有一栋建于1964年的大型车间，建筑面积4212平方米，是大跨度钢结构气楼屋架。

大中华纱厂和华丰纱厂旧址

位于宝山区淞兴西路。建于1919~1932年，占地面积8万平方米，建筑面积75432平方米。大中华纱厂由沪上巨商聂其杰、聂其琨兄弟招股兴办，为当时上海纱厂中生产能力最大的一家。华丰纱厂由沪上巨商王正廷、张英甫等人集资创办，位于大中华纱厂东首。1958年两厂合并后，改称上海第八棉纺织厂。2008年厂区被打造为"半岛1919国际创意产业园"。

现厂区旧址布局、大部分建筑和厂房主体结构、各建筑内部门窗、楼梯等均保存较好。对研究中国民族纺织工业发展历史有着重要的价值。

民生港码头

位于浦东新区洋泾街道。现存历史建筑包括厂房、仓库、别墅、办公室等多种类型，共11栋。民生港码头前身为英商"蓝烟囱"码头，建成于清宣统二年(1910年)。是当时远东设施最先进的码头。上海解放后，民生港码头划归港务局经营。1986年改称民生装卸公司，包括民生港码头、洋泾港码头和朱家门码头。

民生港码头厂区本身面积并不大，但是其历史建筑极为密集，建筑空间形式丰富多样，很能反映当时历史条件下工业建筑特点，是上海市浦江沿岸码头历史发展的见证。

枫泾火车站南岗楼

位于金山区枫泾镇。该防御工事由岗楼、碉堡及平顶工事房组成，总占地面积115平方米。岗楼为1937年日军侵占金山时修筑，高三层，直径为3.7米，辟有射击孔，上为瞭望台；碉堡为砖混结构，高二层，上辟射击孔；平顶工事房砖混结构，上辟有瞭望孔、射击孔，东西墙各辟一门。另在平顶工事房西出入口前有一防护墙。

金山是侵华日军重要的上海登陆地点之一，同时枫泾火车站又是当时江浙进入上海的重要门户。枫泾火车站南岗楼是侵华日军侵略的重要实证。

五原路近代建筑群

位于徐汇区湖南街道五原路。其中的288弄3号，我国著名漫画家张乐平曾于1950年6月至1992年9月在此居住，现由张先生的子女居住。旧居占地面积261平方米，其中建筑占地面积192平方米，为近代独立式花园住宅，砖混结构两层。二楼西房摆设仍保持张先生生前工作室原状，普查发现后被公布为徐汇区文物保护单位，现已成为社区居民学生进行爱国主义、革命传统教育良好场所。

上海重型机器厂旧址

现名"上海重型机器厂有限公司"，位于闵行区江川路街道。占地面积93万平方米，建筑面积33万平方米。工厂前身始建于1934年，1953年更名为"上海矿山机器厂"；1958年在现址建立新厂；1962年被正式命名为"上海重型机器厂"。1961年我国首台自行设计和制造的1200吨水压式锻压机在此诞生。该厂至今仍保留着一定数量的20世纪五六十年代建设的厂房建筑和设备。上海重型机器厂是新中国建立之初的国有机械重工支柱企业，为我国的机电工业和国防事业作出了巨大的贡献。

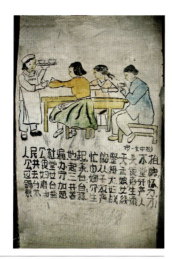

人民公社公共食堂旧址

位于嘉定区娄塘镇。1958年9月起，嘉定县各乡镇相继被新成立的人民公社取代，公共食堂随后应运而生。该食堂时属嘉定县娄塘公社的太平桥大队第四生产队。食堂墙壁上画有三幅反映当时社会状况的彩色壁画："工农商学兵五位一体图"、"祥龙腾云图"和"太平桥食堂用餐图"。食堂占用的朱家住宅建筑，建于1925年，砖木结构，歇山顶，在嘉定农村传统民居中具有一定的代表性，目前已不多见。

影山头遗址

位于江苏省兴化市林湖乡。遗址现存面积约5～7万平方米，在河岸的断面可以清晰地看到文化层。文化层堆积厚度约2米，可分为两层，遗存丰富，普查采集到石斧、石刀、石纺轮、陶鼎、陶釜、陶盉、陶豆、陶三足盘、陶罐、陶壶以及骨笄、骨镞等；另有动物骨骼等。遗址时代距今约6300～5500年，是江淮地区面积最大的一处新石器时代遗址，且保存情况良好。

黄泗浦遗址

位于张家港市杨舍镇。总面积约2平方公里。经两次抢救性考古发掘和全面勘探，共清理灰坑26个、灰沟19条、房址14座、水井13座以及道路4条，出土了陶器、瓷器、铁器、铜器、木器、骨器等文物1500多件。遗存时代以唐代和宋代为主。

发掘表明，黄泗浦遗址主要是唐宋时期长江入海口南岸一个规模较大的集镇港口，遗址内出土了大量日常生活用具，尤其是瓷器的窑口相当多，且"黄泗浦"见于日本僧人著录，足见遗址在唐宋时期繁盛一时。

紫云山墓群

位于宜兴市新街街道。普查发现后进行了勘探发掘，墓地总面积5万平方米，发掘2450平方米，共清理春秋、六朝、明清墓葬28座，以及春秋时期灰坑2个、窑址1座。其中一号墓为带排水沟的四隅券进式穹窿顶单室砖墓，根据墓室后壁砖砌窗格、直墙三顺一丁砌筑方式及人字形铺底砖几个特点判断，其年代为两晋时期。二、三、四号墓特征和一号墓大体接近，年代大体应在东吴至西晋时期。墓葬的形制结构和铭文墓砖对研究宜兴的历史文化有重要价值。

相国圩护堤水牮

位于南京市高淳县砖墙镇，系古人为避皖南山区洪水下泻直冲相国圩而构筑。相国圩为江苏省最早的围湖造田工程，距今已有2000多年。相传水牮系明初朝廷为安民养息、兴修水利时所建。上自水碧桥、下至大花滩约7公里范围内，分别布设"九牮八档"，用土石构筑起挡水之牮，各牮间距150～200余米不等。高淳西部属水网地区，水牮作为古代防洪设施已不多见，对研究古代护堤治水，具有重要意义。

果城里民国建筑群

位于连云港市连云区连云街道果城里巷1～23号。1930年代初由上海中兴公司兴建。占地面积3000平方米，共有四个院落，全石结构、红瓦屋面，对称分布于一条南北向小路两侧，庭院的出入口也相互对称。庭院平面由三合式连体房屋和面向小路的围墙组成，每个小院面阔17.1米，进深21.8米，每幢建筑上下各六间，木质外廊和楼梯，围墙上镶有雕凿精致的石门框，是一组典型的中西合璧式民居建筑群。

1930年代为筹建连云港，当时的民国铁道部、江苏省政府在果城里巷建造了这组建筑群，供荷兰建港专家、经济学家、银行家、高级工程师工作和居住，使这里成为连云港的规划设计和建设指挥中心。是连云港城市建设的最初见证。

国民政府中央广播电台发射台旧址

位于南京市鼓楼区江东门北街。1928年8月1日国民政府中央广播电台正式开播，电台的发射台最初建在丁家桥。1930年在南京江东门外北河口选址建造新电台，并向德国德律风根公司订购了全套无线电广播设备。1932年建成后的发射台，是当年东南亚地区发送功率最大的发射台。

发射台机房为钢混结构，建筑面积约1800平方米。现屋内保存着发射台使用过的各种仪器、设备、电缆等物。院内目前还保留有配电房、警卫营房、碉堡各一，发射铁塔两座，宿舍数幢。发射台由江苏省广播电台使用至今。

韩桥煤矿旧址

位于徐州市贾汪区。贾汪地区最早于清光绪六年（1880年）发现并开采煤炭。韩桥煤矿包括夏桥井（1933年开凿）和韩桥井（1947年开凿），其前身为贾汪煤矿。1964年更名为韩桥煤矿并沿用至今，由于地下煤炭资源枯竭，已于2008年底全面停产。旧址保存了1930年代的石砌水塔、井架和绞车房，1940年代日本人侵占夏桥井时所建的日式办公楼、两座碉堡及建造的学校，1950年代的锅炉房及老烟囱、韩桥矿办公楼等建筑，见证了徐州地区百年煤炭工业发展兴衰的历史进程。

金坛慰安所旧址

位于金坛市金城镇沿河东路火巷，原为地主陈子京的住宅，被日军霸占后成为慰安所。房屋系清代建筑，坐北朝南，可分为二个小院落。东面院落为两进，两进之间为天井；西边院落为三进。建筑现有人居住，保存较好。普查发现后已公布为市级文物保护单位。

1937年"七七"事变后，日机连续三次轰炸金坛城，大部分房屋被毁。日本侵略军入城后，四处烧杀掳掠，并建立三处慰安所。另外两处分别位于花街和丹阳门，现均已被拆除，此处慰安所位于火巷，为仅存的一处，院子西南边的阁楼当时是戒备森严的日军岗楼。该慰安所是日本侵华历史的见证之一。

三河闸

位于洪泽县蒋坝镇，是新中国成立初期我国自行设计、施工的大型水利工程，治理淮河的重要设施之一。

三河闸址在清代曾建有礼字坝，为高家堰五座减水坝之一，后毁于洪水；1935年，国民政府导淮委员会勘定在此处建长750米、60孔活动大坝，1937年底因日军侵华而停工。1952年，经治淮委员会建议、由苏北治淮指挥部设计，动用了近16万人施工，10个月即建成大闸。

三河闸工程的建成，极大地减轻了淮河下游的防洪压力。近60年来，抗御了1954年、1991年、2003年、2007年的淮河流域大洪水，以年均200多亿立方米的泄洪量载入水利史册。

沭阳古栗林

位于沭阳县西部，主要沿虞姬沟一线呈带状分布，其中以新河和颜集两镇最为集中，两镇四村的古栗树多达2000余棵，注册登记的近1500棵，历史都在百年以上。

沭阳县古栗林源于明清时期乡人喜植古栗树的习俗。如新河镇周圈村的古栗林占地8万平方米，有百年以上的古栗树566棵，古银杏172棵；颜集镇花晏村的古栗林约有5.3万平方米，其中一半以上的古栗树是清代鲍姓地主所栽，许口村共有古栗树约千棵，堰下村也有古栗树300多棵。由此形成了独一无二的人为种植的"古树群"景观。不但具有较高的历史文化研究价值，还具有很高的经济价值，更是当地珍贵的生态旅游资源。

方家洲遗址

　　位于浙江省桐庐县瑶琳镇。面积近3万平方米。普查发现后进行了小范围发掘，揭露了与石器加工有关的石片堆、石片面等遗迹，出土了大量石锤、磨石、石砧等石器加工工具、废弃石片和部分半成品、残品等，大批量与制作石锛有关的流纹岩石片，与石英块制作有关的标本20余件等。

　　方家洲遗址的主体年代约当马家浜文化晚期－崧泽文化阶段，是一处距今约5900～5300年间规模较大的玉石加工场所。

青碓遗址

　　位于龙游县龙洲街道。现存遗址文化层最厚处约为1.5米，分布面积约3万平方米，包含新石器时代上山文化、跨湖桥文化两个阶段的文化堆积：下层陶器和磨制石器具有浓郁的上山文化晚期特征，年代约距今9000年；上层陶器与萧山跨湖桥遗址、浦江上山遗址中层的文化面貌基本一致，年代距今约8000年。青碓遗址证明整个钱塘江上游地区是浙江新石器时代文化的发祥地。

彭公水坝遗迹

　　位于杭州市余杭区瓶窑镇。发现包括岗公岭、秋坞、石坞、老虎岭等6处人工堆筑的遗迹。初步判断为良渚时期人工堆筑的水坝遗存，应该与良渚古城外围的防洪治水系统有关。经测定遗存年代为距今4300年左右，其堆筑营建方式为：下部用草裹青淤泥堆筑，上部用黄土堆筑，这种营建的方式是良渚古城莫角山等高台遗迹普遍采用的方法，因此对认识和复原良渚时期大型工程的营建过程具有十分重要的意义。

湖州子城城墙遗址

　　位于湖州市吴兴区爱山街道。大致呈较规则的长方形，现存城门、城墙、附属建筑、排水沟等遗迹，唐代、五代、南宋各时期的遗迹叠压关系清晰。

　　湖州子城遗址，在孙吴时期为吴兴郡治，以后历代都是湖州（郡、州、路、府）衙署所在，子城各部墙体的年代多可以与史载对应。唐宋时期湖州子城东城墙及衙东门遗迹保存完整，在浙江省属首次发现。其唐代的散水形式、两宋时期的排叉柱式样的城门，以及各期城墙的砌筑工艺，对研究中国古代南方城市的建筑技术具有重要价值。

泗洲造纸作坊遗址

　　位于富阳市高桥镇。遗址分作坊区和生活区两大区块，总面积约1.6万平方米。现揭露出的遗迹主要为摊晒场、浸泡原料的沤料池、蒸煮原料的皮镬、浆灰水的灰浆池、抄纸房和焙纸房等；另有石砌的道路、排水沟、水井和灰坑等。还发现1条古河道。遗址最早使用时代可上推到北宋初期，南宋时为全盛期，元代时还在使用，后废弃。

　　泗洲造纸作坊遗址包含的遗迹基本反映了从原料预处理、沤料、煮镬、浆灰、制浆、抄纸、焙纸等造纸工艺流程。

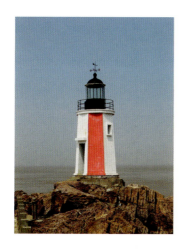

坎门验潮所旧址

位于玉环县坎门办事处灯塔社区。由我国著名的天文与测地界专家曹谟先生主持选址、设计，1929年6月11日由中华民国政府陆地测量总局建设了中国历史上第一座自己的验潮机构——坎门验潮所；1930年5月正式验取潮汐资料，经多年观测，确定了"坎门零点"；1936年1月，"坎门高程"正式启用，并引测到浙江、江苏、北京等17个省市，应用于军事测图等。1959年我国首次向世界公布了"坎门高程"的精确数据。坎门验潮所目前仍是国际海洋水文气象资料交换站。

浙东沿海近代灯塔群

位于宁波市、舟山市，由分布于东海洋面的舟山群岛的嵊泗列岛白节山、半洋礁、唐脑山、鱼腥脑、洛伽山、大菜花山、七里屿，象山石浦海域的东门岛及渔山列岛北渔山等岛屿的13座近现代灯塔所组成。最早的灯塔是始建于1865年的宁波镇海口的七里屿（峙）灯塔。灯塔一般由一座主灯塔和周边的附属控制、生活等设施组成。

浙东沿海灯塔自晚清至民国建立后均由海关管理。新中国成立后，归属交通部管理；1980年后归上海航道局管理。浙东沿海灯塔是我国最早建设的一批现代灯塔，是中国开埠通商的重要见证。

浙江农业大学旧址

位于杭州市江干区凯旋街道。浙江农业大学渊源于清宣统二年（1910年）创建的官立浙江农业教员养成所，后几经变迁。1929年改成浙江大学农学院，并于1934年将学校迁至现址；抗日战争时西迁；抗战胜利后学校在今址得以重建。旧址内现存有先后建造于1940年代至1970年代的建筑共34栋，有西斋，东、西大楼，和平馆、民主馆、团结馆、养虫室等，承担着宿舍、教学、科研等功能，具有仿苏联、新中国成立初期的建筑风格。围绕华家池分布的近现代建（构）筑物群，保存完整、功能明确、分布合理、风格多样，与极其优美的环境互相掩映，形成具有园林特征及深厚历史文化底蕴的人文景观。

浙江省立实验农业学校旧址

位于金华市金东区塘雅镇、法藏寺所在，占地55万平方米，建筑面积22590平方米。1933年由著名土壤学家蓝瑾创办；1942年金华沦陷后一度解散；1949年更名为"浙江省立农业技术学校"直至1967年迁址。现存21幢民国特色建筑：行政楼、教学楼、办公楼、学生宿舍、大礼堂、大膳厅、厨房、教师宿舍、图书馆、仪器室、操场、粮食仓库、实验楼、农社等，保留了民国时期典型的学校建筑风格，更像是座中西合璧的园林。机山之上的唐代法藏寺遗址亦在其中。是规模宏大、保存完好的民国省立学校旧址。

龙泉窑制瓷作坊

位于龙泉市宝溪乡、上垟镇、八都镇。龙泉是著名的青瓷产地，龙泉窑在中国制瓷史上占有十分重要的地位。清代至民国时期，龙泉的传统制瓷业虽几近颓废，但仍变换产品谋求生存，终使传统产业得以延续和传承。宝溪、上垟、八都三个乡镇现存23处龙泉窑生产窑场，保存有23处结构类似的分室龙窑及相配套的水碓房、拉坯房、淘洗池等，修建烧造时代多源自清、民国时期，直至1990年代初。

浦溪河流域遗址群

位于安徽省黄山区甘棠镇、耿城镇。浦溪河流域在黄山主峰之北的皖南山区腹地之中，在河流两岸仅50平方公里范围内共发现12处先秦遗址，包含新石器时代晚期、商代、西周至春秋等时期的遗存。其中以蒋家山遗址面积最大，现存面积超过3万平方米，是皖南山区目前仅见的一处较大型遗址，时代距今5000～4800年左右，遗物以石镞、锛、网坠为主，少量玉饰，发现稻谷痕迹。陶器中的鱼鳍形足与刻划日月符号、小石钺、两侧出角或带短柄石刀，分别反映了与长三角、大汶口及赣北有紧密的文化联系。

新管窑址

位于黄山市歙县桂林镇。依山而建，面积约4000平方米，为龙窑，窑长约30米，由窑棚、窑头、窑体及窑尾、烟囱等组成。窑址地层堆积以废弃的陶瓷器残片和红烧砖、土块为主。该窑主要生产陶器和青瓷，还有部分酱釉。器类有各种窑具以及钵、碗、盏、壶等日用器物，有个别如觚形器等特殊器形。从出土器物和"祥符通宝"钱分析，该窑址年代应为五代末至北宋初，属民窑。该窑产品的外销，为皖南陶瓷外销研究及古徽州经济研究提供了新资料。

东至古徽道

徽道是明、清时期南来北往的徽商贩运商品的咽喉要道。徽商萌生于唐代，明代中叶至清乾隆末年的300余年间是徽商发展的黄金时期，无论是经营行业、经营规模，还是活动范围，都居全国商界之首。

东至县为古徽道途经的重要区域，道上现存有沿途铺设的石板，石亭及建亭碑记，清代修造古徽道的石碑石刻，徽商沿途开掘的泉井，清代禁止在徽道两侧乱砍滥伐、防止水土流失的禁山碑"输山碑"等等，徽道上的14座石拱桥也都由徽商兴建。

双峰寨古遗址

位于金寨县果子园乡，双峰寨因山势得名。山寨海拔825米，平面布局大体呈长方形，墙体由石块砌成，墙高3米，东门、西门、小西门犹存。寨内面积约50万平方米，遗留有石砌房基200余处、古井一口以及石臼等。大别山自古为兵家必争之地，楚汉相交的果子园双峰寨更是首当其冲。此处可能是元末红巾军领袖徐寿辉建立的囤兵处。在土地革命时期、抗日战争时期，成为革命武装和人民群众据关凭险，开展对敌斗争的堡垒。

春秋塘茶林场墓群

位于舒城县城关镇。墓冢两两相对，沿西北—东南方向在一条低矮岗地上排列。该墓地规模较大，目前发现墓葬42座，皆有锥形或圆台形封土，其底径达几十米，高几米至十余米不等。墓葬大都分布在低矮的岗地（山脊）、近水、面临开阔地，同时排列较为有序，形态单一，封土大都保存完好，可能均属春秋时期群舒贵族墓葬。

洪小涛宅

位于黄山市歙县桂林镇。砖木结构，建于明代，坐东北朝西南，两进三开间，三层楼，通面阔10.9米，通进深14.6米，占地面积159平方米，该宅外墙体后期改建过。底层厅堂装修精致，采用方格型天花板；二层则保持明代典型的密栅式楼面结构。整座住宅结构精致，木雕精美。是明代徽派民居精品。

何氏宗祠

位于金寨县古碑镇。建成于1943年，坐北朝南、依山傍水。整个建筑融皖南、赣及皖西建筑风格为一体，两进两包厢结构，共计20间房屋、5个天井院。建筑面积1500余平方米。

何氏宗祠曾在刘邓大军南下时为古南乡工农政府驻地，现由何氏家族使用。它不仅是具有中国传统和地方特色的乡土建筑，也是一处革命旧址。

口子窖酒厂建筑群

位于淮北市濉溪县濉溪镇。口子窖酒遗址由口子窖池、老井及酒厂建筑群构成。口子窖池始建于元末明初，一直沿用至今，已有600余年，形成独特的微生物菌群；口子老井，据传掘于隋唐之际，历代均有修葺，沿用至今；1951年在老濉河东岸"祥兴泰""协源公""协顺""协昌"等老酒坊基础上建设而成的酒厂建筑群，是保存较为完好的中西合璧的现代建筑。

将军山渡槽

位于六安市金安区施桥镇，地处江淮分水岭之间。建于1969年，钢筋混凝土双曲拱结构，跨山而渡，与淠史杭综合利用水利工程联为一体。渡槽全长894米，距地高27米，宽7米，16孔，孔距52.5米，槽底宽6米，壁高2.9米，是目前全国最长的渡槽。是沟通淮河水系和长江水系的重要枢纽，现今依然承担着为杭淠干渠进行水利调节和区域性灌溉任务。

包家村燎原渠

位于岳西县包家乡。1970年代，全国掀起"自力更生，艰苦创业"的热潮，岳西县包家乡人民集全乡之力，历时3年，从山势较高的美丽村凿开一条全长7公里、宽1.3米、深1.2米的渠道，取名"燎原渠"，灌溉农田20万平方米。现"三八洞""友谊洞""青年洞""民兵洞""创业渡槽"等渠道保存完好，至今仍在为下游电站输送发电用水。

第三次全国文物普查百大新发现

黄柏竹林坑遗址

位于福建省武夷山市武夷街道。在山体东坡机耕道断面距地表深度约1米处，发现疑似残破窑炉两座。断面上可见明显的文化层堆积，其中包含较多窑渣、红烧土粒以及原始青瓷残片。初步判定其时代为西周时期。在其不远处还发现另一处遗址。竹林坑遗址发现大量原始青瓷器和可能为烧造该瓷器的窑炉，为研究闽北原始青瓷器的起源和窑业技术提供了第一手田野资料。

塘脚营宫

位于漳浦县绥安镇。坐北朝南，建筑面积256平方米，面宽12.8米，进深19.8米，墙体三合土夯筑，由前殿、天井、左右两廊、正殿组成。前廊粉墙上还保存着清代壁画。塘脚营原为元代军事基点，宫庙虽经历代重修，但基本保存元代木结构，为闽南地区年代最早的古建筑。

黄村值庆桥

位于建瓯市迪口镇。明弘治三年（1490年）始建，最近一次大修为1954年，但整体结构基本保存原貌。桥长30米、宽6米，南北走向，为单孔木伸臂梁廊屋桥。桥藻井内斗拱层层叠叠，廊屋梁架处做大量粗大的丁字形斗拱。该桥是国内现存年代较早的梁式廊桥之一，建造方式上沿用了纯正的宋代营造法式做法，对研究福建明代建筑、梁式木廊桥的演变有着重要意义。

三洲古建筑群

位于长汀县三洲古镇。60多座古家祠家庙、古民宅成片完整保存。其中部分建于明代后期，多数建于清代中后期。规模大、工艺精、环境佳、保留最好的建筑有戴氏家庙等10余座，有一定代表性、具有较高价值的有40余座。其中还有相当一部分的涉台建筑。三洲古建筑群外观高低错落有致，整体建筑高大壮观，有着浓郁的客家建筑风格。

东石玉记群屋

位于晋江市东石镇。玉记号由玉井房十四世章昰（1817~1897年）三兄弟于清咸丰八年（1838年）开创。自1887年起，玉记行在东石海港"玉记坞"北面建大厝8座，占地面积约3000平方米，均为燕尾脊古大厝，砖石木结构，穿斗式木构架。其屋宇墙帽毗连相接，规模宏大，大片的红砖建筑以巷埕相隔，规划齐整。

抗战时期金门县政府办公旧址

位于厦门市翔安区大嶝街道。共7处12栋建筑，仍保存着当年的建筑风貌。其建筑与金门岛上现存的乡村建筑风貌极为相似，多数兴建于清代末年和民国初年，既有闽南传统式民居，也有华侨从南洋借鉴的西洋式民居，成为20世纪初闽南沿海民居建筑的典型代表。经考证，此旧址系1937年至1945年金门岛沦陷期间，金门县政府的办公地点，是海峡两岸抗战历史的重要史迹。

陈塘红军医院旧址

位于宁化县石壁镇。1933年春，原设于江西瑞金的红军第四医院随军在此收治东线战斗中的伤病员。医院按职能分为住院部、后勤部、行政管理部等，另有操演场及红军墓地等革命遗迹及大量红军标语。旧址坐北朝南，占地约850平方米，平面呈长方形。由门楼、下厅、天井、正厅、后厅、雨亭、户盾等组成。是红军在闽西浴血奋战的历史见证，具有革命纪念意义。

坑仔口龙窑窑炉

位于厦门市同安区祥平街道。共有4条斜坡式券顶龙窑，依山坡而建。其中2条保存完整，每条窑炉长达74米，窑床内部高2.4米、宽2米，保存着炉身、窑门、火膛、投柴孔、边门、护窑墙、前后挡火墙、烟囱等完整结构，窑炉上方搭建简易遮篷。产品以日用粗陶为主。据文献记载，此窑创建于清嘉庆二十五年（1820年），后为同安陶器厂，直至2006年停烧。其窑炉结构与古代南方龙窑形制基本一致。

上花人民会场

位于漳州市长泰县陈巷镇。始建于1960年代，坐东南向西北，占地575.95平方米。建筑采用中西合璧式的手法，墙体由红砖垒砌，二层双坡顶，梁架为简易人字架，在会场外檐立面饰有灰塑五角星图案及"上花人民会场"等字样。

连江"海峡之声"广播站

位于福州市连江县黄岐镇。新中国成立初期至1970年代，畚箕山是海防重要战略高地，建有瞭望台、观察哨、营房、碉堡、海峡之声对台广播站、长300米的防空洞。1979年中央军委直接下拨1000万元人民币巨资建造了对台广播站。广播站由坑道和巨型超高音喇叭两部分组成。随着两岸关系的缓和，于1997年陆续撤销。是大陆对台关系的重要历史见证。

包家金矿遗址

位于江西省上饶县茶亭镇。由采矿区、洗矿区、冶炼区、道路桥梁、矿工住区、管理机构区、寺庙、祭祀场、采石场等遗存组成。采矿区面积约14平方公里，选矿区、冶炼区及管理机构区面积约1平方公里。目前已发现古代老窿1112处，唐宋元明四代的炼渣堆积区面积约7500平方米以上。始采年代均为唐代。

华林造纸作坊遗址

位于宜春高安市华林风景名胜区。经考古发掘，在福纸庙作坊区650平方米范围内就发现了各类与造纸相关的遗迹共28个，还在周岭村清理水碓遗迹7座，西溪村清理水碓遗迹7座。揭露出的大批宋、元、明时期与造纸工艺有关的遗迹，时代顺序清楚，功能相互关联。对探讨我国造纸术的发展史有着重要价值。

银山银矿遗址

位于德兴市银城镇。古矿区东西宽约2.1千米，南北长约2.7千米，占地面积约5.67平方千米；冶炼区占地面积约0.33平方千米，古矿区总面积约6平方千米。发现有古矿洞、古巷道194处。开采区有大型露采坑、槽坑和大量废石堆，老窿开采深度达侵蚀基准面100米以下；冶炼区集中在铁石山，炼渣堆积约15760立方米，场面十分壮观。从历史文献记载来看，发现于隋代，开采于唐代，是唐宋时期中国白银生产的重要基地。

恩江古城址

位于永丰县恩江镇。呈东北－西南走向的葫芦形状，南北直线距离1050米，东西直线距离940米，总占地面积约55万平方米。现存城墙2500余米，布局、走势保存完整；墙砖上铭文保留了明至清城墙建设、维修等历史信息。对研究明代城市发展具有重要意义。

李洲坳墓葬

位于宜春市靖安县水口乡。是东周时期一座带封土的大型长方形土坑竖穴，墓室埋葬棺木47具，是我国首次发现的一坑多棺墓葬，为研究东周时期的墓葬制度和社会生活史等提供了新的重要资料。出土文物丰富、种类繁多、技术含量高，在多个方面有着重大突破。其中出土的中国最早方孔纱、面积最大的整幅拼缝织物和中国密度最高、时代最早的织锦实物，为研究古代纺织技术提供了详实资料。

吉安县功名坊

位于吉安县。石溪联科牌楼是吉安县现存最早的木构牌楼之一，建于明天顺六年（1462年），属科举功名牌楼。赤陂科第世家牌坊属功名坊，为清朝中后期建筑，后多有修葺。大栗王家世进士第牌坊为木质牌坊，建于明成化五年（1649年），清雍正十年（1732年）修葺。吉安县功名坊见证了吉安古代人文昌盛，其建筑讲究、雕刻精美。

宜丰培根职业学校旧址

位于宜丰县天宝乡。创建于1919年，为砖木结构两层西式洋楼。坐北朝南，占地面积206平方米。底层正面为七券砖砌拱形门，两边为四券砖砌拱形门，后面二墩砖柱，中间两根石柱，形成四条廊道围住中间的建筑主体结构。二层拱门数量与样式同底层，四边均做木护栏。在南侧砖柱上塑有"宜丰培根职业学校"字样。它是江西省内最早的专门培养农业人才的职业院校。

洪都机械厂八角亭车间旧址

位于南昌市青云谱区洪都街道，洪都集团公司二车间，又称"八角亭"。由意大利工程师设计，于1936年建成，当时名为"中央南昌飞机制造厂"，新中国成立后更名为洪都机械厂。1954年，该车间生产的第一架国产飞机"雅克18"初级教练机试飞成功。该车间保存完好，主体结构为钢筋混凝砖木混合结构，平面呈正八边形，总占地面积5876平方米，分上下两层。它是中国自行制造的第一架飞机的生产车间，见证了中华民族航空工业的发展历程。

广昌大跃进壁画

位于抚州市广昌县驿前镇赖巽家庙内。壁画共有六幅，规格一致，均为高1.82米、宽1.25米。其中有"边收边种""欣欣向荣""大食堂""拾穗图""民兵五好评比台"等内容。壁画绘于1958年，线条清晰，人物造型丰满，色彩艳丽，保存完好。

7501瓷生产基地

位于景德镇市珠山区新厂街道中国轻工业陶瓷研究所。由指挥部（现行政楼）、艺术楼、成型车间（含原料与球磨两个车间）、琢器车间、窑房、窑炉、烟囱（两根）、白瓷仓库等8座建筑构成。始建于1950年代，均为青砖墙体，人字梁木构架，屋顶铺以红色琉璃瓦。整体规模宏大，布局科学，形成了7501瓷研制、成型、彩绘及烧造等一整套专门的生产体系。

黄河三角洲盐业遗址群

位于山东省广饶县、潍坊市滨海开发区、寿光县、昌邑县。黄河三角洲盐业遗址群，分布集中、规模大、数量多，时间跨度从商周到明清，能够完整反映中国海盐生产的发展历程。它的发现和发掘，使人们对当时的盐业遗址的规模、分布情况、堆积形态以及制盐方式有了初步了解，对研究《管子》等文献所呈现的齐国规模化盐业生产水平、制盐方式等有重要意义。

陈庄城址

位于淄博市高青县花沟镇。遗址分东、西两部分。经发掘，确认其为西周时期的城址及东周的环壕，并在城内清理了房基、灰坑、窑穴、道路、水井、陶窑等生活遗迹，并发现了多座贵族墓葬、车马坑以及祭坛。获取了大量的陶器及较多的蚌器、骨器等遗物，墓葬出土了一批重要青铜器及少量精美玉器。此城址是目前山东地区确认最早的西周城址。

琅琊台大台基

位于胶南市琅琊镇。是一处巨大的夯土层遗迹，自然侵蚀严重，残存部分高20米，台基面积在1万平方米以上。台基由不同颜色的质密沉淀物组成，根据填土里的少量陶片初步判定为东周时期的遗存。不远处发现的大小不一的瓦状遗留物，初步断定是秦汉时期的遗物。琅琊台大台基规模大，夯土堆积厚，作为东周至秦汉时期的海防工程或祭祀遗迹，对胶东地区东周至秦汉时期历史的研究有重要意义。

菏泽古代沉船

位于菏泽市开发区。发现的沉船为一木质内河船。船体残长21米、宽4.82米、高1.8米，除去船头、船尾独立船舱外，共分为10个船舱。沉船内及周围共发现文物110余件。包括陶器、瓷器、漆器、玉石、玛瑙、石器、铁器、铜器、金饰等。根据遗物分析，该河船沉没的年代应为元代。根据沉船内的遗物及沉船的形状分析，该船应是当时的官员或商人在内河行驶时使用的船只。

聊城土桥闸遗址

位于聊城市东昌府区梁水镇。始建于明成化七年（1471年），清乾隆二十三年（1758年）拆修。由闸口、迎水、燕翅、分水、燕尾、裹头、东西闸墩及南北侧底部保护石墙和木桩组成。发掘出土了大量遗物，包括明清时期的瓷器、铁器、建筑构件等。该遗址是大运河上完整揭露的第一座船闸，对于研究大运河的水工设施、认识大运河在我国古代交流与沟通中的重要作用具有重要意义。

莱芜山地大型石墙遗迹

位于莱芜市。西起莱城区的崇崖山，东至钢城区的黄羊山与青羊崮一带，全长30余千米。遗迹均位于山岭北侧，由石砌的城墙与城堡组成。附近发现的多处春秋战国时期遗址，为石墙遗迹的年代判定提供了依据。从现存石墙遗迹的建筑方法和高度、宽度判断，可能在春秋晚期、战国早期建成使用不久即被废弃。除了考虑防御北部劲敌齐国之外，可能还具有城墙和城堡的"关口"征税功能。

青州昭德古街建筑群

位于潍坊市青州市云门山街道。发现明清古建筑和传统民居93处，主要分布在东门街、东关街、昭德街、北阁街、粮食街及其两侧街巷。多为四梁八柱式砖木式结构，硬山顶，青砖灰瓦，青石铺地。明、清时期，这里曾是南到临朐、临沂直通南京，北到京城的交通要道，为山东东部著名的商贸中心和宗教活动中心。

胶东海草房

位于烟台荣成、威海、青岛等地区沿海一带。海草房以就近的山石和海石为墙，根据其形状堆砌而成。屋顶为海带草，柔软有韧性，耐腐蚀，不易燃烧。海草房工艺讲究，工序复杂。屋脊显得浑圆，憨态可掬，与墙上棱角分明的石头对比鲜明。据考证，海草房从秦、汉至宋、金逐步形成，元、明、清进入繁荣时期。海草房是胶东沿海地区独有的标志性民俗建筑，为研究胶东沿海的人文居所和建筑特点提供了重要实物依据。

青岛潮连岛灯塔

位于青岛市崂山区潮连岛。建于1899年，是德国海军在青岛海域建造的规模最大的灯塔，至今仍在发挥作用。采用建筑与灯塔连为一体的建筑形式，建筑面积约300平方米，平面呈"工"字形。整栋建筑厚重、坚固，依地势而建，地上一层，有半地下室，红瓦坡屋顶。灯塔地上二层，为八角形石塔，塔高12.8米，灯质闪白10秒，射程24海里。该灯塔既具有艺术性，又具有实用性，对于研究航标历史等有着重要作用。

津浦铁路黄河大桥及机车厂

津浦铁路位于济南市槐荫区中大槐树街道。始建于1908年，1912年全线通车。在山东境内长408.86千米，是我国东部地区一条重要交通枢纽。黄河铁路大桥架于济南市泺口村北黄河上，1909年开工建设，桥长1255.2米、宽9.4米，全钢结构，是当时英德合修的津浦铁路的第一大工程。津浦铁路济南机车厂始建于1910年，现存5幢较典型的日耳曼风格建筑。

"蝙蝠洞"古人类洞穴遗址

位于河南省洛阳市栾川县高崖头村。从洞内采捡到许多牛、马、猪、鹿、熊等等动物骨骼化石，另采捡到有一枚人牙化石及石核、砍砸器、刮削器、尖状器等。由此推断该洞是一处古人类洞穴遗址。据分析，该遗址是晚更新世早期一个保存有人类化石、多种文化遗物和大量动物群化石的重要遗址。

李家沟遗址

位于郑州新密市岳村镇。遗址面积2万多平方米。通过发掘获得了大量的遗物，出土石制品数以千计，还有数量较多的动物骨骼碎片及陶片等遗物。根据地层及出土物，确认李家沟遗址是一处旧石器时代晚期向新石器时代早期过渡的文化遗存。该遗址的发现，为探讨中原地区旧石器时代晚期向新石器时代早期过渡及早期农业起源问题起着重要作用。

敖仓城

位于郑州市黄河游览区及荥阳市桃花峪一带。现存南城墙残长400多米，西墙400多米，东墙百余米，以黄土夯筑而成，夯层厚8～12厘米，平底圆夯，夯径9厘米左右，夯层内含粗绳纹板瓦片，内饰方格纹。文献记载，秦置敖仓于此，曰敖仓城，在秦统一六国和汉兴起中在粮食供应上起到重要作用。运河鸿沟开通后，敖仓城处在南北大运河和西通洛阳的交通要道上，地理位置优越。

月台瓷窑遗址

位于新密市牛店镇。遗址东西长1000米、南北长1500米，总面积150万平方米。中部被月台河分割，瓷窑遗址就分布在月台河两岸和与月台河相连的沟壑两侧。从遗址文化堆积情况看，为五代至宋的瓷窑遗址。为研究河南瓷窑由北向南发展，及钧窑、汝窑的发展源头等具有重要意义。

重丘故城

位于驻马店市泌阳县付庄乡。整个城址平面呈拐尺形，面积约0.7平方千米，采用堆筑和夯筑两种筑法。从发现的陶器口沿、绳纹陶片看属东周时期。公元前301年，楚国败于垂沙之战，重丘故城被秦齐韩魏联军侵占，从此失去了整个泌阳地域，致使楚长城的防御体系不复存在。重丘故城的发现和研究对于探讨楚国在整个泌阳县境内的防御体系，乃至楚长城在南阳盆地东沿的防御体系都具有重要意义。

平岭楚长城遗址

位于舞钢市杨楼乡。从发掘情况看，人工墙体的修筑是将自然山体稍加平整后修建南北两道石砌墙体。其中北侧墙体较规整，宽约2.25～2.35米，残高约1.15米。南侧墙体下部较规整，宽约1.85米，残高约0.74米，上部石头已凌乱。结合此次发掘的平岭长城墙体的结构特点及年代看，该段长城是不晚于战国时期修筑的，并显示出防御北方的特点。

寺坡汉代崖墓群

位于南阳市淅川县寺湾镇。悬崖高6～15米，面积21万平方米，悬崖上墓群分布较密集。根据墓穴形制及出土器物、花纹砖推断为汉代。这是中原地区首次发现崖墓，为研究丹江、汉水流域汉代时期社会、政治、经济、文化、丧葬习俗等提供了难得的实物资料，进一步证明了当时中原地区和西南地区(特别是四川盆地、重庆地区）的文化交流融合。

闰楼墓群

位于驻马店市正阳县付寨乡。墓地面积较大，分为东、西和中部三个区，总面积为20万平方米，发现有墓葬近300余座。发掘商周、唐、宋、明、清古墓葬149座，发掘总面积1.8万平方米。出土青铜器、玉器、陶器、骨器、石器共275件，发现遗迹有房基、灰坑、井、窑30余处。为商周时期贵族及贫民墓群。该墓群的发现为研究豫南地区淮河流域上游晚商文化及淮夷集团的政治、经济、文化具有重要价值。

凤凰岭三皇殿

位于济源市五龙口镇，为明代道教建筑。面阔三间（10.94米），进深一间（6.68米），系单檐歇山式无梁殿建筑，灰色筒板瓦覆顶。属典型的中原地区明代中期地方建筑手法"无梁殿式建筑"。檐下斗拱、拱眼壁、大额枋、平板枋、挑檐檩、檐椽、飞椽、角梁、耍头等砖雕图案精美，在河南现存明代砖石无梁殿建筑中实属少见，具有重要的建筑艺术价值。

岩刻岩画

位于新郑市、禹州市、叶县、方城县等。主要分布在中岳嵩山东南余脉的具茨山，豫南地区的伏牛山顶、桐柏山余脉，东西长约40千米。据初步统计，具茨山岩画的存量达3000多处，方城县境内的岩画分布面积约2000平方千米，主要以巨石文化遗迹、星象图案为主。这些图案与中原上古文化有密切的渊源关系。具茨山古代岩画的确认填补了以往我国中原地区岩画考古发现的空白，为研究包括传说的黄帝文化在内的中原上古文化提供了一类新的实物资料。

蔡桥遗址

位于湖北省荆州市荆州区马山镇。南北长约3.5千米，东西宽约2千米，东北部有夯土城垣，城外有护城河遗迹。遗址东约5千米处有一烽火台遗址。城内有台基12座。遗址范围内有大量泥质陶和夹砂陶器物残片，器型可辨的有鬲、盂、盆、豆、纺轮等。根据遗址内台基的选址、形状、构筑、方向、布局、采集标本及台基附近的古河道、城垣、烽火台等分析，该遗址应属于春秋时期楚国都城，为探索早期楚郢都提供了重要线索。

青山遗址

位于荆州市江陵县资市镇。分布范围约20万平方米，现存长方形建筑基址8个，保存较好的有4个，形制相近，东西长约120米，南北宽约70米，顶部平整，高出周围地面约3米，边缘及周围有大量灰陶绳纹筒瓦、板瓦等建筑遗物和泥质灰陶盆、豆、鬲、盂等器物残片。据分析，该遗址是继潜江龙湾章华台宫殿基址群之后新发现的一处楚国游宫遗址群，为进一步探索和研究东周时期楚国的宫室营建制度提供了新的实物资料。

南漳古山寨群

位于襄樊市南漳县板桥镇。南漳山寨群共有300多座，始建时间不详。现存建筑主要为明清时期遗存，其中大部分为进剿白莲教起义而筑，多依山取势，修筑在临河、三面陡峭的绝壁峰顶以及关卡要塞处，布局严谨，设计巧妙。寨墙由片石或条石垒砌，设有马道、瞭望孔、箭垛等军事设施，功能齐全。堪称山地建筑之奇观，反映了古人的聪明才智和高超的建筑艺术水平。

五峰古茶道

位于宜昌市五峰土家族自治县采花乡。是明清时期五峰外运茶叶、山漆、药材等货物的主要通道。现存有石板古道、古桥、路碑、骡马店遗址和摩崖石刻等遗迹。它是湖北现存线路最长、覆盖地域最广、道路设施最齐全、遗存类型最丰富、保存最完好的商贸贸易古道，对于研究土家族地区对外经济发展、文化交流具有重要价值。

武当山窑址群

集中分布于十堰市武当山旅游经济特区，丹江口市习家店镇，占地总面积约30万平方米。是明代敕建武当山时的重要遗存，主要为武当山皇家庙观烧制建筑构件。现已发现87座单体窑址，其中14座保存较为完整。出土有花砖、吻兽、脊饰等建筑构件百余件。它的发现，对研究武当山古建筑群的建筑材料来源、工艺制作技术等提供了实物资料。

天子岩手印岩画

位于恩施土家族苗族自治州巴东县官渡口镇。岩画地处天子岩数百米高的岩壁上，横向分布着近400个褐红色手印纹。岩画幅面长约20米，宽1.4米，分左右两部分。天子岩手印岩画是长江中游地区目前已知唯一一处岩画，有助于阐释三峡原始艺术与古老的风俗，包括人类迁徙的路程、图腾等。同时，也为研究三峡乃至我国西南地区早期人类活动提供了新的依据。

板桥乡公所旧址

位于襄樊市南漳县板桥镇。始建于1921年。旧址依山势而建，坐北朝南，为四合院式，自南向北渐高沿十字线对称布局，占地约2000平方米，建筑面积约700平方米，土木结构，悬山小青瓦顶，采用当地传统工艺干打垒法砌筑而成。碉堡高14米，单檐悬山青瓦顶，三层以上四面均设有瞭望和射击孔。是湖北省目前已知规模最大、保存最完好的民国时期基层政权旧址。

中华全国文艺界抗敌协会成立旧址

位于武汉市江汉区中山大道。占地面积约400平方米，是一栋现代风格的古典主义建筑，砖混结构，平面呈矩形，共4层。旧址原为汉口市商会大礼堂，建成于1921年。次年，在此召开了第四届全国商会联合会代表大会。1938年3月27日，中华全国文艺界抗敌协会在此召开成立大会。该旧址作为武汉商业发达的标志性建筑，不仅见证了汉口总商会光荣传统，更见证了抗战初期武汉作为全国文化中心的地位。

武昌表烈祠

位于武汉市武昌区首义路街道。1938年初，国民政府18军工程营在其驻地左侧的蛇山南坡建成了这座表彰先烈、供奉阵亡将士的祠堂——表烈祠。该祠坐北朝南，中轴线上依次为牌楼、神道、主楼。它在吸收西方先进技术的基础上采用中国古典式建筑形制和布局建成。该祠作为武汉会战的重要遗存、保存最完整的抗战烈士纪念建筑之一，是中国人民抵御外辱、争取民族独立和维护国家主权的重要见证。

华新水泥厂旧址

位于黄石市黄石港区红旗桥街道。创建于1907年，是中国近代最早开办的三家水泥厂之一。旧址占地面积约5.4万平方米，现存湿法水泥窑、四嘴装包机、高耙机、低耙机等生产设施及生产线、运输线等配套设施。湿法水泥窑3台，其中1、2号窑始建于1946年，配备有美国原装进口设备。其"湿法水泥生产工艺"，代表了当时水泥行业先进的生产力。华新水泥厂从清末创建一直沿用至今，为研究我国水泥工业的发展史提供了详实的实物资料。

鲁家山遗址

位于湖南省澧县涔南乡。分布在一块高出四周约1米的台地上。遗址分布范围呈椭圆形，东西长约130米，南北宽约85米，总面积约1万平方米。采集到夹砂红陶、泥质灰陶等石家河文化时期的陶片。该遗址是澧阳平原史前遗址群中一座小型环壕聚落遗址，对了解澧阳平原新石器时代晚期文化分期序列具有重要价值。

坐果山遗址

位于永州市东安县大庙口镇。总面积达2万平方米，文化遗存厚达3米。现发掘面积约1000平方米，发现一组完整的山地居住遗迹，共有柱洞100多个，灰坑（包括火塘）10余个，以及大量陶器、石器、青铜器与玉器等遗物。反映了商周时期人类生活的自然环境、建筑居室的情形，这在湘南地区尚属首次。该遗址是南溪河流域古代遗址群的中心遗址，对于建立这一地区商周时期的文化序列具有重要价值。

鬼仔石像遗址群

位于江永县、道县、江华瑶族自治县。鬼仔石像遗址可分为两大类：第一类为分布于旷野中，石像多背倚土山；第二类为岩穴型，石山嶙峋，洞穴深邃，昔日多有暗河。经比较分析，初步确认，鬼仔石像均系地表式供奉而非坎坑式埋藏，绝大多数石像可见地面高度；石像原材料大多为本地河床中随处可见的砾石，加工粗放，雕制简约。初步研究，其产生及变迁，跟瑶族文化相关。

沩山窑

位于醴陵市东堡乡。分布范围达129平方公里，现存自宋以来的窑址60座，与窑相关的瓷泥矿井、瓷器运输故道、生活设施、古塔庙宇等49处遗存。该窑口在宋元时期生产白瓷、青瓷和酱色瓷，明清时期烧制青花瓷，至清末民初成功烧制出釉下五彩瓷，成为中国釉下五彩瓷器的发源地。

汉代长沙王陵墓群

位于长沙市岳麓区及望城县。主要分布于岳麓山、谷山二处山系临湘江的低矮山丘和台地上，南北长约12千米，东西宽约6千米。墓群包括公元前202年～公元37年间长沙王（或王后）的陵园建筑遗迹。迄今为止共计发现25处陵墓遗迹点（已发掘5座）。汉代长沙王陵墓群墓主身份等级高，且数量多、分布集中、保存相对完整，对研究汉代诸侯王葬制、汉代长沙国历史乃至汉代政治、经济、军事、文化等方面具有重要价值。

大园苗寨古村寨

位于邵阳市绥宁县关峡苗族乡。占地面积6平方公里，由四个聚居点组成，总面积3.82万平方米。大园苗寨始建于宋太平年间（976～984年），明代初具村寨雏形，清代为发展的鼎盛时期。寨内不同时期的古建筑类型丰富，公共建筑大都完整，祭祀性建筑别具一格，防护性设施臻于完善。以民居建筑为主体的苗寨建筑群具有典型苗区特色。

红二军团长征司令部旧址

位于娄底市新化县奉家镇。旧址始建于清末，坐北朝南，为四合大宅院，抬梁式砖木架构，上覆小青瓦。占地面积约7000平方米。建筑墙体上多处保留了非常清晰的毛主席语录和大跃进时期的绘画。旧址反映了中国工农红军第二军团在长征途中从事"反围剿"斗争，由湘西转战贵州建立红色革命根据地中的一段珍贵历史。同时又是一座保存完整具有浓郁地方特色的古民居。

安江纺织厂

位于洪江市安江镇。1921年建于长沙市银盆岭湘江河畔，1940年迁至现址。现保留了抗战时期的碉堡楼、苏式专家楼及电影院、职工食堂、职工医院、托儿所、八角亭等苏式建筑；以及动力、准备、前纺、细纱、织布、机修、印染等车间以及部分英国进口织布机。经过近百年的迁徙变迁，整体风貌格局保存完整，是湖南目前保存最完好、最早的工业遗产之一，对研究近代湖南纺织工业具有重要价值。

安化古道

位于益阳市安化县东坪镇、江南镇、田庄乡。是明清时期安化黑茶生产、运输、销售活动留存至今的历史痕迹，是安化黑茶文化的一个缩影。现存安化古道沿线保存了大量与黑茶相关的文化遗存包括古茶园、古道（风雨桥、茶亭）、黑茶加工作坊、古街古集市、船码头等。安化古道是安化黑茶文化的重要物质载体，是我国明清时期南方山区繁华经贸活动的缩影。

黄金寨古茶园

位于保靖县葫芦镇（原堂朗乡）。黄金一名来自苗语地名"苟贡"。黄金古茶树属乔木型茶树，目前分布较集中的共有7大古茶园，年代在明清及民国，面积约14.86万平方米，其中围径在30厘米以上的占茶树有2057余株。黄金古茶树是湘西大山中古老、特异、珍稀的地方茶树资源，历史悠久，品质独特，是我国古茶历史中的活化石。

松岗窑址

位于广东省东莞市清溪镇。年代为明清时期，延续至民国。分布范围较大。目前可见的遗迹有窑炉2座，均为龙窑。残留有夯土墙体或墙基的房址6间，灰砂构筑的淘洗池（炼泥池）2处，石块构筑的圆形池1处，以及取土的原生高岭岩矿。遗址中有大量废弃堆积，采集到大量的青花瓷器、青釉瓷器和褐釉瓷器残件。是青花瓷窑系从粤东向珠江三角洲地区发展的实证。

邓邦鑑夫妇墓

位于湛江市徐闻县城北乡。坐东北向西南，为交椅形墓，宽5米，深10.3米，占地面积为88平方米。青石砌筑。坟包前有墓志铭碑二通，保存完整，墓碑正文为"皇清颐化例授布政使司经历纯正邓大府君之墓"，墓主为邓邦鑑（清乾隆乙戌年～道光庚戌），享年92岁。其右侧5米处有邓公原配夫人墓一座。

邓邦鑑夫妇墓构造奇特，富有地方特色，是研究粤西地区埋葬习俗的实物例证。

通真岩岩画

位于阳江阳春市春湾镇，具体年代不详。岩画向南，宽0.8米，残高0.5米，墨绘线描佛教初祖达摩"只履西归"的故事。画中达摩祖师额头高广，双目炯然，锡杖倚肩，梵相俱现，正悠然坐于西归途中石上小憩，回眸东顾。人物头部及衣衫涂红彩，线条简括飘逸，禅意盎然。这种以古代摩崖岩画形式出现的达摩像在广东地区比较少见。

长围村围屋

位于韶关市始兴县罗坝镇。由围楼和民居组成，坐北向南，建于清代。面阔52米，进深92.2米。围楼呈长方形，四层高15米。整座民居河石瓦木构筑。围内中间天井，二层四周出靠栏（走廊）。有木梯可登楼。围墙牢固结实，底层外墙厚1米。民居青砖瓦木构筑。中间祖堂，三厅二井。两侧民居，二厅四房组合，地面铺青砖。整组建筑保存完好，是典型的客家围屋。

南沙陈氏宗祠

位于佛山市南海区丹灶镇。始建于清乾隆三十九年（1774年），同治九年（1870年）维修扩建。坐东北向西南。广三路，深五进，总面阔29.4米，总进深83米，面积2440.2平方米。中路三间三进，抬梁式木构架，硬山顶，素胎"金玉满堂"瓦当。

整座建筑木雕、砖雕、石雕精美，规模宏伟，保存较完整，总体布局巧妙，空间开合有序，保留了明代、清代、民国三个时期建筑风格。

281

黄沙塘高桥

位于惠州市惠东县白花镇。为清代四跨式石梁桥，东西走向，横跨黄沙塘沥，全部用花岗岩石打制而成，桥面长21.57米、宽0.8米，桥高3.8米。石桥结构简单坚固，既省材省料，又便于排洪，造型简洁，且坚固实用。是研究惠州地区古代石桥的实物资料，也是研究岭南乡村桥梁发展历史的珍贵资料。

广九铁路石龙南桥

位于东莞市石龙镇，横跨东江。1907年8月动工，1911年建成通车。广九铁路石龙南桥原为广九铁路单线铁路大桥，钢石木混凝土混合结构。桥设5孔，第1～4孔为70米下承桁梁，第5孔为20米上承钢板梁，全长324.8米。

广九铁路石龙南桥曾为广九铁路重要组成部分，在保障香港物质供应和促进粤港经济社会发展方面发挥了重要作用。

潘氏宅院

位于广州市海珠区南华中路。为龙溪潘氏私宅，坐北朝南，占地面积为714平方米。院内主楼居中巍然兀立，宽12米、深12米、高10米。为西式混凝土结构两层楼房，带半地下室，折中主义风格。

潘氏宅院是较早吸收西方建筑艺术，采用西方建筑技术和建筑材料建造的欧式洋楼。

季立居

位于梅州市梅江区三角镇。据季立居资料载：1913年马六甲华侨应贤公返乡购地建成。坐西北向东南，由牌坊式外门楼、禾坪、水井、堂屋、化胎、围龙、左右横屋、杂间（距主体建筑50米左右）等组成，总面阔36.33米，总进深49.04米，共30个房间，占地面积约1790平方米。

季立居祖祠合一、古朴典雅，体现了客家人聚族而居、敦亲睦邻、和谐的生活形态，对于研究梅州城区传统民居建筑文化具有较高价值。

顺德糖厂旧址

位于佛山市顺德区大良街道。1934年建成，由捷克斯可达工厂连工包料承建，制糖设备来自捷克。尚存四栋早期厂房：制糖车间、压榨车间和成品糖仓库两间；以及助晶箱、桔水罐等早期设施。建筑为钢框架结构，大跨度钢桁架上盖铁皮顶，空心红砖墙。砖身有"永业砖窑""永""河南小港"等铭文。

顺德旧糖厂是近代中国第一代机械化甘蔗糖厂，见证了中国制糖行业史与广东近代工业发展史。

都乐洞穴遗址群

分布于广西壮族自治区柳州市鱼峰区、柳南区都乐河流域。该遗址群由10处遗址组成，均位于石灰岩洞穴中，为岩厦式洞穴。遗址多背山面水，洞前地势开阔。所在洞口朝南，高出附近地面3～10米，遗址面积约30～250平方米不等，均为灰黄色含螺壳的文化堆积。

都乐洞穴遗址群的发现，进一步丰富了柳州史前文化内涵，为探讨柳州乃至西江流域史前文化的演化、建立柳州史前文化序列提供了十分珍贵的资料。

大清国钦州界碑

位于防城港市防城区、东兴市中越边境一带。清光绪十六年闰二月廿六（1890年4月14日），由钦州知州李受彤与法使四画官拉巴第等签定了《广东越南第一图界约》，约定防城境内的两国边界从竹山北仑河口至峒中北岗隘的200多公里，全段以石碑为标志，一面书写"大清国钦州界"（当时防城属钦州府辖），一面书写"大南"二字。

现已找到并登记的大清国钦州界碑共24块，大部分碑体保持完整，具有极其重要的历史文物价值，其余的将继续寻找。

282

梧州近代军事设施遗址

位于梧州市。建于清末至民国时期，包括碉堡、炮台、瞭望台、指挥所、隐蔽所等设施，现存55座，主要分布在梧州市区制高点，以及桂江、西江沿岸，尤以白云山、锦屏山一带最为集中，保存也最为完整。

这些军事设施遗址，为研究广西乃至整个西南地区人民抗击外来侵略史、军事史、近代社会史、建筑史等方面提供了重要的实物资料。

桂林三花酒酒窖

位于桂林市象山区象鼻山岩洞内，是桂林历史最悠久、条件最优越、规模最大的天然酒窖。象鼻山下岩洞作为酒窖的历史可追溯至明代，直至今日，该酒窖仍然是桂林三花酒酒窖所在地。酒窖分为上洞（云峰岩）和下洞两部分，洞宽3～8.6米，高2～8.5米，蜿蜒往复盘踞于象鼻山山底，总面积2300多平方米，可以储藏白酒数千吨。桂林三花酒酒窖是广西最著名的老字号酒窖，具有特有的深厚历史文化底蕴和文化价值。

乐湾古建筑群

位于桂林市恭城瑶族自治县恭城镇，由乐湾大屋、陈氏宗祠、陈四庆宗祠、陈五福宗祠、乐湾炮楼及乐湾大墓等组成，分布面积约1平方千米。

乐湾古建筑群是桂北地区保存较完整、规模较大、由不同类型的建筑组成的一组清代客家人的家族建筑群，风格独特。

蛮降屯白裤瑶族古村寨

位于河池市南丹县里湖乡。寨内有古树古藤、古井古道，有用石块堆砌而成的寨门寨墙遗址，寨门保存完整。蛮降屯地属岩溶峰丛地貌，寨子被茂密的植被和参天古树环绕，房屋错落有序，多为干栏式建筑。蛮降屯是白裤瑶民族文化保留最完整的一个村落。

天峨县拉汪壮族传统民居

位于河池市天峨县三堡乡三堡村拉汪屯。拉汪壮族传统民居修建于清末民初，现存建筑32间。民居大多为木瓦二层楼结构，内部为穿斗台梁混合结构。窗花装饰多用木板透雕花草、凤凰、骏马、梅花鹿等吉祥花卉和吉祥动物。拉汪壮族传统民居风格独特。

南宁育才学校旧址

位于南宁市西乡塘区心圩街道。该址原为黄氏宗祠，建于清道光十九年（1839年），坐西北向东南，占地面积340平方米，建筑面积255.4平方米。整个建筑为硬山顶砖木结构，青砖青瓦清水墙，地面青砖铺砌，建筑呈两进两廊中座拜亭的围合布局。越南中央学舍区（广西南宁育才学校）总部创办于1951年7月。

该旧址是在特殊的历史条件下设立的，不仅是越南革命干部的摇篮，也是培植中越两国人民友谊的园地。

广西土改工作团第二团团部旧址

位于南宁市江南区江西镇。团部旧址现保存的6处房屋均为清末年间所建，青砖青瓦面，硬山顶，抬梁式砖木结构，各栋的建筑形式基本相同，进深约9.5米，面阔约10米。1951年末至1952年夏，中央派来的广西土改工作二团进驻麻子畬，成员多是中国文化、教育、理论界的名人。这批中国文化名人曾集中在此工作、生活达半年之久。

贡陂堰

位于桂林市全州县龙水镇。该堰堰堤用条石砌筑，并做成台阶状，下宽上窄，逐级内收，可缓和下泄水流的冲击力度，确保堤坝的安全稳固；条石下面用松木纵向铺垫，既可确保堰堤基础牢固，又大大增强了抵抗洪水冲击的能力；堰堤做成拱形，并在上部设置多处大小不一的泄水天平；堰堤下方河滩大量种植柳树。贡陂堰自南宋始一直得到有效的维护和管理，沿用至今，发挥着重要的灌溉防洪作用，具有较高的实用价值。

乌烈新石器时代遗址

位于海南省昌江县乌烈镇。在遗址地表采集到新石器时代石制工具和装饰用具147件，这些石器用途主要用以砍伐、削割和渔猎及装饰用具等。另采集到新石器时代夹砂粗陶器残片56件，均为手制，是当时的生活用具。

遗址的新石器时代文化内涵比较丰富，为海南西部新石器时代文化分布、区域类型、文化谱系等研究提供了新的资料。

峨蔓古盐田

位于儋州市峨蔓镇。在细沙、盐丁、灵返、小迪4个自然村均有盐田，其中最大的要数盐丁村盐田。

盐丁村盐田面积约16.5万平方米。盐田中共有5000多个形态各异砚式石盐槽，大的直径达3米，小的直径为0.5米，均以黑色的火山石依其自然形状凿刻而成，每个盐槽普遍有1~2厘米的沿边；26间石砌盐房坐落在盐田中央，用以存放工具和储蓄盐粒。

盐丁、灵返和细沙村的盐田，虽然面积及砚式石槽大小各不相同，但制盐工序是一样的。峨蔓古盐田完整保留了海南省先民们土法制盐的传统技艺和大量的古法生产器具、生产工地遗存。

排坡莫氏宗祠

位于定安县定城镇。占地1585平方米，至今已有400多年历史。排坡莫氏宗祠是定安境内规模庞大的一座古建筑群，因其历史悠久，建筑宏丽，颇具特色而闻名遐迩。排坡莫氏宗祠共有两座，分别为排坡村合族宗祠、大宗宗祠，均保存完好。其记录了海南先民开疆扩土的不懈努力。

林氏古民居建筑群

位于万宁市后安镇。为林姓其洲公于清代乾隆年间所建，现保存较完整的九套房屋，硬山顶，为砖木结构（正室正厅两侧均为木柱木板壁结构）。建筑群呈横向三排分布，其中前排三套、中排四套、后排二套，共九套，平面呈"兴"字布局。有门巷互通相连，布局严谨，前庭后院左右相通。该建筑群具备典型的南方古建筑特点，保存状况良好。

保平民居建筑群

位于三亚市崖城镇。该建筑群大部分始建于清代，沿用至今。整个村落共有42户、200多间房屋，占地面积达0.25平方千米。

该古民居院落朝向不定，大都有门楼、照壁、左右厢房、正屋等组成；屋顶较低，举折不高，廊外垒墙，墙外再建廊；梁架结构均为穿斗式，木质隔板；几乎所有的墙楣上都有彩绘。

保平村的民居建筑群是迄今为止在海南省内发现的最大规模的民居建筑群。

陈策将军故居

位于文昌市会文镇，建于清末。故居坐西北朝东南，占地面积约530平方米，为砖木建筑结构。故居为海南琼北农村地区传统的民居建筑，其布局形式呈二进格局。陈策（1893~1949年），原名陈明唐，字筹硕，原任国民党海军上将总司令。

白查黎族船形屋

位于东方市江边乡。白查村黎族船形屋是黎族的传统民居，村中至今保存着81间船形屋。

黎族船形屋用藤条、树枝、木棍扎制屋架，用茅草覆顶，屋檐接地，檐墙合一，远看像船底，因而被称为船形屋。白查村是中国最后的一个黎族古村落，被誉为"黎族最后的精神家园"。对研究少数民族建筑文化、生存方式等有重要意义。

俄歪岭日军侵琼据点旧址

位于白沙县阜龙乡，当地农民称日本岭。1943年，日军从琼文地区转向西线，推行堡垒政策，并在可任村的南面俄歪岭上设据点，修道路建战壕，设瞭望台等掩体设施。1944年秋在我军的打击下，俄歪岭的日军据点被迫撤走。现岭上还残存有公路、战壕、掩体等建筑物，遗物有泥砖、啤酒瓶等。该遗存基本完整。

符家宅

位于文昌市文城镇。该民宅是由松树村村民符永质、符永潮和符永秩三位同胞兄弟于1915年共同出资所建，历时三年建成。占地面积近1738平方米，坐东南向西北，整体建筑呈海南传统的单纵轴线多进式布局，由围墙、三间正屋、八间横屋组成。其中三间正屋建筑布局结构严谨，宏伟壮观，通风透气，木质门窗大部分都装饰有精美雕刻。后排八间横屋均由后围墙相连，后墙中部开有一小门。

符家宅对研究海南民国初期华侨住宅的建筑特点和风格具有重要价值。

海南石碌钢铁厂旧址

位于昌江县石碌镇。1958年6月创办，建有28立方米高炉群3座和4座焦炉群。1969年重建，修复28立方米高炉和50立方米高炉。1975年在原来设备基础上改造配套，扩建为年产生铁5万吨、钢2.4万、钢材1.5吨的规模。1986年，第二座50立方高炉建成投产。2007年7月停产。现厂里还保留原有的厂房及生产设备机器等工业遗产。

老鼓楼衙署遗址

位于重庆市渝中区望龙门街道。2010年4～7月，重庆市文物考古所对其进行了清理揭露，发现有宋元至明清时期的房址、道路、水井、灰坑、灰沟及礌石堆等遗迹25处，出土了一批保存较好的瓷器、瓦当、礌石、坩埚等遗物。老鼓楼衙署遗址建筑规模宏大，纪年明确，推测可能是南宋四川制置使余玠组织抗蒙时期的衙署遗址。它的发现不仅填补了重庆城市考古的重要空白，而且对研究重庆城市沿革变迁、川渝地区古代建筑及宋蒙战争具有重要的学术研究价值。

钓鱼城蒙军攻城隧洞遗址

位于合川区钓鱼城办事处，建于南宋。整条隧洞从距出奇门约200米处的山下开挖，顺山势抬升挖至出奇门城墙内，形成约20度坡度，开出口洞3个，总长约200米，宽1.3米，高1.5米。该遗址是南宋时期一处重要的战事工程，其发现为研究蒙军攻打钓鱼城这段历史，了解古代战争和战事工程修建技术等提供了更为翔实可靠的资料。

龙洞湾冶锌遗址（群）

位于石柱县龙潭乡，石柱与丰都交界处的七耀山西南麓，遗址面积共约150万平方米。时代为明代晚期至清代。遗址地表随处可见冶锌炼渣，调查中采集到冶锌反应罐残片，冶炼工具等。发现了尚存的古代石板道路，碑刻一通，矿井若干。在试掘中发现冶炼炉一座，两端用土坯筑墙，炉床上用砖砌墙，形成一个宽约0.6米、长约10米的"马槽"，上可置反应罐。

龙洞湾冶锌遗址反映了非常成熟的冶锌技术，表现了明清冶锌业的繁荣景象。

龙溪古镇建筑群

位于巫山县龙溪镇。占地面积2.53万平方米，传统街巷1040米，现存建筑最早建造于清朝末年。街道为青石板铺就，小巷木楼，古朴宁静，民风淳朴，保存着清代以来各个历史时期的文化印记。对于研究川东地区清代以后建筑发展、演变过程和趋势，了解地处巫山、奉节、巫溪三县结合部的龙溪在社会、经济、文化等方面的发展具有重要的价值。

重庆国民政府军事委员会旧址

位于渝中区解放西路，建于1935年底。为三幢两楼一底的砖木结构建筑群，坐东南朝西北，建筑面积1991.14平方米。外墙为小青砖勾缝，建筑屋顶为歇山与悬山两种，周围有封火墙。建筑内设壁炉、砖柱台灯、地下室、哨台、雕花扇门等，至今保存完好。

国民政府军事委员会旧址是重庆作为战时首都在抗日战争这段历史中的重要实物载体，是中国人民英勇抗战的重要标识。

李子坝公园抗战遗址群

位于渝中区李子坝，于1938年落成，总面积达8000平方米。包含5组（9栋）抗战历史文物建筑，分别是高公馆、李根固旧居、刘湘公馆、国民政府军事参议院旧址、交通银行旧址。

该抗战遗址群充分展现了抗战期间重庆作为陪都，在反法西斯斗争中发挥的重要作用。集中反映了民国时期重庆地区建筑风格、建筑形式和建筑技术。

万县盐井人民公社旧址

位于万州区新田镇，修建于1937～1939年。该楼坐西向东，占地面积160平方米，建筑面积300平方米。为土木结构，三楼一底，青瓦庑殿式屋顶。楼面阔15米，进深11米，通高约15米。房基四周有阶基，东西面宽1.5米，南北宽1.8米。1958年11月，万县成立盐井人民公社，楼子正门上方现存三合土堆塑的凸出于墙面的"万县盐井人民公社"八字牌匾和五角星图案。

盐井人民公社旧址无论是对于研究近现代重庆地区碉楼一类建筑形式和技术，还是对于研究新中国成立初期重庆农村地区社会、经济发展状况都具有重要价值。

涪陵816工程遗址

位于涪陵区白涛街道。从1966年9月开始修建，经过17年建设完工，整个洞体总建筑面积10.4万平方米，洞内建成大型洞18个。洞体内厂房进洞深度400米左右，顶部覆盖层最厚达200米。洞体可以承受100万吨氢弹空中爆炸冲击，还能抵抗8级地震的破坏，是一处理想的战备工程。

816工程遗址对于研究我国1960年代，毛泽东同志提出的"深挖洞，广积粮，不称霸"的战略方针和全面三线建设，国防战备的特殊时代提供了非常重要的实物资料。

红卫兵墓园

位于沙坪坝区沙坪公园。占地4324.5平方米，131座坟墓里掩埋了573名在1966～1968年在武斗中丧生的红卫兵。墓园呈西高东低、多级阶梯状，一道高高的围墙将整个墓园围成一个船形，隐含"大海航行靠舵手"之意。墓群坐西朝东。红卫兵墓园是特定历史时期历史事件的重要见证，是一个时代的缩影。

南沱红星渡槽

位于涪陵区南沱乡。建于20世纪50年代至70年代。整个渡槽占地面积31500平方米，横卧连丰、关东、焦岩、南沱、沿坪、石佛6个村，西北东南走向，长达9000余米，高架槽基础宽3.5米。渡槽单拱最大跨度49米，最高处约20余米。槽内为三合泥地坪，内宽1米，内空高0.88米，槽沿0.3米。

该渡槽对于研究建国后工农业生产的发展状况，国家对农村生产发展的规划与农村水利工程建造技术等具有重要的实物参考价值。

阿梢脑遗址

位于四川省阿坝藏族羌族自治州九寨沟县漳扎镇。遗址呈扇形分布，北宽南窄，东西长900米，南北宽150米，总面积13.5万平方米。在阶地各处断面上可见房屋墙体痕迹、灰坑、踏面、灰烬层等文化堆积遗存。调查发现大量遗迹现象，并采集到大量陶片。初步认为该遗址是一处具有一定规模的汉代聚落遗址，是迄今为止在九寨沟藏羌地区调查发现最早的遗址。

郝家河郝氏家族墓地

位于广元市旺苍县张华镇。长36米、宽40米，面积1440平方米。共有清代墓葬10座，均坐北向南。墓地墓园结构保存完整，墓前的建筑雕刻为当地盛产的青砂石。建筑结构稳定，建筑上大量采用高浮雕和透雕的工艺雕刻出戏剧、人物、动物、花草等图案。这处家族墓地为研究晚清时期四川农村经济发展、文化艺术、建筑工艺和丧葬习俗提供了较好的实物资料。

木雅藏寨

位于甘孜藏族自治州康定县沙德乡、甲根坝乡、贡嘎山乡。该藏寨（经堂）群主要包括沙德乡俄巴绒一村西南、甲根坝乡阿加上村南、贡嘎山乡六巴村和沙德乡瓦约村。从这四座经堂、民居的建筑风格以及壁画的绘画方式判断，经堂建造年代较为久远。

经堂壁画所绘内容为藏传佛教本尊、护法及传记故事，其壁画颜色、绘画内容、方法是研究藏传佛教各画派及其绘画技法的重要实物资料，同时也是研究当时藏传佛教在川西片区传播、发展的重要依据。经堂内的彩绘佛龛、佛像、经书、印经版以及白海螺、皮鼓等文物具有重要的历史价值。

清溪古建筑群

位于犍为县清溪镇。现存建筑大都建于明至民国时期。分布面积0.48平方千米，由24条街道构成，街面多为青石板铺筑。经调查认定的不可移动文物共有257处。有祠堂8处，会馆4处，寺庙3处，民居221处，牌坊1处。另有码头遗址和抗战时期国民职业学校旧址、水利设施清溪渠等近现代重要史迹及代表性建筑。对于研究古代城镇的兴起与发展以及古代社会、经济、文化生活等方面具有重要的价值。

佛尔岩塄石窟寺

位于巴中市通江县杨柏乡。佛尔岩塄崖壁高约25米。石窟寺坐东向西，共有唐、宋造像4龛14尊，分南北两区，相距50米。1～3号龛分布在北区，造像11尊；4号龛分布在南区，造像3尊。龛外留有圆形、方形孔和沟槽，当为窟檐建筑遗迹。石窟造像有七尊、三尊、单尊三种。

佛尔岩塄石窟造像数量虽不多，但龛窟造像布局严谨，构思奇巧，雕刻刀法洗练，风格富于变化，人物神形交融，栩栩如生。

灵游院石窟寺

位于资阳市安岳县岳阳镇。开凿于五代，清代续凿。共有龛窟17个，造像913尊，碑刻题记20通。龛窟多为方形双层平顶，具有较为典型的五代时期造像特点。造像内容主要有观无量寿经变、一佛二菩萨、一佛二弟子四菩萨、罗汉、地藏、观音、佛道合龛等。题材丰富，艺术风格具有四川地域特点，保存状况较好。

永利川厂旧址

位于乐山市五通桥区桥沟镇，创建于1939年。该旧址由生产区的建筑物、构筑物和碑碣，生活区的建筑物以及生产生活水源"百亩湖"构成。生产区包括实验室、炼冰室、纯碱厂、山洞厂房、机械厂、发电厂、抽水房、办公室、现场指挥调度室、地下防空隧洞和"新塘沽"石刻。生活区包括公馆楼、专家楼、员工楼和炮楼。建筑物为砖木结构和石木结构。在我国民族工业的发展史上具有特殊的地位。

嘉阳煤矿芭沟近现代典型风格建筑群

位于乐山市犍为县芭沟镇。建筑群占地面积5.5万平方米，建筑面积24078.78平方米，建筑年代上起1938年，下迄1958年。主要有英式民居、苏式民居、苏式行政办公楼、苏式党群办公楼、中式传统民居以及黄村矿井办公楼、大礼堂、中英街、孙越崎旧居等建筑，另有黄村矿井等工业遗产。部分近现代典型建筑尚存文革时期的标语、宣传画等。既是中外合资企业的历史遗存，也是民族工业发展进程的历史记录。

中国工程物理研究院旧址

位于绵阳市梓潼县长卿镇，建于1965~1993年。院部占地面积581,418平方米，有砖混建筑163栋和防空洞1处。办公楼、大礼堂、图书室、档案室、情报室、通讯站、模型厂、邮局、防空洞、诊所、中小学、邓稼先旧居，以及其他科学家居住的别墅区、家属宿舍、招待所基本保持原状。在办公楼墙体上有"团结起来争取更大的胜利"等文革标语13幅。是我国尖端科学技术发展的历史见证。

碧山大队毛主席著作学习室

位于绵阳市三台县柳池镇清溪村四队土桥沟。建于清末至中华民国，1967年被辟为毛主席著作学习室。建筑面积174.44平方米，坐东向西，四合院布局。现存正房三间、南北耳房各一间。土木结构，单檐悬山顶，小青瓦屋面，叠瓦正脊抹灰装饰，脊头微翘。学习室至今基本保存当时的原貌，墙壁上仍完整保存有文革时期的标语、毛主席语录及学习园地专刊等史迹。

渔溪洞遗址

位于贵州省习水县东皇镇。渔溪洞实为两个天然洞穴，1号洞洞厅宽敞干燥，洞口向南；2号洞洞内较为阴暗潮湿，洞口向西。在洞前台地和洞内人为扰乱的角砾堆积之中采集到一批石制品、动物化石、烧骨等，同时还发现夹砂陶片和后期瓷片等遗物。为贵州考古学研究从旧石器时代晚期向新石器时代过渡提供了重要的实物证据。

锦江谷岸遗址群

位于铜仁地区铜仁市。主体应为商周时期遗址。主要包括落鹅遗址、坳田董遗址、黄腊关遗址、落箭坪遗址、坳上坪遗址、新屋遗址、笔架冲遗址、磨刀湾遗址、茅溪遗址、锡堡遗址、宋家坝遗址、方田坝遗址等，共计17处（包括器物采集点3处）。采集石制品、陶片数百件，征集铜钲1件。

遗存群填补了铜仁地区考古发现的空白，将铜仁地区有史可考的历史大大提前，为深入探讨商周前后锦江流域的考古学文化及其演进提供了重要的实物资料。

鲍家屯水利工程

位于安顺市西秀区大西桥镇。建于明洪武二年（1369年），距今已有630余年。鲍家屯古水利工程属引蓄结合的塘坝式水利形式，它由横坝、顺坝和高低龙口组成，可以满足丰水与枯水期的引水、水量调节等功用，整个工程系统布局合理，设施简洁且功能完备，除灌溉外还有供水、排洪、水力利用等功能。是研究我国水利和农业科技史的实物资料。

大利村古建筑群

位于黔东南苗族侗族自治州榕江县栽麻乡。始建于明、清时代。共发现百年以上民居建筑29幢、花桥4座、鼓楼1座、萨坛1座、石板道3条（含碑3通）、古墓葬1座、古井6眼、古粮仓12座，村寨四周百年以上古树128株。大利村古建筑群顺溪流、依山就势而建，将建筑融于自然环境之中，构成独具特色的人文景观，充分体现了人与自然和谐相处的建筑思想和理念。

客兰寨古建筑群

位于铜仁市瓦屋乡。始建于明代，占地面积15万平方米。民居具有典型民族和地域特点，至今仍较好地保存有"三合院"、"四合院"建筑12座，宗祠3座。除此之外还有手工作坊、码头、古井、学馆、庙宇、营盘、神道碑、司前屯堡、保寨楼（碉堡）、公墓以及井边龙巷、三房龙巷、绍文龙巷、庙宇龙巷、大房龙巷、满房龙巷六条巷道等。傩堂戏、阳戏等民族民间文化仍在传承。客兰寨古建筑群是黔东地区民族文化与当地汉族文化融合的代表。

水塘李氏民居

位于盘县水塘下伍屯。由11座四合院组成，整体坐西朝东。建成时间主要为清嘉庆和道光年间，光绪年间增建部分厢房和偏房。总占地面积8600平方米，总建筑面积2475平方米，四合院天井总面积723平方米。

水塘李氏民居由正房、左右厢房构成，部分四合院于正房对面设置照壁。正房为穿斗式梁架，硬山式屋顶。大门均为门楼式，门楼垂瓜均为镂空雕，门墩做成须弥式。台明、踏跺、地坪等石作工艺精细，至今仍保完好。是研究西南清代建筑技术和区域建筑装饰文化不可多得的实物资料。

独坡脚岩画

位于惠水县大龙乡。该洞洞口西南向，底部为石板，基本没有泥土堆积，洞宽15米、高5米。该岩画系用赭红色矿物质颜料绘制而成，现存图案150个。图案内容有"人骑马"、"人持物"、单体动物和方格状、点状符号等，并以人骑马图案为最多，马头多朝向洞外。

独坡脚岩画同附近的龙里巫山岩画、长顺付家院子岩画共同形成黔中地区规模庞大的岩画群，为探讨中国南方岩画的内容题材、作画手法和目的等提供了新的资料。

茅台酒厂历史建筑群

位于遵义仁怀市茅台镇。建于明代，清同治元年(1862年)恢复重建，加上后来国营茅台酒厂时期修建的共计10处，占地面积约20余亩。包括茅台酒厂的前身——成义烧房旧址，恒兴烧坊旧址，荣和烧坊旧址及其踩曲仓旧址和干曲仓旧址、二片区制曲石磨坊旧址、干曲仓旧址、踩曲仓旧址、发酵仓旧址，一片区发酵仓旧址，下酒库第八栋和第五栋酒库。

茅台酒厂历史建筑群作为国酒茅台从两汉迄今为止的最早酿造体系的实物见证，具有极高的历史研究价值和传统酿造工艺价值。

红林机械厂主厂房旧址

位于黔西县红林彝族苗族乡。建于1966年，1970年建成投产。由主厂房、制氧站、相关生产配套设施和生活设施构成。主厂房位于穿洞之中，洞长200米、高20米、宽30米，整个厂房共有215栋房屋。红林机械厂见证我国航空工业的发展历程，是中国航空工业发展的一个缩影，是西部开发的重要见证。

苗族加榜梯田

位于从江县加榜乡。最初开垦年代无从考证，主要分布在2007年新辟的党扭至加榜的简易公路沿线，总长25公里。梯田从海拔709.04米至901.09米，坡度在45～75度之间。加榜梯田总亩数暂无确切数据。梯田、村落、山川、溪流集于一体，保留着传统的梯田耕作模式，民族风情浓郁，是加榜苗族适应自然、改造自然而形成的文化景观，是当地农耕文化的核心代表。

水塘坝古生物化石遗址

位于云南省昭通市昭阳区太平办事处。原为褐煤场，面积为3万平方米。出土大量的古生物化石，其中最重要的是发现了猴子、古猿的化石。经古地磁测定，化石群距今六百万年。对研究东亚地区晚新生代时期脊椎动物的进化、古环境的变迁、中国南方中上新世中地层的研究具有重要的学术价值。

学山遗址

位于玉溪市澄江县右所镇。除明清时期的晚期建筑基址外，发现了石寨山文化的建筑基址，有半地穴式和干栏式的房屋，还有连接房屋的道路、灰坑等遗迹。是目前云南发现的唯一一处保存完好的青铜时代的聚落遗址，为研究石寨山文化的属性、特点和渊源提供了重要的资料和依据，对研究滇文化的村落形态和布局以及其他地区滇文化的演变和流向具有重要的意义。

小田坝营盘遗址

位于曲靖市会泽县火红乡。是曲靖乃至云南规模最大、保存最为完好的军事设施遗址，年代大约为明代至清代同治时期，系采用当地规则山石堆垒而成，总面积9252.6平方米。遗址所处区域系云贵交界处的高山峡谷地段，地势险峻，是研究云贵交界地区明清时期政治、军事、民族及交通状况的重要实物资料。

城子村土掌房

位于红河哈尼族彝族自治州泸西县永宁乡。是迄今为止国内保存最为完整、规模较为宏大的汉彝建筑风格结合的古建筑群。占地面积15.8万平方米，共有土掌房1000多栋。整个建筑群依山而建，坐南朝北，一排排土库平顶房参差错落。此村原是彝族先民白勺部的聚居地，明朝成化年间，土司昂贵在这里建造了土司衙门，城子村为"永安府"，土掌房规模得到大规模扩展，形成府城格局。

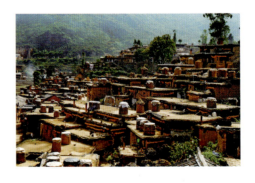

古墨水磨房群

位于临沧市凤庆县诗礼乡。最早的水磨房建于清嘉庆年间，现有水磨房27间，其中可以使用的21间，水磨房遗址3间，碾子房遗址3间。水磨房由引水道、水轮、磨盘和磨轴等部分组成。建筑格局由水渠、磨房、畜圈、厕所等组成。每座水磨房面积大约在15~30平方米，石条为基，垒石为墙，青石板当瓦覆顶。磨房前河面上共有石桥9座。水磨房四周分布着高大的核桃树林，直径0.3米以上的古核桃树200株。

翁丁佤族古村寨

位于临沧市沧源佤族自治县勐角乡。始建于清代，村落沿袭佤族父系氏族时期的头人制，同时具有从原始公有制向私有制过渡的特征，保留了古老的生产生活方式及古老的民居建筑，整个村落由干栏式乡土建筑群及寨门、寨桩、粮仓房、神林、图腾柱、撒拉房、祭祀房、木鼓房、剽牛桩、牛头桩等组成，寨内设有佤王府，是佤族传统建筑风格保留最完整的原始村落。是研究佤族文化、佤族历史乃至远古人类社会的活化石。

金沙江岩画

集中分布于迪庆州香格里拉县，丽江市玉龙县、宁蒗县。属旧石器时代至新石器时代遗存。岩画多绘画于岩厦的石壁上，内容有野牛、野羊、鹿、猴、人物、狩猎工具及一些符号和图案。岩画的技法主要有描绘和凿刻两种，描绘岩画占绝大多数，其颜色多为土红色。专家认为是云南境内目前发现的最为古老的岩画，为云南原始艺术史和金沙江流域远古时期生态环境的研究提供了难得的实物资料。

腊者布依族民居建筑群

位于罗平县鲁布革乡。总分布面积约2.7平方千米，年代为晚清以来。是迄今为止云南省发现的建筑数量最多、保存最为完整的布依族建筑，是融民居、古道、桥梁、宗教遗址、树木景观、生产生活用具为一体的文化景观，真实反映了布依族依托自然、利用自然、和谐共生的文化价值理念。

同乐傈僳族村寨

位于维西傈僳族自治县叶枝镇。建筑均为井干式结构板房，以木楞为墙，木板为瓦，层层叠叠，一栋连一栋。村里历史最久的民居已有190多年，但大多数民居为三四十年前所建。是云南傈僳族乡土建筑群中保存最完好的建筑群，充分体现了傈僳族依山、临水、就林的建村理念，完整地保留了傈僳族居住、生产生活、社会活动设施的传统风貌。

红河县哈尼梯田

位于红河哈尼族彝族自治州红河县哀牢山南部，是哈尼族人世世代代留下的杰作。红河县所有的梯田都修筑在山坡上。以一座山坡而论，梯田最高级数达3000级，梯田大者有数亩、小者仅有一平方米，往往一坡就有成千上万亩。红河哈尼梯田主要有3个重点保护区:甲寅乡他撒村委会西南部梯田、宝华乡朝阳村委会朝阳村北部撒玛坝梯田、乐育乡尼美村委会尼美村东北部尼美梯田。红河县哈尼梯田主要耕种水稻，田中央也围池养鱼，梯田周围种有棕树和樱桃树。

达律王府

位于西藏自治区昌都地区贡觉县莫洛镇。该建筑建于吐蕃时期（约九世纪）。后在八思巴前往元大都时进行了重建，系当时贡觉首领达律·阿尼森培的城堡。占地面积400平方米。前部为夯土砌筑围墙形成的庭院。主体建筑位于后部，为二楼一底藏式土木石结构，底层为监狱和"勇士决斗室"；第二层为居住区；第三层为拉康。四壁及望板上绘有大量壁画，从画风判断为元代壁画。内容主要为释迦牟尼、佛本生传等。

地曲古栈道

位于昌都地区类乌齐县滨达乡。据《西藏图考》、《西藏志》等史料记载，栈道遗址所在地位于川藏古道（又称茶马古道）线上，该栈道始建年代应为清代。现存栈道长207米、宽2米。栈道为木架结构。该古道是自古以来藏族同胞与祖国各民族之间长期交往的见证，对于研究藏地与内地之间的联系具有重要的历史和研究价值。

唐加寺

位于拉萨市墨竹工卡县唐加乡。据记载，寺庙始建于公元7世纪初，由松赞干布妃芒萨赤姜创建，原名尼玛拉康。后有所增建。18世纪准噶尔部入侵西藏时，寺庙改宗格鲁派，更名唐加寺。文革期间佛像和僧舍以及壁画遭到严重毁损。

寺院的集会大殿，为二层藏式石木结构建筑，四面墙壁上彩绘佛本生故事等。尼玛拉康四壁彩绘千尊无量寿佛，西南面外墙彩绘有壁画，共有13幅。对研究11世纪西藏壁画艺术史及绘画风格演变过程提供了新的实物材料。

帕当巴拉康

位于山南地区贡嘎县杰德秀镇。据传，由云游西藏的印度高度帕当巴桑杰于公元11世纪末至12世纪初修建了八相合塔，后来修建了周围的拉康建筑。佛塔由塔基、塔身、塔刹三部分构成，是西藏现存建筑塔类中仅有的一座"八相合塔"造型的佛塔，对研究佛塔建筑具有一定的价值。

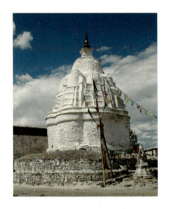

恰芒波拉康

位于日喀则地区吉隆县差那乡。相传，该拉康最初建筑是由藏医大师新宇拓·云登贡波（1126~1201年）出资，恰芒波地方的恰·桑杰噶玛伏藏师修建。现存恰芒波拉康建筑以东西向分布，主要由一座殿堂、两间储藏室和一间厨房组成，建筑分布面积558平方米，门向正东。殿堂由后庭佛堂（主供殿）及前庭经堂（集会殿）构成。木构架雕刻保存较好，具有12~13世纪时期的风格特征。

朵日坚岩画群

位于阿里地区札达县托林镇。岩画刻在大小不一的岩块上，共发现有48组画面。该岩画群所有图像均用敲琢法完成。岩画题材主要有动物、人物、器物、符号和佛塔以及藏文等。藏文中还出现"古格"的缩写和六字真言等。车辆岩画的发现是该岩画最大的特点，共发现两幅车辆图，一辆车为两轮、一舆、一十字辕，另外一辆为两个紧连的轮子和一个人形，似人在推车轮。

纳曲宗普石窟

位于阿里地区普兰县普兰镇。约有20多座石窟，分布面积大约为500平方米。石窟形状有单室、双室、多室之分，还有上下分层贯通的台梯式石窟，其中一双室的内室绘有藏族传统"乡布"。台梯式顶层石窟四壁绘有壁画，大致年代约12世纪。北壁中间金刚萨埵为石窟内主佛，其腹部位置的壁面后制作有小石板固砌的方龛供"装藏"，已被盗。该壁画石窟的发现对研究藏传佛教壁画的供奉形式及其内涵具有重要的价值。

恰姆石窟寺

位于日喀则地区定结县琼孜乡。有3座洞窟。1号窟内有泥塑佛像背光，残体泥塑镀金粉像。2号窟为三间窟相通的"套间窟"，有用彩粉绘制坛城的长方形台座一个、供佛台和残佛像四个；3号洞窟，窟顶有模糊不清的原壁画，四壁绘满清晰的后期壁画。恰姆石窟寺是日喀则地区发现的第二座石窟寺。

中央人民政府驻藏代表楼

位于拉萨市城关区功德林街道。1964年由中央人民政府拨专款修建，1965年建成使用。整个建筑群体现了我国早期现代建筑风格，为砖石结构，东西对称分布，内部房间紧凑，设施齐备。该楼涉及历史事件和人物众多，是西藏革命历史的重要实物例证。

热色多让列石群

位于那曲地区尼玛县尼玛镇。分布面积约200平方米。遗迹由天然石块堆砌成外围边框，中间填充不规则石块，边框平面基本呈长方形，东西长7.4米、南北宽10米；遗迹西侧、北侧共立有18根石柱，个别立石上刻有六字真言及莲花生咒等。是藏北那曲地方保存最为完整、规模最大的立石地点(列石群遗址)之一，对研究青藏高原藏北无人区相关历史、立石文化等有着较高价值。

桥镇遗址

位于陕西省宝鸡市陈仓区桥镇。遗址平面略呈椭圆形，面积约15万平方米。发现文化层1处、灰坑1座、陶窑1座、房址2座。遗址区域内采集有仰韶文化半坡晚期泥质红陶尖底瓶、钵等陶器残片；龙山文化泥质红陶、夹砂红褐陶篮纹罐以及筒瓦、板瓦、槽型瓦等建筑材料残片；还发现西周时期夹砂灰陶鬲等陶器残片。

桥镇遗址面积大，内涵丰富，特别是发现了龙山时期的筒瓦、板瓦、槽型瓦，为研究黄河流域新石器时代文化提供了重要实物资料。

尚家岭宫殿遗址

位于宝鸡市千阳县南寨镇。面积约12万平方米。遗址北部断面有夯土台基，西部断面上暴露有厚约0.4米的文化层，有大型不规则形柱础石。采集有战国晚期至汉代的板瓦、筒瓦、空心砖等残片。2006年遗址区内曾清理出陶下水道一件和陶水管一节。根据陶下水道出土时与陶水管连接在一起，均压在夯土层下，推断该陶下水道为排水设施。遗址规模大，内涵丰富，是宝鸡西部罕见的战国至汉代的大型宫殿遗址，很可能是回中道沿线的附属皇家设施，遗址中发现丰富的战国素面半瓦当，在陕西秦汉宫殿遗址中也属罕见。

蒋家庙城址

位于宝鸡市金台区金河乡。平面呈梯形，面积约40万平方米。城墙沿陡峭的断崖而筑，防御功能显而易见；其建筑方法特殊，即在断崖处夯土紧贴崖面，在平缓地带挖槽筑基筑墙，墙基宽约6米。夯土土质较纯，极为坚硬，板筑夯层清晰。城址最高处为西北角，海拔926米，最低处为东北角，海拔625米，两者相对高差达301米。城墙叠压在"红腰带"土（春秋战国时期形成的）之下，在其北墙东段的夯土层下发现先周时期的灰坑。也就是说，此城的形成年代应在商代（先周）至春秋时期，初步推断为西周时期。

镇坪盐道遗址

位于镇坪县。是古代四川巫溪宁昌井盐运销陕南、鄂西北等地的重要通道。盐道最早开通于商周时期，1970年代废弃。盐道起于重庆巫溪县大宁厂，翻越陕渝交界鸡心岭后，在镇坪县境内沿南江河及其主要支流两侧分布，属秦巴古盐道起点，沿途有数处店铺、寺庙遗迹。它的发现不仅说明了这一地区盐业开发和利用的悠久历史，为陕西、鄂西北地区食盐运销及其沿革研究提供了重要资料，而且也为研究三省市交界地区经济文化交往、民俗风情及地域文化形成等方面有一定学术价值。

杏园沟口崖墓

位于柞水县下梁镇。商洛市六县一区调查发现的崖墓有4000余座，杏园沟口崖墓共分布崖墓6座。6座崖墓均为双室墓和多室墓，"永和"年号题记墓位于第二层，编号ZXM4。是迄今为止发现的商洛地区唯一一座带有年号题记的崖墓，对于商洛崖墓的年代推断、具有标尺性的意义。也为探索陕西南部汉水流域地区崖墓的起源、传播，演变与发展，具有十分重要的考古学价值。

宁强县古代羌人石板墓葬

主要分布于宁强县境内的嘉陵江及其支流白水江流域。墓葬群达10处之多，已发掘50多座墓葬。墓葬多选址于山坡中上部向阳地带。墓室结构基本一样，都是由多块石板搭建而成一个长方体，顶部正中开凿有藻井，部分墓室后部正中凿有圭形龛。墓室立板大都雕刻人物、动物、植物、器物、云纹等图案。为研究古代羌族史、民族迁徙、民族融合、民族文化、习俗，特别是白马羌提供了宝贵的考古学资料。

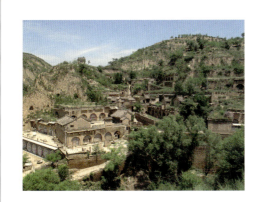

袁庄砖雕壁画墓

位于甘泉县城关镇。为长方形仿木结构砖砌单室墓，墓室东西长2.17米，南北宽2.14米，高2.58米，叠涩覆斗形墓顶。墓室砖上面彩绘壁画。部分壁画砖被撬破坏，大部分壁画保存尚完整。墓室现存有壁画9幅。东壁中为老年夫妇对坐饮宴图，右上方题"明昌四年十一月初一日工毕"。其余壁画内容所描述的都为孝行故事。

该墓题记时代确切，人物关系清楚，壁画内容丰富。题记中还反映了金明昌年间的经济状况。

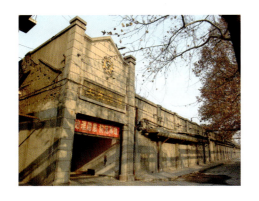

贺家石党氏庄园

位于绥德县白家硷乡。建于清嘉庆年间，历时近百年，占地面积约6.7万平方米，是黄土高原乃至全国最大、最完整、最具有特色的城堡式特色民宅，砖石结构，以窑洞为主体。其中尤以大门、影壁墙的设计，造型、图案、雕刻堪称一绝。整个建筑坚固，布局合理。上下相通，左右相连，属传统的三明两暗两厢房的典型建筑。此民居修造豪华、铺设讲究、石窑靠山、冬暖夏凉、明路暗道通畅方便。整个建筑与地形相随，布局合理，是陕北窑洞建筑的典型代表。

297

大华纱厂旧址

位于西安市新城区太华南路。大华纱厂是中国西北地区首家机械纺织企业和近现代工业基地。创建于1935年。历史上各时期都在这里留下了具有时代烙印的建筑。这些建筑包括生产车间、仓储库房等工业建筑，也有民宅似的管理用房。既有民国时期的青砖小院，也有新中国成立后的红砖建筑，还有改革开放以来的钢筋混凝土车间。其中最有价值的是民国时期的纺织车间厂房，单体钢结构，由原上海象新公司包建。

汉阴凤堰梯田

位于汉阴县漩涡镇。由凤江、堰坪梯田和茨沟吴氏民居、太平堡遗址四部分组成。凤江梯田和堰坪梯田相距不足10千米，各自连绵成片。梯田主要沿汉江北岸凤凰山南麓浅山丘陵修建成梯状水田，海拔高差约50～100米。根据当地现存清代民居以及吴氏家谱记载，梯田是清代湖南长沙府善化县移民吴氏家族垦建，始于清乾隆二十一年(1756年)，大规模建于咸同时期，兹后历有增修。是目前秦巴山区发现的面积最大，保存完整的清代梯田。

一棵树烽燧遗址

位于甘肃省酒泉敦煌市南湖乡。烽燧用土坯夹芦苇砌筑，附近地面有大量汉代灰陶片。发现有简牍12枚，无字素简4枚，还有木器残件、丝绸、麻布、毡片、麻、苇编绳等物。其中出土简牍中有纪年的2枚，为西汉宣帝元康三年（公元前63年）封检、西汉元帝初元四年（公元前45年）木简。封检简文所及文字对于探讨汉代边郡符信的种类、形制及使用和汉代龙勒县大煎都候官的候望燧次问题有重要研究价值，是研究汉代丝绸之路南道、北道的交汇和军事防御体系的最新资料。

地埂坡墓群

位于张掖市高台县罗城乡。分布面积32万平方米，墓葬30座。清理发掘5座，基本由墓道、照壁、墓门、前甬道、前室、后甬道、后室等构成，其中2座以原生黄土雕出仿木结构的梁架、屋顶、立柱、斗拱等，3座绘壁画。出土金博山、铜连枝灯构件、铜车马器构件、石龟、骨尺等。为研究河西地区魏晋时期的中西文化交流、民族融合、丧葬礼俗等提供了珍贵资料。

298

金崖古建筑群

位于兰州市榆中县金崖镇。分布于苑川河两岸的河谷阶地上绵延12千米的范围内，现存古建筑16处，集中分布的古民居50院，多建于清晚期。金崖是丝路古道上货通东西的旱码头。明清以降，逐渐成为兰州水烟的主产区和集散地。金崖古建筑及民居群较为全面的反映了千年丝路古镇所特有的地域文化，尤其是对研究地方宗族传承演变、商旅经济、民俗文化及近代手工业发展历史和建筑文化等有着重要意义。

马家梁摩崖石刻

位于陇南市徽县虞关乡。题记阴刻，录文："虞关巡检许清文（字）澄因/……见山路数 延崎岖陡峻往来乘驴□/车马驮轻负重挨排难行坠没崖河/伤死者甚多澄发心令□许琳许/璘司吏卜连率领兵牌人等用工开修/更异坪坦立石为铭者矣………/岂成化三年岁次丁亥三月吉日就石/"。为明代虞关巡检许清文在虞关古渡主持开修道路的记事摩崖题记。此道是甘肃进入四川、陕西道路的青泥古道，题刻是研究茶马古道的重要资料。

荒草梁汉蒙分界碑

位于白银市景泰县红水镇，甘肃景泰与内蒙古阿左旗勘定呈东南-西北走向的边界线上。正文楷书阴刻，碑阳："於道光二十七年蒙、陕甘制台布大人，布政司宝大人饬派宁夏府岳，委员彭，指定按照嘉庆六年旧界，碑南民地，碑北蒙地"，计六行47字。碑阴："道光二十九年闰四月二十六日/中卫县、皋兰县、红水县丞□眼同筑立/蒙员格林三音错格图/潘台达索"，东西各竖行阴刻蒙文。该碑是清代道光年间汉地与蒙地边界划分的重要实物资料。

金川镍矿露天矿老坑遗址

位于金昌市金川区宁远堡镇。1958年金川镍矿发现，使我国的镍资源储量一跃而居世界前列，为我国现代工业发展奠定了重要基础。1990年7月停采。在地球上留下了一个长1300米、宽700米、深310余米的椭圆形人造天坑，它以310米的矿坑深度居国内同类矿山之首，堪称中国最深的人造天坑。是中国镍钴工业从无到有、从小到大的见证，反映了新中国镍钴工业的发展历史。

兰州第一水厂旧址

位于兰州市西固工业区。是国家"一五"时期156项重点工程配套项目，建成后是当时国内规模最大、设备最新的现代化自来水厂，时有"亚洲第一大水厂"之称。厂区占地面积65万平方米，建筑面积20.67万平方米。主要生产构筑物有上下游斗槽式预沉池、上下游一级取水泵房、上下游操纵室、加药间；18座直径100米辐流式沉淀池，其中上游取水构筑物始建于1950年代，全部由前苏联设计援建并提供主要大型供水设备。真实地反映了我国"一五"时期工业建设的成就。

泉坪猛犸象化石点

位于白银市会宁县新庄乡。发掘出土的象化石为头骨和下颌骨，及部分肋骨、肢骨残片。象头骨长1.35米，最宽处0.9米，下颌骨长0.87米，最宽处0.65米。两门齿残缺仅留存根部，上下四颗臼齿保存完好。该象头骨和下颌骨化石为早期猛犸象类，时代可能为上新世，距今约300万年。据悉，这是国内发现的第一具完整的早期猛犸象头骨化石，在世界也很罕见，具有非常重要的科学研究价值，特别是为研究猛犸象类群在欧亚大陆的起源和演化提供了最好的材料。

多儿水磨坊群

位于甘南藏族自治州迭部县多儿乡。建于清代，沿用至今。11座水磨坊，集中分布在长不过150米、坡度陡降约15%的多儿河之上。每个磨坊长约7.5米，宽约5.6米不等，高约6~7米，主体木结构，外层部分由泥石构筑，人字型顶建筑。是甘南藏区保存至今，集中成片呈规模的水磨坊分布群，具有鲜明的地域文化特点，体现了藏区传统的生产生活方式。

庄浪梯田

位于庄浪县。开垦于1964年至今，分布在18个乡镇，总面积1500多平方千米的山巅梁峁。其中榆林沟、庙隆沟、岔李沟、堡子沟等10条重点流域为其代表。梯田为多级地块依山就势而建，各山脉间连绵起伏，相互缠绕，形成以小流域为单元，以梁峁、沟道坝系为主线的有机结合，有效保护水土资源生态的综合治理。是黄土高原梯田生态环境与自然的和谐统一理念的最佳体现。

酒坊坪遗址

位于青海省海东地区民和回族土族自治县转导乡。面积约20万平方米，台地呈长方形，东南部断崖上暴露有文化层，内含有木炭、陶片等遗物，地面散布有马家窑类型绳纹灰陶罐、泥质彩陶罐、夹砂粗陶罐、半山类型网格纹泥质彩陶罐、马厂类型泥质彩陶罐等器物残片。属于新石器时代马家窑文化马家窑类型、半山类型和马厂类型阶段。为研究该地区新石器时代文化聚落分布、区域类型、文化谱系和文化关系等方面提供了新的资料。

尕队遗址

位于黄南藏族自治州同仁县保安镇。地表散布有大量的彩陶和泥质红陶、夹砂红陶，纹样有漩涡横条纹、粗绳纹等，器型有钵、罐、瓶等。并采集到一块磨研石。东南角和北边有暴露的文化层40～50厘米。周围的断崖上有环壕遗迹。遗址应属新石器时代马家窑类型、卡约类型，对同仁地区各族人民在隆务河流域繁衍生息的历史具有重要的研究价值。

夏尔雅玛可布遗址

位于海西蒙古族藏族自治州都兰县巴隆乡。平面呈南北狭长的椭圆形，面积为1.2万平方米。发现有用河卵石堆砌的宽1米、高0.5米石墙。文化层厚0.6～0.9厘米，地表采集有夹砂红陶、灰陶等残片、石器及兽骨等，可辨器形有罐、盆及石斧等，属于青铜时代的诺木洪文化遗址。诺木洪文化的来龙去脉目前仍然是一个谜。这处遗址为研究柴达木盆地古代文明的兴衰与气候变迁、民族迁徙的关系提供了重要线索。

上草褡裢湖西遗址

位于海北藏族自治州海晏县甘子河乡。遗址依上草褡裢湖西岸建址，呈弧形状；自东向西有清晰可辨的人工堆积墙体，墙体长约1100米，高5～8米。以遗址为中心，湖岸西侧呈现两处高低错落的半圆形类似于广场的台地，台地边缘有墙体根基痕迹，多处暴露石砌地基；地表散布大量不同时代的碎陶片、兽骨等；暴露有大面积的灰坑和灰层。

此遗址范围大，保存完整，结构布局独特，是一处较大的卡约文化聚落群，填补了四五千年前人类在青海湖一带生产生活的空白。

根顿群培故居

位于黄南藏族自治州同仁县双朋西乡。有土木结构的四合院21间，院门一间，建筑面积475平方米。根顿群培1903年诞生此地，1951年去世于拉萨嘎日西。他是一位著名的藏学家，精通藏、英、梵等语种，对藏族历史、文学、佛教、哲学、美术、逻辑学、语言学、地理学等均有研究，著有《白史》、《龙村贡坚》等。

加卜着藏式古建筑群

位于果洛藏族自治州班玛县灯塔乡。由21户藏式古建筑组成，占地面积1.8万平方米。清中（晚）期由于长期的战争以及部落之间的争斗，使得班玛境内特别是玛柯河流域建起了大量的藏族民居。这些藏族民居一般都建在高的台地上或山顶上，建筑材质以石块为主，木料为辅，石砌高墙，易守难攻，以保平安。对研究古代藏族群体生活习性和藏式建筑工艺方面具有重要价值。

巴嘎萨岩画

位于德令哈市怀头他拉镇。岩画所在巴嘎萨山沟口有8处独立的岩画，最大的一块约为1.5×1.5米，打制技法采用敲凿、磨刻、磨划的手法制作，图案有牛、马、骆驼、大角鹿等动物个体形象和骑马、骑骆驼、双驾马车、放牧等生活场面。岩画年代应为秦汉至南北朝时期，揭示了当地的人文、动植物甚至气象环境。

多日桑茶玛木桥

位于玉树藏族自治州囊谦县吉曲乡。建于民国时期。木桥长97米、宽6米。有4个用木桩压叠形成空心正方形、中间装满石头的桥墩，桥面是将长短一致的木桩用钢丝紧紧绑牢，木桥保存完好。所使用的建筑材料就地取材，利用附近林区所产松木木材和河滩中的河卵石，结构上以木材作为外围框架，前端采用三角形式便于河水分流，以减少冲击压力，符合力学原理，木框内填充卵石，以增加桥墩的稳定性。

英雄地中四井

位于海西蒙古族藏族自治州冷湖行政委员会。1958年8月21日，青海石油局派出石油勘探大队1219钻井队开始在该地区钻探寻找石油资源，1958年9月13日，由1219钻井队钻至650米后发生井涌，继而出现井喷，喷势异常猛烈，原油连续畅喷3天3夜，油井附近成为一片油海，日喷原油高达800吨左右，从此冷湖油田第一口油井诞生。地中四油井喷油标志着全国四大油田的冷湖油田正式诞生，是青海柴达木地区石油早期开发活动的直观反映。

多伦多盐场

位于玉树藏族自治州囊谦县娘拉乡。整个盐场总面积达66975平方米，盐泉来自北山的山腰上，盐田北高南低，按地形走势分割成1000多个区块，是一座古老的保持传统制盐工艺的民族轻工业作坊。盐场的制盐技术至今依然保持着原始的以人工集体作业方式。盐场附近有一个安静和谐的自然村落，当地居民均为藏族，盐业是当地村民世世代代从事的一项重要产业。多伦多盐场对探索玉树地区古老制盐产业及民族轻工业作坊具有很高的研究价值。

小河湾遗址

位于宁夏回族自治区彭阳县新集乡。面积约48万平方米，地表散见大量文化遗存。2009年7月，发掘面积3000平方米，清理墓葬4座。发现遗迹主要有房址、灰坑、陶窑、水井、道路、壕沟等；出土有陶器和铜器等，同时出土少量的带有"陶文"的器物。是宁夏首次发现的面积较大的秦汉遗址。

对今后研究战国至汉代王国制向郡县制的转变和宁夏彭阳地区秦汉时期的县置情况，探寻该地区秦戎文化面貌以及秦文化与西戎文化、北方草原文化的关系提供珍贵的线索。

青羊沟遗址

位于银川市西夏区贺兰山东麓。总体呈坐西北向东南分布，间由二道人工便道将洪积扇分成三级台地，形成一个规模宏大的遗址区，总面积330,125平方米。主要有依地势而建的时代不同的石砌台阶、便道、石墙、高台建筑、石料加工区、烽火台建筑及石圈遗址，是目前为止贺兰山东麓发现规模最大、保存最好的大型古遗址之一。遗址距离西夏都城和陵园都不远，对于研究西夏的历史文化具有重要的意义。

黄羊滩边墙（长城）

位于永宁县黄羊滩农场。边墙长16.1千米，均已坍塌呈斜坡状，底宽13米、残高1.5～1.2米，边墙利用在墙体西侧开挖宽约6米、1.2米深的砂石土堆积而成，现可见土棱。沿途可见边墙墙体、烽火台、营堡等遗迹，保存较好。黄羊滩边墙在宁夏地区尚属首次发现，为我国长城资源增添了新的内容，尤其为明代长城提供了新的资料和增添了新的长度。

麦垛山清真寺

位于同心县窑山管委会，为清代建筑。清真寺建在石块及青砖垒砌的台基上，占地580平方米，仅有礼拜大殿和南北厢房。采用四合院布局，使用大木起脊式的礼拜大殿。由前卷棚、殿身、后窑殿三部分组成，上面用勾连搭的形式连在一起，形成一座完整统一的大殿。庭院富有中国传统风格。这种运用中西合璧的建筑装饰，将伊斯兰风格与中国传统建筑手法融会贯通，是研究宁夏早期宗教建筑难得的实物。

双疙瘩岩画

位于石嘴山市大武口区石炭井。该岩画点共有三块巨石，面积约30平方米，三块巨石分别有岩画224幅、48幅、24幅。

画面多为造型生动的动物、骑士、符号等，最为奇特的是有数量相当、不同造型的麦穗、农作物等画面，岩画中的各种动物形象生动、活灵活现，骑士线条粗犷、神态矫健，农作物更是生机盎然、颗粒饱满。极好地反映了我国北方地区游牧文化与农耕文化和谐交融的一派盛景。

中卫酿酒作坊

位于中卫市沙坡头区滨河镇。据调查，该酿酒作坊的前身，为清同治七年至光绪二十四年(1868~1898年)烧办，当时称为"义隆源"烧坊。现保留着20世纪50~70年代的建筑，包括储酒仓库、酿酒老窑坊、面粉楼及包装车间10栋，均为砖混结构。其中5栋双曲拱顶式仓库建于1958年，设计科学、风格特殊。对研究酿酒工艺传承及保护与利用良性发展具有较高的价值。

青铜峡黄河铁桥

位于吴忠市青铜峡市青铜峡镇。1959年7月1日正式竣工通车。主要是为青铜峡水利枢纽工程及黄河两岸运输物资而建。建成后的青铜峡铁桥是一座综合利用的桥，是包兰线青铜峡车站至余桥12公里专用线之间的咽喉。该桥为半永久性桥梁，桥长292.3米，桥身由七孔折穿式花梁和折装式桥梁等组成，桥墩采用木桩及铁丝笼片石结构。是宁夏第一座黄河桥梁。

青铜峡双曲砖拱形粮仓

位于吴忠青铜峡市青铜峡镇。建于1960年代。现存的两排粮仓占地面积为2802平方米，每排仓房由4个单体库组成，单体仓房高7.2米、宽13米。大跨度砖拱屋面除在横轴做拱外，在纵轴向由8个小型拱连拱，呈现双曲拱，大拱跨度在14米，拱高3.7米；小拱跨度2.4~2.6米。展现了20世纪五六十年代的建筑艺术。

兰州军区守备第一师师部旧址

位于石嘴山市大武口区石炭井。1969年10月兰州军区骑兵2师改编为步兵第20师（代号5310部队），11月从甘南移防宁夏进驻石嘴山地区。1985年9月6日，奉中央军委命令，撤销全师建制。以师直机关为基础改编为陆军第47集团军坦克旅旅部。

师部旧址坐落在贺兰山之中，依山而建。有办公楼、营房、电影院、篮球场等设施。目前整个军营建筑群体闲置无人使用，建筑损坏严重。

红山口遗址

位于新疆维吾尔自治区哈密地区巴里坤哈萨克自治县红山农场。该处居址较集中，数量很多，规模很大，多是双层石块堆积，也有单层石块堆积的，还有多层石圈的。另外，在遗址区周围还发现有很多的墓葬和岩画。墓葬以起封堆的中心凹陷的土石混合圆形封堆墓为主，不起封堆的围一圈石块的方形墓圹墓和不起封堆的围一圈石块的圆形墓圹墓较少。岩画内容雕刻的以山羊为主。

红山口遗址是新疆早期的一处聚落遗址，种类丰富，对于哈密早期考古学文化研究有着重要的意义，尤其对古代游牧文化的研究，开拓了新的视野。

托呼其佛寺遗址

位于哈密地区哈密市柳树泉农场。为隋唐时期时期佛寺建筑。土坯结构建筑，平面呈长方形，坐西朝东，东西长8.15米，南北宽7米。主室平面呈正方形，边长2.5米，穹窿顶，顶部部分坍塌，回廊顶及回廊西墙、回廊北墙部分已倒塌。在内墙壁仅见有少量的彩绘壁画痕迹。对于研究古代哈密的佛教文化有着重要意义。

阿克吐木休克烽燧

位于哈密地区哈密市沁城乡。修建于清代。主体建筑保存完好，由外侧围墙和内侧的塔楼两部分构成。外墙与塔楼的墙基均为石块垒砌而成，在墙基之上为土坯墙体，土坯墙体的构筑方式为，将土夯筑呈砖块的形状，再将土块层层交错排列砌成墙体。在烽燧四周的墙体上发现有15个射击孔。在烽燧周边分布有4座石围建筑遗迹。对于研究清代哈密军事、政治制度有着重要的意义。

塔勒德布拉克墓地

位于塔城地区裕民县江格斯乡。发现墓葬4座，由东北向西南呈链状排列。其中石圈墓2座，封堆外缘围有石圈，中部填黄土，石圈带宽约1米，封堆高0.4~0.5米、直径12~15米。土堆墓2座，封堆系黑土加少量沙石堆积而成，封堆高0.4~1.3米、直径24~30米。墓地年代待定。

前山墓葬

位于哈密地区伊吾县前山乡。现存大型贵族墓葬9座，面积约18万平方米。主墓直径46米，中央凹陷直径约24米，深3米。封堆外沿为圆角方形带状环壕，宽约15米，深0.5米。墓葬西北侧环绕分布殉葬坑21个。封堆南北两侧共分布祭祀石堆7处。墓葬东侧有东西向间距2~5米的立石142块。8座陪葬墓分布于主墓西侧约120米，南北排列紧密。

前山大墓是一处典型的隋唐时期突厥人的古墓葬，对于研究古代突厥人在哈密的活动和生活有着重要的意义。

比特库勒岩画

位于阿勒泰地区哈巴河县铁热克提乡。以红色颜料绘于一处较大的独立岩石上，由于年代久远，色彩暗淡。主画面位于岩体顶部，画面右侧为一人物半身像，左侧刻有一人物头像。岩体左下角有画面较模糊，仅中部有一把短剑可辨，画面左上角有两个叠加的V字形图案。岩画彩绘人像与阿勒泰其他地区一些石人比较相像。

五一农场酒花烘烤房

位于乌鲁木齐市头屯河区农十二师五一农场社区。建于1964年，为砖混结构，高13米，共4层，1层为烘烤炉，2、3层为烘干室，4层为风机室。是新疆第一座加工啤酒花的车间。反映了当时乌鲁木齐市工业化的发展进程。

老龙口

位于阿拉尔市农一师四团团部。由引水口、闸门、护栏组成，均为钢筋混凝土建筑。闸门为三孔闸，上有三组控闸设备。闸门北侧护栏下端有"向伟大的中国共产党第九次全国代表大会献礼"、"向伟大的中华人民共和国建国二十周年献礼"等标语。该龙口1969年延用民渠进水口建成，1979年在上游500米处新建协合拉新分水闸后，该龙口停止使用。老龙口是当时兴修水利，促进农业发展建设的历史见证，建筑风格时代特征明显。

萨尔乔克像塔

位于哈密地区巴里坤哈萨克自治县萨尔乔克乡。修建于1966～1967年间，平面为南北两个梯形相对，中间为一长方形，总长15米、宽3.6米。东面顶部写有"毛主席万岁"五个大字，下部为毛主席立像，已模糊不清。两侧屏风写有毛主席的《题庐山仙人洞》诗，主体为毛主席关于农业的语录。西面顶部用新哈文写有"毛主席万岁"几个字，下部为毛主席手背后立像。两侧屏风写有毛主席的《送瘟神》诗。像塔南北两侧各画有一个工农形象，已模糊不清。萨尔乔克像塔时代特征明显。

农一师五团玉尔滚俱乐部

位于阿拉尔市五团民族分场。1971年11月始建，1973年10月竣工，为当时阿克苏地区最大的俱乐部。建筑坐东朝西，占地约1140平方米，呈"工"字形，土木结构，苏式建筑。中间为礼堂，东、西两侧为办公室。正面门额上有"农一师五团玉尔滚俱乐部"字样，下为"1973.10.1"，南墙西侧上部有俄文。建筑四面墙体上部均有标语。反映了当时开垦边疆、建设新疆的时代风貌。现礼堂已成危房。

特约编辑　张双敏　孙秀丽　文 丹　徐秀丽　张 冲
特约审稿　刘小和　乔 梁　王立平
英文翻译　李新伟　刘红艳　聂江波
装帧设计　甘婷婷

责任印制　王少华
责任编辑　张广然

图书在版编目（ＣＩＰ）数据

第三次全国文物普查百大新发现 / 国家文物局编.
— 北京：文物出版社，2011.11
ISBN 978-7-5010-3340-9

Ⅰ．①第… Ⅱ．①国… Ⅲ．①文物－考古发现－中国
Ⅳ．①K87

中国版本图书馆CIP数据核字(2011)第231152号

第三次全国文物普查百大新发现
100 New Discoveries of the Third Nationwide Surveys of Cultural Heritage

编　　著　国家文物局
出版发行　文物出版社
地　　址　北京市东直门内北小街2号楼
邮　　编　100007
网　　址　www.wenwu.com
电子邮箱　web@wenwu.com
经　　销　新华书店
印　　刷　东莞新扬印刷有限公司
开　　本　889×1194毫米　1/16
印　　张　19.25
版　　次　2011年11月第1版　2011年11月第1次印刷
书　　号　ISBN 978-7-5010-3340-9
定　　价　300.00 元